THE LOW SALT, LOW CHOLESTEROL COOKBOOK

The Low Salt, Low Cholesterol Cookbook

Myra Waldo

BERKLEY BOOKS, NEW YORK

*The author wishes to express her thanks to the late
Dr. Seymour Rinzler for introducing her to the problem of
dietary fat and its relation to heart attacks and for
permitting her to attend the sessions of the New York
Anti-Coronary Club and to participate in its meetings and services.*

Diet and Heart Disease copyright © 1968 by the
American Heart Association
Portions of this book appeared previously in
COOKING FOR YOUR HEART AND HEALTH

This Berkley book contains the complete
text of the original hardcover edition.
It has been completely reset in a type face
designed for easy reading, and was printed
from new film.

THE LOW SALT, LOW CHOLESTEROL COOKBOOK

A Berkley Book / published by arrangement with
G. P. Putnam's Sons

PRINTING HISTORY
G. P. Putnam's Sons edition published 1961
Berkley edition / May 1974
Tenth printing / April 1981

A BERKLEY BOOK ® TM 757,375
Berkley Books are published by Berkley Publishing Corporation,
200 Madison Avenue, New York, New York 10016.
PRINTED IN THE UNITED STATES OF AMERICA

Contents

"Diet and Heart Disease"

A statement developed by the Committee on Nutrition of the American Heart Association.

The development of atherosclerotic coronary artery disease is influenced by many factors; among the factors associated with an increase in this disease are:

1. A familial history of coronary heart disease; the presence of diabetes mellitus, hyperlipidemia, gout, hypertension, obesity, and certain personality characteristics.
2. Sex and age: Men are generally more susceptible than women and both become increasingly susceptible with advancing years.
3. Environmental factors such as a diet rich in saturated fat and cholesterol, cigarette smoking, and habitual physical inactivity.

There is growing evidence that the early identification and correction of these risk factors may favorably influence the course of coronary disease. For this reason, the American Heart Association has urged the implementation of risk factor identification programs.

The fact that control of diet is one method of correcting or modifying some of these risk factors led the American Heart Association to release two previous reports (1961 and 1965) on the relationships between diet and atherosclerosis. Since that time, additional supporting data have been accumulated, particularly on the effects of diet on the occurrence rate of myocardial infarction. Accordingly, the American Heart Association, through its advisors, has revised its Statement on Diet and Heart Disease to include these reports.

It is most important to note that much of the data currently available on the relationship of diet to coronary artery disease are from studies using subjects unusually susceptible to coronary disease or atypical of the general population of the United States. There is an urgent need for more tightly designed, prospective studies involving larger numbers of healthy subjects so as to provide an unequivocal answer. A report on the feasibility of the dietary modifications for such a study has been published.

It has been repeatedly documented that in populations with high concentrations of serum cholesterol, the frequency of atherosclerotic coronary heart disease is high, whereas in populations with lower concentrations of cholesterol in their serum, the frequency of coronary disease is lower. The evidence now indicates that avoidance of prolonged elevations of serum cholesterol can decrease the hazard of developing premature coronary disease.

It has already been shown that in most (but not all) persons, elevated concentrations of cholesterol in the serum *can be decreased* significantly and *can be maintained* at a lower level by conscientious and sustained adherence to a nutritionally sound, modified fat diet. It has been suggested, but it has not been proven, that this type of diet will minimize the progressive rise in serum cholesterol concentration that generally occurs in most adults.

DIETARY RECOMMENDATIONS

Although the dietary recommendations in this statement are designed for ''healthy'' individuals to reduce the risk factors influenced by diet, they are particularly applicable to individuals who are shown to have increased risk as determined by plasma lipid or lipoprotein concentrations. In general, a diet designed to decrease the risk of coronary heart disease involves the following recommendations:

1. *A caloric intake adjusted to achieve and maintain proper weight.* Obesity is statistically associated with both hypertension and diabetes, and secondarily, with coronary heart dis-

ease. Correction of obesity may also reduce elevated serum lipid concentrations.

2. *A decrease in the intake of saturated fats, and an increase in the intake of polyunsaturated fats.* This will lower increased concentrations of cholesterol in the serum of most people. The ideal quantity of fat needed in the diet is not known, but an intake of less than 40% of calories from fat is considered desirable. Of this total, polyunsaturated fats should probably comprise twice the quantity of saturated fats. Many studies have shown that saturated fats elevate the serum cholesterol of man and that polyunsaturated fats lower serum cholesterol. The cholesterol-elevating effect of saturated fats is about twice as great as the cholesterol-lowering effect of polyunsaturated fats.

Considerable confusion has resulted from the regulation forbidding manufacturers to label vegetable oil products with their actual polyunsaturated fatty acid content. This has made it difficult to distinguish between a product "made with vegetable oil," but heavily hydrogenated (saturated) in manufacture, and one retaining a high content of polyunsaturates in the final product. Since 1961, many manufacturers have made a substantial effort to increase the polyunsaturate content of vegetable oil shortenings, the lightly-hydrogenated salad and cooking oils, and especially, the tub-type margarines. Accurate labelling would make it possible to identify the brands with a high-polyunsaturated fat content. For the present, margarines that are high in polyunsaturates usually can be identified by the listing of a "liquid oil" first among the ingredients. Margarines and shortenings that are heavily hydrogenated or contain coconut oil, which is quite saturated, are ineffective in lowering the serum cholesterol.

It should be noted that quite commonly, diets severely restricted in fats, with carbohydrate filling out the caloric requirement, may accentuate hypertriglyceridemia. Although the exact role of the triglycerides in atherogenesis is not clearly established, there is increasing evidence that hypertriglyceridemia is associated with an increased incidence of coronary disease in younger men.

3. *A substantial reduction of cholesterol in diet.* The average daily diet in the United States contains approximately 600 mg. of cholesterol. Sharp reduction in the amount of cholesterol in the diet has been found to lower the concentration of cholesterol in the serum of most people. In hypercholesterolemic individuals, reduction of dietary cholesterol to less than 300 mg. daily is recommended. Because cholesterol is abundant in many protein foods of high biological quality, careful planning is necessary to lower the intake of cholesterol without impairing the intake of foods high in protein.

Other dietary factors: Although there is a great deal of interest in the possible role of other dietary factors (simple sugars vs. complex carbohydrates, alcohol, coffee and artificial sweeteners, such as the cyclamates and saccharin) in the development of coronary heart disease, the available evidence is incomplete. Dependence on foods such as vegetables, cereals and fruits to supply most of the dietary carbohydrates is preferable to excessive use of sugar including candy, soft drinks and other sweets.

In the application of these recommendations to family groups with a high incidence of coronary disease and/or with risk factors, any change in the diet must preserve the principles of good nutrition. Although nutritional requirements differ during certain periods of the normal life cycle, the demands of optimal nutrition during periods of growth and development of infants, children and adolescents, and of pregnant and lactating women can be met by appropriate modifications of the recommendations under these dietary principles. Dietary habits which are formed during the developing years may continue life-long and influence the severity of atherosclerosis in later life. Diets similar to those recommended herein have been consumed by many persons for periods of more than ten years without any evidence, clinical or biochemical, of deleterious effects.

As already mentioned, coronary heart disease is a result of many factors. Diets rich in saturated fat and cholesterol represent one important risk factor that can be safely modified. Dietary management does not exclude appropriate use of drugs and other measures for control of risk factors.

12

Introduction

Everyone wants to live as long as possible, and in general, people are living longer than ever before. In recent years, however, one killer has come forth to supplant wars, traffic accidents and cancer. This killer is coronary occlusion, or "heart attacks," as they are commonly called. It not only kills the elderly, as might be expected, but also takes a heavy toll of the middle-aged, whom we customarily regard as being in the prime of life.

Most people don't care for statistics—they don't make very interesting reading. But the chances are better than even that any given American will die of heart disease. What is particularly disturbing is the steady increase in the *rate* of deaths from coronary heart disease over the years per 100,000.

Year	Rate
1920	283
1930	328
1940	407
1950	494
1960	513
1967	598

What causes heart disease?

Coronary heart disease, according to many researchers, is apparently associated in a strong measure with our diet. Many doctors now believe that this disease is the result of a lifetime of eating the typical American unbalanced diet—too many fats, mostly dairy products, rich desserts and fatty meats.

Of all the major killers, heart disease is the one disease in which hope has been given that the individual has at least a measure of control over his destiny and life expectancy.

By changing your diet, you may and probably will lower your cholesterol level (which we'll presently discuss) and, in turn, lessen your chances of becoming the victim of a heart attack. The vast majority of American men, from the time they are forty years old, have some fatty deposits in their coronary arteries and are particularly susceptible to this disease. For men between forty and sixty-two, the death rate is startlingly high. Howard Sprague, a former president of the American Heart Association, stated that 40 percent of all men over forty years of age have a definite degree of obstruction in their arteries.

A wide range of studies indicates clearly that the fats we eat are directly implicated in the problem of heart disease. It has also been shown that the various *types* of fats differ greatly in their effect. Tests made on four continents indicate that where the diet is high in butter, milk, eggs and meat, the heart disease rate is high. The most recent surveys .hroughout the world show that where people follow a low-fat diet, heart disease is comparatively rare.

It may be flatly stated when a race or nation consumes a diet high in fat and cholesterol, that race or nation will be troubled by coronary heart disease or atherosclerosis. Of all the races and nations of the world, American men have the highest cholesterol levels and the highest incidence of heart disease.

Remember: Coronary heart disease is, as its name implies, a disease, and from all that has been learned, it is not necessarily inevitable. It is preventable in a large proportion of cases and it may often be curable.

It has often been said that the life expectancy of the average American has greatly increased over the past half century. So it has, having risen by about twenty years since the year 1900. But life expectancy for a fifty-year-old person has increased by only 2.2 years in all that time. Most of the increased life expectancy is the result of preventing childhood and infectious diseases.

WORLD DEATH RATES FOR STROKE AND CORONARY HEART DISEASE AMONG MALES 45-64
1965-67 AVERAGE

Country	Death Rate Per 100,000 Population	
	Stroke	Coronary Heart Disease
United States	75.3	598.4
Australia	108.4	587.1
New Zealand	90.8	572.9
United Kingdom	118.7	541.1
Canada	65.4	525.7
Belgium	86.7	324.7
Austria	117.0	332.4
West Germany	115.8	379.8
Czechoslovakia	96.2	323.6
Israel	83.2	406.9
Hungary	124.7	311.2
Denmark	59.1	378.7
Japan	321.1	100.6
Italy	113.2	244.0
Norway	69.6	364.6
Netherlands	60.2	330.8
Rumania	137.8	162.4
Sweden	61.8	299.1
Switzerland	62.0	257.4
Chile	140.1	184.9

Much of the causal relationship between cholesterol and the incidence of heart disease has not been fully proved; the complete research picture will surely take a generation. To prove all the points involved to a 100-percent certainty will take time, much time. Meanwhile, heart disease fatalities will continue. But almost all forward steps in the medical field have been made by men of courage who have dared try new techniques and methods to illustrate their beliefs. Think of the fatalities that would have occurred if everyone had waited for 100-

percent certainty in the use of insulin (in diabetes), surgical anesthesia, quinine in the control of malaria. There is enough evidence on hand *now* to warrant the use of dietary control, in an effort to assay its role in coronary heart disease.

The heart

The human heart is an extraordinary mechanism. This remarkable muscle is about five inches long and weighs slightly more than a half pound; it is not situated on the left side of the body, as some people believe, but almost in the center of the chest, and is only slightly to the left of center. The chief function of the heart, of course, is pumping blood to the aorta, which sends it throughout the body. When the blood fails to reach the heart muscle through the coronary arteries in adequate amounts, damage occurs, resulting in what is commonly called a heart attack. Sometimes it is called a coronary, a coronary thrombosis, a coronary occlusion, coronary disease, or the like, but any one of these terms means that blood is not reaching the heart muscle.

The body requires a constant supply of oxygen circulating through the system, accomplished by means of the bloodstream which carries oxygen to all parts of the body. In common with all other tissues of the human body, the heart requires a constant flow of fresh blood bringing with it a supply of oxygen. Without this fresh oxygenated blood, the heart will fail.

Blood travels throughout the body by means of arteries. We all know the familiar sensation called pins and needles caused by pressure on a hand or foot, the result of temporary interference with the circulation.

The pipelike arteries are composed of a set of fibrous, muscular and elastic layers. A child's arteries are supple and completely flexible, becoming firmer during later years. As with almost all other parts of the body, arteries are subject to disease, and one of the most common is known as *arteriosclerosis*. In medicine, a "sclerosis" refers to a hardening; of course, arteriosclerosis means hardening of the arteries. Many elderly persons, and some younger ones, are affected by hardening of the arteries of the extremities, notably the legs and arms. But our discussion is not concerned so much with arteriosclerosis as with the specific condition known as *atherosclerosis*. The "athero" portion of the word is derived from the Greek term for "porridge" or "mush"; this word was first coined by early scientists who found deposits of small particles of a yellowish, wax-fatty substance (cholesterol) in the arteries, which they thought resembled porridge.

Although the expression "hardening of the arteries" is frequently used, actually the fatty deposits are comparatively soft. These deposits cause a gradual narrowing of the arteries, thus limiting the flow of blood. The healthy condition and the partially blocked artery are seen in the two illustrations. Combined with the narrowing, there is another danger—that of a sudden interruption in the flow of blood through the arteries by blood clotting. A clot is a form of solidification of the blood, which, when it reaches a narrowed artery, is likely to cause a stoppage and bring about a "heart attack." Obviously this second danger—that of blood clotting—would not be nearly so great a danger if the arteries were not constricted by fatty deposits. Therefore, the problem is, essentially, to prevent deposits from forming in the arteries.

The human heart is fed by a system of arteries which must remain open in order to supply the necessary blood with which the heart operates. These arteries seem to form a crown (Latin: *corona*) around the heart; for this reason they are called coronary arteries.

Early research

More than a century ago, scientists began to wonder if the fatty deposits in coronary arteries were not responsible for blood stoppages and heart attacks. By a series of experiments (begun about 1910) it was shown that fatty foods produced arterial disease in rabbits, normally free of it because of their all-vegetable diet. Research has further shown that the fatty substance deposited on the walls of the arteries was not a true fat, but a waxy substance resembling fat. If one takes a small

Blood Passage

Fibrous Outer Layer (Serosa)

Inner Lining (Intima)

Muscular Middle Lining (Media)

A healthy artery with a normal passage for the flow of blood.

An artery showing a considerable amount of cholesterol deposits; note the narrowed passage.

amount of fresh candle wax which has dripped down the sides of a lighted candle and rubs it between the fingers for a short time, it will very roughly resemble the texture of cholesterol. The precise reason *why* cholesterol is found in patches on the artery walls may be subject to argument, but the fact that it *is* there is incontrovertible.

Cholesterol

Cholesterol is not poisonous and is an inactive substance. Scientists believe it does damage by merely being deposited on the arterial walls. Incidentally, cholesterol must be distinguished from fat, which it resembles in many ways. Fat is a food and is used by the body for fuel, but cholesterol has no food-energy value. However, the body requires cholesterol, *in suitable amounts*, even manufacturing it when lacking in the diet.

It should be borne in mind that certain foods naturally contain cholesterol, and recent studies show that it may be very important to limit the intake of such foods. Until the past few years, scientists did not give much consideration to the amount of dietary cholesterol consumed, preferring to give their attention chiefly to the matter of limiting fats, particularly saturated fats. However, it now appears that even comparatively small amounts of dietary cholesterol, as little as 1 gram per day, show a strong tendency toward raising the cholesterol level of the blood in most people. When you realize that even a medium-sized steak or 4 eggs have cholesterol enough in either food to equal ·or exceed 1 gram, it is obvious that dietary control becomes an important matter. There seems to be agreement among researchers that the dietary intake of cholesterol-rich foods should be limited, usually to as little as 300 milligrams per day. Of course, once the serum cholesterol level has been reduced to a completely satisfactory level (say, under 210 milligrams), then the 300-milligram restriction may be eased, although even then it is best to reduce the total fat intake and make sure that more unsaturated fat than saturated fat is consumed in the daily diet.

For your assistance, the following tables indicate the cholesterol content of selected foods. Bear in mind that 1 ounce of food has about 30 grams. Therefore, it is necessary to multiply the number of ounces of food consumed in a portion to obtain the total quantity of milligrams of cholesterol. For example, using the first food item (beef), it may be readily observed that there are 21 milligrams of cholesterol in 1 ounce. If you eat 3 ounces of beef as a serving, it will contain 63 milligrams of cholesterol, this figure being obtained from the extreme right-hand column. If you eat 6 ounces of beef, it will have twice as many, or 126 milligrams of cholesterol.

Among the foods lowest in cholesterol are fruits, vegetables (if prepared and served without butter or other saturated fats), breads and cereals, vegetable oils (except coconut oil), nuts (particularly low are almonds, pecans, peanuts, and walnuts), and the legumes, such as dried peas, lentils, and beans.

CHOLESTEROL CONTENT IN FOODS USED IN FAT-CONTROLLED DIETS

Food Items	mg. cholesterol per ounce (30 grams)	Approximate weight or measure of average serving (ounces)	(measures)	(gram weight)	mg. cholesterol average serving
Beef, lamb, or pork	21	3 oz.		90	63
Veal	27	3 oz.		90	81
Chicken	18	3 oz.		90	54
Fish (steaks or fillets)	21	3 oz.		90	63
Cottage Cheese (creamed)	5	2 oz.	½ cup	60	10
Milk (skimmed)	1	8 oz.	1 cup	240	8
Shellfish:			Approximate measures as substitute for one egg.		mg. of Cholesterol
Crab or shrimp	38	2 oz.	½ cup	60	76
Lobster	60	2 oz.	½ cup	60	120
Oysters	60	2 oz.	6-8 each (medium)	60	120
Organ Meats:					
Liver	90	2 oz.		60	180
Heart	48	2 oz.		60	96
Sweetbread (thymus)	75	2 oz.		60	150
Egg (whole)	165	1½ oz.	1 whole	50	275

Cholesterol and Fat in Selected Foods

Foods with very little or no cholesterol and saturated fat
Breads
Cereals
Cottage cheese
Fruits (avocado is in this category if in limited amounts)
Gelatin desserts
Pasta
Pretzels
Rice
Skim milk
Skim milk yogurt
Vegetables

Foods low in cholesterol
Ice milk
Nuts
Peanut butter
Sherbet

Foods low in cholesterol and high in unsaturated fats
Margarines (if liquid oil is listed first in label indicating ingredients)
Oils (except coconut oil)

Foods low in saturated fats and moderate in cholesterol
Fish
Poultry
Shellfish
Veal

Foods low in saturated fats and high in cholesterol
All organ meats (including kidneys, liver)

Foods moderate in cholesterol and high in saturated fats
Beef
Lamb
Ham
Pork

Foods high in cholesterol and high in saturated fats
Bacon
Butter
Cheese
Chocolate
Commercial baked goods (pies, cakes, etc.)
Cream (sweet and sour)
Cream substitutes
Egg yolks
Frankfurters
Ice cream
Milk, whole

Most people are interested in knowing the level of cholesterol in their blood. To obtain a reading, the physician takes a small blood sample. The amount of cholesterol in the blood is given in milligrams for each 100 cubic centimeters of blood, usually set forth as "mg. percent." In the United States, a reading of 225 or less is considered low; from 226 to 259 is medium; over 260 is high. Some researchers, including those at Harvard Medical School, believe that 210 and above should be reduced. Tests indicate that middle-aged men with cholesterol readings over 260 have *six* times the incidence of heart attacks than do men with less than 225.

Early chemistry studies showed that when walls of the arteries were found to be in a thickened condition, the thickening substance consisted of quantities of fat and cholesterol. As both fat and cholesterol are carried in the blood coursing through the arteries, it was only reasonable to assume that the "plaques" (patches) found on the arterial walls were caused by deposits left by the blood as it traveled about the body. The early scientists reasoned that if a person had a high cholesterol level and more than an average amount of deposits on his arteries, he should be a prime candidate for a heart attack.

But how could this theory be investigated? The test for cholesterol in the blood was easily accomplished, but no suitable way could be devised to examine the coronary arteries of a living person. However, researchers hit upon the idea of making comparison tests between those who had died of heart attacks and people who were accidentally killed. It was found that there was a considerably greater degree of narrowing in the arteries of heart attack victims than in those who had died from accidental causes. Furthermore, when it was learned that the level of fatty substances in the blood of the accident victims was lower than in those who had died of heart attacks, the pattern of research was soon established and verified.

What is cholesterol? Is it truly harmful on the artery walls, or is it merely circumstantial evidence of disease? Hundreds of researchers have devoted their efforts to discover the answers to these questions, and while much remains to be ascertained, certain facts (some proved, some half-proved) have emerged.

Triglycerides

In addition to cholesterol in the blood, doctors are now testing for what are called triglycerides. Recent studies have shown that the triglyceride level may be very important. As you know, the blood carries fats, and it is important to learn how these are altered and stored in the body. It should be remembered that fats do not dissolve by themselves in the blood; in order for them to become soluble, they must join up with what are known as *alpha* and *beta* proteins. When this takes place, the combinations of fats, together with the two types of proteins, become soluble, and they are technically known as lipoproteins. It is apparently true that many people lack these alpha and beta proteins, or their number is insufficient. For these people, the normal joining up and metabolization of fats in the bloodstream does not properly take place. The precise reason for this defect is not currently known. But the appropriate inheritance of fat-carrying proteins is undoubtedly of great importance to the individual.

It is now regarded as essential for physicians to check not only the cholesterol level of their patients but the triglyceride level as well. At present, it is believed that the highest proper triglyceride level is a reading of 160. When combined with a cholesterol level not exceeding 220, it may then be assumed that there is no undisclosed threat; of course, this assumes that the remainder of the physical examination is normal.

The foods we eat

Everything we eat fits into one of these categories: carbohydrate, protein or fat. Carbohydrates include the sugars and starches that make up such a large part of our everyday diet and which tend to add those extra calories; typical carbohydrate foods are table sugar, cereals, potatoes and bread. Proteins are something quite different; these are complex foods that are absolutely essential to the body, being required to restore body tissue used up in the normal wear and tear of daily life. Meat, fish, eggs, milk and cheese are the most usual protein foods.

Now we come to fats, and here our discussion will become more specific because fats are deeply implicated in any discussion of cholesterol and coronary heart disease.

Most people eat fatty foods because they like them; the human body can probably manage with comparatively fewer of them in the diet. Fats are of two types: the visible fats such as butter and edible oils and the invisible fats such as those in milk and cream. But many people do not realize that fats may be completely hidden; even the leanest meat, for example, consists of only two-thirds protein; and there still remains one-third fat, although the visible fat has been removed.

Fat is extensively used in the American (and European) style of cooking. Frying foods and serving them with sauces and gravies are typical of fats added to those normally contained in the food itself. Of the total caloric intake in the diet of Americans, about 40 percent (and sometimes more) consists of fat. Diet experts agree that this percentage is far too high.

Edible fats are also of liquid and solid types. Liquid fats include olive oil, corn oil and others that ordinarily flow at room temperature. Solid fats are those that retain their more or less solid state at room temperature; the typical solid fats we all know are butter, ordinary margarine, solid vegetable shortenings and lard.

Saturated and unsaturated fats

Chemically, edible fats consist of combinations of four molecules; three of these are called fatty acid molecules, and the fourth is glycerol. Since the glycerol molecule is unlikely to have anything to do with our problem, we can disregard it and concern ourselves with the fatty acids which make up three-quarters of the fat molecule. Fats differ from one another because of the various types of fatty acids they contain. Probably everyone has heard talk about the degree of saturation of fats, but most discussions and reports generally fail to explain the difference between the so-called saturated and unsaturated fats.

About 1915, the process of commercial hydrogenation came into use in order to change liquid fats (chiefly cottonseed and soybean oils) into solids, because these were more suitable for table use and because they would keep longer without turning rancid. At the present time, a substantial percentage of the shortenings and table spreads consumed in the United States are of the hydrogenated type.

The chemistry of fats

The chemical structure of the fatty acids reveals a sort of "backbone" of carbon atoms, depending on the type of fatty acid involved; there may be as few as four or as many as twenty (or more) carbon atoms forming the backbone. Based on the number of carbon atoms, a minimum and maximum number of hydrogen atoms may be combined with the carbon. The fewer the number of hydrogen atoms found in the fatty acids, the lower the degree of saturation—that is, the saturation of hydrogen atoms in conjunction with the carbon atoms. The converse is also true: The more hydrogen atoms that are combined with the carbon, the greater the degree of saturation.

Satfats (saturated fats)

We can now begin to understand the commercial hydrogenation process. Taking a natural, liquid oil (cottonseed, for example), the processors convert the liquid oil into a more solid form by chemically combining hydrogen atoms with the original carbon atoms. The actual hydrogenation process consists of sending hydrogen bubbles, in the form of gas, through the liquid fat. The hydrogen is thereby forced into a chemical union with the carbon naturally contained in the fatty acids.

To the eye, the most noticeable change is from a liquid oil to a solid fat. What has occurred is the saturation of the carbon atoms with more hydrogen atoms than are normally present in nature. The commercial process need not *completely* saturate the carbon; that is, the carbon atoms need not be forced to combine with the *maximum* number of hydrogen atoms. Therefore, there may be varying degrees of saturation. In the process, as pointed out in the previous paragraph, the liquid oil becomes solid because it is the nature of highly saturated fats to become somewhat firm at room temperature. In the same way, if the hydrogen atoms were removed from ordinary saturated fats, they would become liquid. For convenience, we'll call saturated fats satfats, and unsaturated fats linfats because of the linoleic acid (which we'll discuss later).

Naturally, a method of measuring the degree of saturation of fats was required, and it was discovered that measurements could be made with iodine, and the "iodine number" is now the standard way of measuring. The iodine joins with the carbon atoms, and the lower iodine numbers indicate a high degree of saturation, because little of the iodine combines with the carbon of saturated fats. Those fats with a high degree of saturation have low iodine numbers, whereas those with low saturation have the highest numbers. Here are some typical examples:

Natural Fat	Iodine Numbers	Classification
Coconut oil	8 to 10	
Butter fat	32 to 39	Low
Lamb fat	32 to 45	
Beef fat	35 to 47	
Lard	51 to 89	
Olive oil	79 to 90	Generally
Peanut oil	58 to 100	neutral
Cottonseed oil	105 to 115	
Corn oil	115 to 124	High
Sunflower seed oil	130 to 138	
Safflower oil	144 to 146	

The great significance of the process of hydrogenation of fats is in the consistent scientific reports indicating that highly saturated fats produce undesirable, high cholesterol levels in the blood. Continuing studies by scientists all over the world show a close correlation between not only the quantity but the *type* of fat consumed in the daily diet. It has been determined that unsaturated liquid oils (those with iodine numbers over 100) generally do not raise the cholesterol level. On the other hand, solid fats which are highly saturated (such as butter and animal fats) have a strong tendency to increase the cholesterol level. Even more fascinating is the almost proved indication that high iodine number fats not only do not increase but may succeed in lowering the cholesterol level.

We've discussed fatty acids, those which make up most of the fats we ordinarily eat. Scientists have given names to these fatty acids, and the one with which we are most concerned is called *linoleic acid*, which has a quite low degree of saturation. This valuable fatty acid is most commonly found in corn oil, cottonseed and linseed oil; being of vegetable origin (rather than animal), it has the desirable effect of tending to lower the cholesterol level.

Oleic acid, also a fatty acid, is another term to remember. It is in an intermediary position, most scientists believing that it neither tends to increase nor decrease the cholesterol level. In this neutral category, a typical example is olive oil, which is high in oleic acid but comparatively low in linoleic acid. Research is being undertaken to determine the importance of various combinations of oleic and linoleic acid on cholesterol, but nothing affirmative has yet developed.

Now what happens to linoleic and oleic acid when they undergo the hydrogenation process? As a rule, each of these fatty acids moves one step toward saturation. That is, the highly desirable, unsaturated linoleic acid is changed into a partially saturated fat in the general class of oleic acid, and neutral oleic acid becomes completely saturated. After the usual hydrogenation process, the linoleic acid is reduced, on the average, from an important, valuable 50 percent to about 5 percent of the total fat. It is believed that more than 500,000 tons of linoleic acid are destroyed each year by the hydrogenation process, thus depriving the American public of an essential fatty acid so important to life and health.

Since there is apparently such an important correlation between the fats we eat and the cholesterol in the blood and arteries, we should pay close attention to this remarkable substance. Although associated with fats in the body, cholesterol is not actually a fat; it is classified as an alcohol. Those who may find this fact strange should not be disturbed because many familiar substances can be separated chemically into categories different from their obvious appearance.

Cholesterol has the texture and appearance of a fatty wax, as mentioned previously, and is insoluble in water, although soluble in alcohol. Like a true fat, which cholesterol seems to mimic, it floats on the surface of watery substances. From what has been said of the dangers of cholesterol, many people equate it with an evil like cancer. In normal circumstances, cholesterol is a useful and desirable substance in the human body. It is found in all parts of the body, including the brain and blood, and undoubtedly serves vital bodily needs. Only when abnormal quantities collect in areas like the arteries does it assume an evil aspect. If cholesterol is lacking in the diet, the body will manufacture it in the liver; thus it is apparent that cholesterol is normal and proper in *moderate* amounts.

How the body utilizes the fat we eat

With this brief background of fats, fatty acids and cholesterol, consideration may be given to what happens to the fats we eat in our ordinary diet. As previously mentioned, fats are utilized by the body for quick energy; if excess fats are eaten, the liver stores them temporarily so that the fats may be gradually released over a period of time. The bloodstream is the mechanism utilized by the body for distributing this energy throughout the system. Research chemists were puzzled about how the blood conveyed fat, since it was known that fat does not dissolve in watery substances such as blood. Research revealed the secret. The body creates what scientists call *lipoproteins*,—that is, combinations of fats, protein and cholesterol—because lipoproteins can and do dissolve in the blood.

The body creates these lipoproteins—the combinations of fat, protein and cholesterol—primarily to transport the energy foods in solution in the bloodstream. After the lipoproteins are formed, they flow out into the blood and are carried through the body. The fats, now in solution in the blood, burn readily and are soon disposed of. The proteins are soluble in the blood and are also easily used up. The remaining constituent of the lipoprotein is the cholesterol. Until very recently, it was assumed that the body could not use up cholesterol, for it was not a type of food, such as fat, protein or carbohydrate. But the last few years of study indicate that the consumption of cholesterol in foods *does* have an effect on the serum cholesterol level, tending to raise it in most persons. That is true in even comparatively modest amounts of dietary cholesterol; for example, three-quarters of a pound of steak with fatty marbling, containing 1gram, eaten daily will increase the cholesterol level in the vast majority of individuals. Therefore, it is suggested that the daily consumption of cholesterol should be lowered to not more than 300 milligrams per day. Later on, when the cholesterol level is reduced to 210 or less, it should be possible to relax the restriction, if the intake of polyunsaturates to saturates remains proportionately high. Obviously, this discussion is an oversimplification of the problem, with the more technical details being limited or omitted for the sake of clarity.

Other factors

Is diet the sole cause of coronary heart disease? It would appear that diet is vitally related to atherosclerosis, but many other factors remain to be resolved. Conclusions regarding certain unsolved factors may require many, many years. Some factors may be given increased importance as investigations and research continue, whereas others may eventually be eliminated from consideration. These factors include other diseases, the sex differential, overweight, heredity and family history, emotions and stress, age, occupation, exercise, salt in the diet, tobacco and alcohol, and starches.

Salt

The intake of salt (sodium) also has been implicated in heart disease and strokes.

First, what is sodium? It's a mineral essential to life and is derived from the foods we eat, whether animal or vegetable. Sodium is present in most foods, although it generally can't be seen, felt, or even tasted. Generally speaking, fruits have comparatively little sodium. However, poultry, fish, meat, milk and eggs are comparatively high in sodium. Vegetables cover a wide range, extending from very little to a considerable amount. Too much or, contrarily, too little can cause ill effects.

Excess amounts are normally excreted by the healthy person, but in certain illnesses, the body retains sodium and water as well. Such persons are often placed on sodium-free or low-sodium diets of 500 to 1,000 milligrams a day.

In this book, the various illnesses can't be considered, for they require constant medical supervision. Instead, acknowledging the implications of sodium in heart disease and stroke, a mild restriction of salt intake is indicated, and that advice is suggested for everyone.

To explain the terms "sodium" and "salt," let us consider some of the finer points. Sodium is not salt, but salt contains a quantity of sodium, almost half in fact. Thus, we find the basic reason for restricting salt in the diet is to limit and control the intake of sodium.

All the receipes in this book use less salt than found in most cookbooks and also as prepared in most American homes. Other flavors, introduced by the use of herbs and spices, make the dishes quite palatable nonetheless, which helps compensate for the lack of salt. When dining out in restaurants or in the homes of friends, be sure never to use the additional salt found on the table. Remember that one teaspoon of salt has 2,300 milligrams of sodium.

It's definitely advisable to restrict the intake of salt as a precautionary measure, so forget the salt shaker.

OTHER DISEASES

There are certain illnesses that almost without question seem directly to affect heart disease. Hypertension, which alone causes 75,000 deaths a year in the United States, is a disease wherein the arteries are drawn together and constricted; the blood pressure increases in order to force the blood through the narrower passageways of the arteries. In turn, the increased pressure puts additional demands on the heart, increasing its size, with possible damage to the arteries and kidneys. Other diseases which are related to our problem include diabetes, thyroid deficiencies, and kidney disease. *Conclusion:* There is a well-defined relationship between hypertension (increased

31

blood pressure) and atherosclerosis which cannot be disregarded in any serious discussion of this problem.

THE SEX DIFFERENTIAL

One of the melancholy facts of life that every married couple must face is the probability that the majority of wives will outlive their husbands. The frequency of heart attacks in middle-aged men and their comparative infrequency in women of similar age is an accepted fact in our country. To illustrate, here are some statistics on fatal heart attack rates each year in the United States:

Age decade	Men (per 100,000)	Women (per 100,000)
30-39	49	11
40-49	180	47
50-59	610	191
60-69	1,211	535

It is obvious from these figures that there is a definite and marked difference between the sexes in the probability of coronary heart disease.

Clinical tests indicate that young and middle-aged women are remarkably resistant to atherosclerosis until the menopause, after which women apparently lose their natural immunity and the incidence of heart disease increases so swiftly that by the time the sexes reach their seventies, they are on a par. A fatty, high-cholesterol diet is particularly risky for women after the menopause.

The enigma remains as to why men have more lipoproteins and higher cholesterol levels than women, on the average, for their respective age groups. At first, it was thought that there might be inherent structural differences in the arterial walls of men and women, but this theory is still conjectural. Of course, scientists naturally turned to the innate sexual differences between the two groups, putting forth the view that female hormones offered a certain degree of protection to women. This theory was further strengthened by the fact that women apparently lost their immunity or protection immediately after the menopause, when female hormones ceased to be manufactured at the former rate.

In this regard, under special circumstances, researchers have given female hormones to men with high cholesterol levels and noted a strong tendency for the lipoprotein and cholesterol level to decrease. Of course this therapy can scarcely be recommended to the public because of its obvious drawbacks. Tests have been made with chickens, rabbits and rats which were fed high dosages of cholesterol-fat foods and soon developed coronary atherosclerosis. Later, these same animals were given estrogens (female hormones), which resulted in reductions of the induced conditions.

Here for the first time in these tests was the startling fact that cholesterol deposits could be "reversed." Arterial deposits which had formed in the animals because of their fatty diet exhibited a tendency to disappear, at least in part. Needless to say, these results must be regarded as only experimental because the diet was fed to chickens over a period of just eight weeks, so the deposits of cholesterol on the arteries were comparatively fresh. In human beings, the diet would cover many decades and the cholesterol deposits almost an equal time. Furthermore, human beings may or may not respond in the same way as chickens.

Conclusion: There is a marked sex differential between men and women in their susceptibility to atherosclerosis during the middle years; this apparent "immunity" disappears after the menopause. At present, it appears that there is an undeniable relation between female sex hormones and atherosclerosis. Women, as well as men, would be well advised to keep their cholesterol levels at a moderate figure because they tend to develop even higher cholesterol readings than men in later years.

OVERWEIGHT

For many years, Americans have become accustomed to reading statistics from life insurance companies indicating that overweight increases the mortality rate, particularly of middle-aged men. These figures have repeated themselves consistently over the years and their conclusiveness can no longer be doubted. They indicate that among persons 30 percent overweight, the heart attack rate is one and a half times that of persons with normal weight. More recent studies show that there is some sort of correlation between obesity and high cholesterol, but the interplay is not absolutely conclusive. Inasmuch as other factors enter into the problem, a person who brings his weight down to normal does not automatically gain freedom from the possibility of heart attacks, although the chances are diminished. But as we shall see, the importance of overweight, in the presence of other conditions, cannot be minimized.

In considering how persons became overweight, is it not likely that they both overate and ate too much fat in the process, which combined to cause the overweight along with a high cholesterol level? In other words, is it not possible that a person who is overweight and has a high cholesterol level reached that stage because of too much fat in his diet, which resulted in the overweight and high cholesterol? Furthermore, when the insurance companies state that obesity increases the heart attack rate by one and a half times, it is possible that the overweight is concomitant with the high cholesterol, and it is the latter, not the overweight, which increases the rate of heart attack incidence. In this regard, it has been shown that when overweight persons bring their weight down to normal, their chances of having a heart attack are also brought down to about the same as those who were of normal weight originally. But, in turn, this revives the previous point that people who are overweight have probably consumed too much fat. The probabilities are strong that by reducing their weight, such persons are reducing their fat intake and probably bringing down their cholesterol level at the same time their weight is reduced.

Conclusion: The precise correlation between overweight

and heart disease has yet to be proved, but what has been learned clearly shows that normal weight (or even slightly less) is essential for all persons in middle or late years. If you are overweight, immediately begin your reducing and don't stop until your weight is down to normal. The danger of overweight in relation to the chance of a heart attack indicates that this should be given immediate priority.

HEREDITY AND FAMILY HISTORY

One of the most puzzling questions yet to be solved by researchers is the individual difference between apparently similar human beings. Placed in direct focus, the question is whether people tend to inherit a predisposition toward high cholesterol, overweight and high blood pressure. It must be remembered that this subject has only recently been under investigation with regard to potential heart disease and little conclusive information is at hand. It is within the bounds of possibility that some persons may inherit a *tendency* to high cholesterol levels; some scientists even now think the disease called essential hypercholesterolemia may be inherited.

The heredity problem seems to be receiving comparatively little support, however. Tests indicate that no race or group of people is necessarily more susceptible than another in the matter of cholesterol. Readings made all over the world indicate that newborn infants have similar cholesterol levels, with changes occurring much later as the years go by. It seems more likely that the changes are the result of diet rather than any racial characteristics.

Everyone knows a family in which heart attacks have stricken several members. It seems only natural to assume that such families have a predilection or susceptibility to heart attacks.

The studies that have been made at the present time indicate that where coronary heart disease strikes several members of a family, the likelihood is that they all had high blood cholesterol levels. Usually, in families of this type, even the women tend to lose their female "immunity" and show high cholesterol levels.

It is believed that all members of a family have high cholesterol because they all eat similar foods, high in fat. But, then, what of certain members of these families who have normal blood cholesterol levels and apparently escape the family tendency? Therefore, because members of your family have a "predisposition" toward heart disease, there is no reason to despair.

A prudent person would give serious heed to following whatever precautionary steps seem advisable, particularly adherence to a diet limited in fats. As food patterns are probably set in childhood, it is not unusual for men to talk fondly of food that Mother used to make; if Mother's family menus were high in fats, it is probable that the current high cholesterol level of her son represents years of a fatty diet. Inasmuch as members of the family usually follow the same diet together, the predisposition to heart attacks may chiefly represent a family liking for considerable quantities of fat in the diet.

Conclusion: Whether there is a family predisposition to heart attacks has not been verified, nor is it known whether there is a tendency to pass along to succeeding generations an inability to cope successfully with fats. The same uncertainty exists regarding structural defects in the arterial walls and also with family traits concerning hypertension. Since no one can change his heredity, positive measures seem in order. Chiefly, this means proper diet.

EMOTIONS AND STRESS

According to popular but unverified belief, this is a cause of heart disease. Everyone knows of a man who has apparently overworked himself and ultimately succumbed to a heart attack. "Overwork," "too much tension," and similar comments are made in sympathy by the friend to the grieving widow and believed by both. Evidence to sustain this belief is lacking, however.

We all believe that our present hectic times are the tensest in all history; of course, every generation over the past thousand years also considered its period as the most stress-laden. Of all factors which may contribute to heart attacks, stress and emotion are the most difficult to measure. What is the gauge or measuring unit? Obviously there is none. People vary greatly in their personality makeup, and one person's stress is just the ordinary run of daily life to another.

Moreover, does business stress affect a person during working hours only? Big-city life, with its fierce competition, the difficulties of commuting, rearing children, all contribute to tension and emotion, according to those who argue that urban life is likely to increase the risk of heart attacks. But the heart attack rate in easygoing South Carolina is higher than in New York City. Surveys in Japan indicate that the farmer-peasant (living with little tension) has a heart disease rate similar to that of a city dweller in Tokyo.

The general inclination to proclaim stress and tension as an important factor in heart disease is natural and inevitable, but not necessarily correct. Whenever we read that an important executive or official has died of a heart attack, it seems only natural to think in terms of that person's career and work; we tend to forget that thousands and thousands of other persons die every day. Another reason has been suggested: The physician is inevitably asked by the family why his patient should have died of a heart attack. It seems only reasonable to satisfy the family with a flattering statement that his patient had been overworking rather than tell them the harsh truth that he had been overeating.

Of particular interest in this regard are the results of studies made during the war years in England and occupied Norway, when tensions and stress presumably were very high. It was found that the coronary mortality rate *decreased* during those trying years when England was being severely bombed and Norway was in the harsh hands of the Germans. Although life was extremely trying, heart attack incidence dropped at the same time that the amount of fat in the daily diet was stringently reduced. In Norway, the death rate for coronary disease increased as soon as the war was over and the food supply returned to normal. In England, a similar increase occurred when American lend-lease shipments of edible fats reached that beleaguered country.

Undoubtedly, stress and emotion can strongly affect us, some people completely losing the desire to eat, while others are perversely driven to compulsive eating. Strong emotional events, excitement, danger and fear definitely operate to alter the pulse rate, elevate blood pressure, and may temporarily affect the action of the heart; but there is as yet no proof that they otherwise harm or adversely affect it. Short-lived emotions and reactions must be separated from long-term, more or less regular stress and emotion. If having an excitable nature or emotional personality predisposes an individual to the likelihood of a heart attack, how do we reconcile this with the excitable Spanish and Italians, who have quite low coronary disease rates?

Despite conflicting opinions with respect to stress and emotions, a strong body of opinion has developed which now believes these factors are important. They reason that high blood pressure on the walls of the arteries, as well as the pressure caused by the flow of blood, is directly associated with the progression of depositing cholesterol on the walls of the arteries. It has been shown that extreme fear, rage, or anger releases hormones into the bloodstream, and this increases the coagulability of the blood.

Conclusion: It seems fairly certain that some people are subject to stresses and strains to a greater degree than other individuals. These people may strongly react to stress (often psychic in nature), which may increase their cholesterol levels. Of course, individuals vary considerably in their personality makeups and react differently in matters of emotions and stress. People engaged in difficult, tense or extremely tiring occupations are well advised to use common sense and restraint about overlong working hours and also to avoid excessive tension. This, however, is good advice for everyone.

AGE

As remarked previously, infants throughout the world are born with similar cholesterol levels. Cholesterol is deposited on the arteries beginning about the tenth year of life. From seventeen to twenty-five, men's readings are moderate, but then begin to climb, reaching high figures at about forty. After sixty-two or so, there is apparently a decline in the cholesterol level, with the figures often becoming lower in persons of advanced years. It is therefore apparent that the forties and fifties are particularly important (and crucial) for men and that the thirties are also vital because these are the years in which the cholesterol level rises rapidly.

Conclusion: From the age of thirty years, care should be taken to see that the cholesterol level is kept within safe bounds.

OCCUPATION

Many doctors and laymen wonder whether particular occupations tend to increase the incidence of heart disease. In a series of tests conducted in Chicago and London, results were somewhat inconclusive, although they pointed to the possibility that the chief differences among respective heart attack rates for various occupations were directly influenced by the work involved, the amount and regularity of physical activity. In general, it was found that those occupations involving strenuous physical labor had the lowest incidence of heart disease.

Conclusion: It would appear that any occupation involving regular, continuous physical activity is less likely to lead to a heart attack than a sedentary occupation.

EXERCISE

Those who believe that regular exercise prevents heart disease always point to figures indicative of a lower incidence among physically active workers. This point was discussed earlier. However, from tests made in several Scandinavian countries, the reverse was found to be true, with hardworking rural laborers having higher heart disease incidence than the sedentary city folk.

Many scientists fail to find a precise correlation between exercise and coronary heart disease. A comprehensive investigation made simultaneously in the United States, Europe and South Africa did not disclose sufficient facts to support such a connection. Although opinions differ, there is negligible proof that exercise lowers cholesterol levels; nevertheless this remains a subject for future research.

However—and this is important—physical activity does tend in general to reduce weight, and weight reduction (with or without special low-fat diets) tends to decrease cholesterol levels. There can also be no doubt that exercise promotes the circulation of the blood; inasmuch as good blood circulation is primary in the problem of heart disease, it may well be that physical activity is desirable. Mere desultory knee bending is not enough; a minimum of an hour's daily walking at a brisk (not gentle) pace is required.

At the other extreme are those who believe that physical activity is harmful. They argue that heart attacks often occur after physical activity, and they are prepared to cite numerous illustrations to prove their point. The fact is that exercise will not cause a heart attack. Most heart attacks occur while people are sitting still, or even sleeping. Important, too, is the fact that a large number of attacks occur four or five hours after dinner, showing that the bloodstream may be overloaded with fat, thus increasing the chance of blood clotting.

Conclusion: Experts differ on the relationship between exercise and heart attacks. It seems desirable, if only for general health, improved circulation and a good figure, to exercise with some degree of regularity.

SALT IN THE DIET

The body holds in solution a more or less fixed percentage of fluids to dilute the amount of salt in the system. Those who habitually salt everything they eat may have a dozen or more pounds of water weight in their system. Surveys indicate that excessive users of salt tend toward higher than average blood pressure; inasmuch as high blood pressure is a clear danger signal on the road to possible heart disease, this condition should be corrected. In the event of a heart attack, the body will be required to pump extra fluids through the body.

Conclusion: It would seem reasonable to lower (although not to eliminate completely) salt intake; this in turn will result in a loss of weight, which is also desirable.

TOBACCO AND ALCOHOL

Some scientists maintain that cigarette smoking increases the heart disease rate in direct proportion to the quantity smoked. In one report, it was stated that coronary heart disease was 68 percent higher for regular cigarette smokers than for nonsmokers. This increased rate did not seem to apply with equal force to cigar or pipe smokers, though why is not yet known. One factor that is definitely known is that cigarette smoking temporarily increases the blood pressure; it is also known that elevated blood pressure is harmful.

With regard to alcohol, there was nothing shown to prove that the regular consumption of alcohol had any connection with the heart disease rate. For most persons, alcohol in moderate amounts has a relaxing effect, but it is fattening—extremely so.

Conclusion: Those who have high blood pressure or high cholesterol levels should definitely limit their cigarette smoking or, even better, stop it completely. The same suggestion applies to alcohol.

STARCH AND OTHER CARBOHYDRATES

Another missing link in the continuing study of heart disease is the possible effect of starch and other carbohydrates. Studies of starch in the diet tend to indicate that persons with high starch diets show comparatively low incidence of heart disease.

41

Of course, scientists immediately turned to the three countries where starch intake is high—Italy, Japan and China. In the first two countries, coronary disease rates are very low; figures for China are unavailable.

Japan consumed about 78 percent of calories in the form of starch, Italy about 62 percent, and the United States a mere 32 percent. The heart disease death rate per 100,000 in Japan is 100.6; 244 in Italy; and 598.4 in the United States. It is not known whether the starch itself is effective in lowering cholesterol and heart disease incidence, or if the starch merely serves as a cheap substitute for the more expensive, fatty animal proteins. In both Japan and Italy, the per capita protein consumption is about the same as in the United States, but the diet contains much less animal protein and animal fat. In addition, the Italians like the neutral olive oil, and the Japanese use the beneficial fish oils.

In certain countries the diet is low in fatty meats and dairy products but high in carbohydrates (such as grains, cereals and potatoes). Such countries inevitably have extremely low coronary disease rates, perhaps because the diet is basically low in fats and cholesterol. Research emphasizes that the more prosperous and developed countries always have high cholesterol levels and heart attack incidence, whereas the underdeveloped countries do not.

Sugar, too, seems implicated in the overall picture of heart disease; countries which consume large quantities of sugar usually show higher death rates for heart attacks than do the low-sugar-consumption countries. As might be expected, Japan and Italy consume very little sugar in their diet—Japan only 4 percent, Italy 6 percent and the United States a whopping 16 percent.

Conclusion: Definite evidence is lacking to form a clear conclusion; starches and sugars may or may not be involved in the overall picture of heart disease.

PUTTING THE FACTS TOGETHER

From all the welter of facts, speculations and contradictions, certain basic premises appear. The relevant factors surely seem to include (1) high cholesterol, (2) high blood pressure and (3) overweight; it also appears that there is one additional factor, which we'll call the X factor and discuss later.

(1) High cholesterol

The blood consists of corpuscles suspended in a watery fluid. When the blood is allowed to clot, the solid corpuscles are held in the clot and a liquid, which is called the serum, can be separated. Although all portions of the blood contain cholesterol, references in this book to cholesterol levels refer only to the portion of cholesterol in the blood serum.

There is only one way of obtaining a cholesterol reading of one's blood: by having a doctor take a blood sample for analysis. When you are having the test made, be sure to ask for an exact reading, rather than a report that the cholesterol level is "low," "average," or "high." Now, what are the average cholesterol levels of American men? Although there is a wide spread, the average American male has a reading between 225 and 255, but these two figures represent the highest average in the world. To have an average American reading is scarcely any cause for complacency. In Peru, the average is a mere 137; 146 in India; 163 in Japan; and 175 in Italy. In the United States, the average is a rather high 240. These investigations go back a number of years, and even then the investigators were quick to point out that countries with cholesterol averages below 200 had a basic diet of vegetable fats rather than animal fats.

(2) High blood pressure

Scientists agree that there is a close correlation between elevated blood pressure and heart disease. High blood pressure tends to increase the development of atherosclerosis, although the precise reason *why* this occurs is subject to additional confirmation. A fascinating experiment made with animals showed the proof of this theory and also that a variation was

43

true: Where rabbits were free of cholesterol deposits on their arteries, increased blood pressure (artificially produced) did not result in increased cholesterol levels or deposits in the arteries.

Everyone should have his blood pressure checked at reasonable intervals. The fortunate ones will find themselves with low pressure readings; medium pressure is satisfactory; and those with high pressure readings should immediately be placed on their guard to keep weight and cholesterol at normal levels. Normal blood pressure is usually defined as consistently below 140 over 90, whereas 160 (or over) systolic and 95 (or over) diastolic is considered high.

The connection between high blood pressure and heart disease cannot be overlooked. Salt restriction is particularly important in cases of hypertension.

(3) Overweight

As previously noted, some scientists believe that the direct relationship between overweight and heart disease has not been completely proved. Even these dissenters *unanimously* agree that overweight is always *potentially* dangerous and increases the possibility of heart attacks. Weight reduction results in an average lower cholesterol level regardless of the type of diet used to lower weight, so weight should always be kept at the proper level.

It is worth restating that although the reasons why overweight increases the chance of heart disease are not fully known or agreed on, the percentile figures are not in doubt. Assuming that the normal-weight person has a certain mortality rate, one who is overweight has a greatly increased rate. This should give pause to any overweight person, particularly the middle-aged American male. However where an average obese person brings his weight back to normal, the average death rate for heart disease decreases, and his chances of having a heart attack are lessened.

Certain unchangeable factors—heredity, age, sex and previous medical history—plus certain unknown, not completely determined factors such as tobacco, starches and sugar in the diet, exercise, stress and emotion make the sum total of the X factor. Obviously we cannot change what we are; our sex, age and heredity are incontrovertible. The importance of some of the factors has yet to be completely fixed or evaluated. The X factor therefore exists but cannot be included in future discussions pending scientific confirmation.

But the basic, proven dangers are three in number: high cholesterol, high blood pressure, and overweight. Singly, they increase the risk of heart attack; in combination they are truly worrisome.

THE TYPES OF FAT

For several decades, it has been known that the consumption of fats had a definite association with the cholesterol level. However, it was not until 1952 that Dr. Laurance Kinsell, a California research scientist, observed that there was a strong difference between the effects of animal fats and vegetable fats on the cholesterol level. Kinsell found that when patients were placed on diets with vegetable fats predominating, blood cholesterol dropped and consistently remained below those of patients whose diets contained animal fats, the saturated fats. A result of these tests was the speculation that animal fats might contain some component which tended to raise cholesterol levels.

These tests of Kinsell were the important breakthrough which has led to our present-day knowledge concerning the inherent differences between satfats (generally animals fats) and linfats (unsaturated vegetable fats) and their effect on cholesterol. Soon independent researchers all over the world confirmed Kinsell's findings: that satfats have a tendency to increase cholesterol levels, whereas unsaturated fats do not.

The research picture is far from complete. There are no

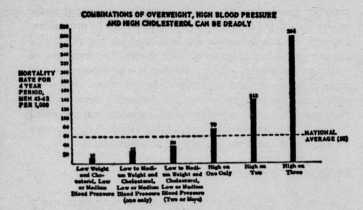

COMBINATIONS OF OVERWEIGHT, HIGH BLOOD PRESSURE AND HIGH CHOLESTEROL CAN BE DEADLY

MORTALITY RATE FOR 4 YEAR PERIOD, MEN 45-62 PER 1,000

NATIONAL AVERAGE (58)

Low Weight and Cholesterol, Low or Medium Blood Pressure — Low to Medium Weight and Cholesterol, Low or Medium Blood Pressure (one only) — Low to Medium Weight and Cholesterol, Low or Medium Blood Pressure (Two or More) — High on One Only — High on Two — High on Three

This chart illustrates the fact that those who have low weight and low cholesterol and low or medium blood pressure have extremely low rates of heart disease incidence. In a 16-year period, the rate will be only 40 in 1,000 or one chance in 25. A person who is high on all three factors is almost certain, statistically, to experience a heart attack. (*Data from the Framingham Report.*)

lifetime studies available because it was only in 1952 that the importance of unsaturated fats was first discovered. Regular, continued tests made by scientists around the globe have proved Kinsell's original point. In checking the value of unsaturated fats, corn oil and fish oils were the ones chiefly used for the experiments. Corn oil is acceptable to the palate of Americans and Europeans; the fish oils are not, being acceptable only to those who are familiar with them, like the Japanese.

Tests tended to show that when corn oil, for example, is added to the normal diet, cholesterol levels are lowered; on the other hand, other experiments indicated that merely *adding* such unsaturated oil does not significantly change the cholesterol level and that corn oil must actually *take the place* of the saturated, animal fat.

Many physicians working on the problem of high cholesterol agree on the fact that the outstanding treatment for atherosclerosis and high cholesterol levels is the *substitution* of unsaturated vegetable fats for saturated fats. It is recognized that the effective lowering of cholesterol by means of unsaturated oils in the diet may be a great step forward in the search for a cure for atherosclerosis, or possibly its prevention, although the precise connection between lowering cholesterol and atherosclerosis is yet to be fully shown. The technique of taking an unsaturated oil into the diet is a correlation of two research advances: first, that diet alone can reduce cholesterol levels, and, second, the potential relationship between high cholesterol and atherosclerosis. It also appears that continued intake of a diet high in both calories and saturated fat increases the cholesterol level and probably atherosclerosis.

TESTING UNSATURATED FATS

Scientists were, of course, anxious to test their newly discovered theories about low-fat low-cholesterol diets not only on healthy individuals but also on those who had experienced heart attacks. Two similar groups of fifty persons each (all with records of previous heart attacks) were checked for eight years. One group of fifty followed their normal diet pattern; the other fifty were placed on a special diet consisting of about 1,600 calories per day with 20-25 grams of fat. Their respective records at the end of three and eight years showed decisively that the low-fat low-cholesterol group had significantly lower mortality rates than had the group following their normal diet pattern.

In another test, three groups were given three different diets: The first group had no meat or dairy products except a small amount of milk; the second group had very moderate amounts of meat and fish plus some cheese and eggs; the third group ate very large amounts of meat and cheese plus two eggs daily. The results showed that the first group (on the vegetable-fat diet) had lower cholesterol levels than those on the high protein, animal-fat diet. The results were somewhat inconclusive on the second diet. From these tests, scientists have continued further in similar directions, and almost all agree that the cholesterol level responds readily to changes in the diet alone.

THE AMERICAN DIET PATTERN

The researchers wondered whether Americans, accustomed to eating as their palates and habits dictated, would change from their usual high saturated fat diet to a diet lower in saturated fats and higher in unsaturated oils, even though it was one that would tend to lower their cholesterol level and prolong their lives. In New York City in the middle 1950's a project was undertaken involving some six hundred men in all walks of life, aged twenty to fifty-nine. This group, called the Anti-Coronary Club, was originated by Dr. Norman Joliffe, a strong campaigner for cutting down on saturated fats. After six months, members in the fifty- to fifty-nine-year category dropped about 30 points from their original cholesterol average of about 250. Similar lowering of the cholesterol level was achieved with younger members, and even those with "normal" averages succeeded in lowering their cholesterol level.

It should be remembered that the normal American standards are considered too high in almost every other country in the world. Similar results, and success in lowering cholesterol by means of unsaturated oils, have been achieved by Dr. Jeremiah Stamler working with the Chicago Board of Health and by Dr. Ancel Keys of the University of Minnesota.

The successful activities of these experimental groups indicate that Americans *can and will* (and often must) change their dietary patterns. According to their relative state of prosperity, Americans have shown an increasing intake of fat calories, so that at the present time, from 40 percent to possibly even 50 percent of all calories consumed are fat.

FAT QUALITY

With the increase in fat consumption that has taken place in the past fifty years or so, there has also come a change in the type and quality of fat consumed. Americans seem to prefer a high-protein high-fat diet. As their ability to pay increases, most people seek richer foods, heavier cream, pastry and ice cream, thick fatty steaks, heavily marbled roasts—all of which

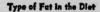

Type of Fat in the Diet

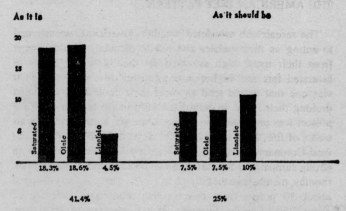

On the left, we see that of a total of 41.4% of fat (in relation to total calories), 18.3% are saturated fats, 18.6% are oleic, and only 4.5% are linoleic acid. According to the various "Anti-Coronary" diets, the total fat intake should be reduced to about 25% of the total caloric intake. Of this lesser percentage, about 7.5% should be saturated, another 7.5% oleic, and 10% of linoleic acid.

are high in saturated fats. Of course, in the process, the intake of unsaturated fats is lowered. Because of these two factors (increased total fat consumption and change of fat quality), Americans today are eating a higher proportion of saturated fats compared with fifty years ago.

From all information currently available, it would appear prudent for any middle-aged adult to lower his intake of saturated fats, particularly if confronted with overweight, high blood pressure or high cholesterol. This means much less butter and cheese, fatty meats and fried foods. But primarily it means revision of eating habits so as to avoid excess quantities of saturated fat in the everyday diet. In addition, for those with high cholesterol levels, it means cooking with unsaturated fat, so as to reduce the cholesterol level. Salt intake must be limited as well.

There are certain foods that Americans will eat, and others they will not. For every American who will eat snails, there are a hundred who will shudder at the very thought. While octopus is an everyday food for many Italians, it is not acceptable food to the average American. Therefore, the American palate must be taken into account in prescribing a diet. Novelties are usually soon abandoned. Inasmuch as we are not proposing a temporary change such as a weight-reducing diet, but rather a more or less permanent change in eating and cooking habits, clearly the change in diet must be suitable and acceptable to the American taste on a long-range basis. As we know from what has gone before, the paramount issue is cutting down on satfat (animal fats) and adding in their stead, linfats (unsaturated vegetable fats with a high iodine number and a high percentage of linoleic acid). And a close secondary issue is the limiting of salt intake.

FINDING A SUITABLE UNSATURATED FAT

Thus it is necessary to find a satisfactory linfat suitable to the American palate and generally available in stores throughout the country. The chart below sets forth the composition of typical fats and oils to which the American consumer has access.

Fat or Oil	Iodine Value	Fatty Acids Saturated	(Percent of total) Oleic	Linoleic
Beef tallow	46.8	48	50	2
Butter	32	55	33	3
Chicken fat	86.5	23	53	24
Cocoa butter	36.6	60	37	3
Coconut oil	9.7	91	7	2
Corn oil	126.8	10	28	53
Cottonseed oil	108	25	21	50
Lard	70	38	46	10
Margarine	39	26	57	9
Olive oil	89.7	11	76	7
Palm oil	53.1	45	40	8
Peanut oil	93	18	47	29
Safflower oil	144	8	15	72
Sunflower oil	131	12	20	63

Source: USDA: *Fatty Acids in Food Fats*

In the chart below, most of the fats are arranged in their order of "iodine number," as previously discussed.

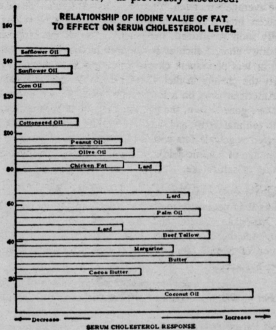

RELATIONSHIP OF IODINE VALUE OF FAT
TO EFFECT ON SERUM CHOLESTEROL LEVEL

160

Safflower Oil
140
Sunflower Oil

Corn Oil
120

Cottonseed Oil
100
Peanut Oil
Olive Oil
80   Chicken Fat   Lard

Lard
60
Palm Oil
Lard   Beef Tallow
40
Margarine
Butter
30   Cocoa Butter

Coconut Oil

◄— Decrease   Increase —►
SERUM CHOLESTEROL RESPONSE

Concerning this chart, it may be said that all oils having iodine numbers above 100 act in the same general way and tend to decrease the cholesterol level. Iodine numbers from 90 to 100 are more or less neutral, having but little effect on cholesterol. However, most oils and fats having iodine numbers below 90 tend to increase cholesterol levels. It should be noted that iodine values do not precisely correlate to the cholesterol response. Note that lard appears at several different places, but the cholesterol-producing effects are not identical. Also, safflower oil has a greater iodine number than corn oil, but it is no more successful in lowering cholesterol.

SAFFLOWER, SUNFLOWER, COTTONSEED, SESAME AND CORN OILS

In the classification above 100 (iodine number), we find

five fats: safflower, sunflower, cottonseed, sesame and corn oils.

Safflower oil is made from the safflower plant and has a very pleasant taste. It is now widely available in most food stores.

Sunflower oil is made by pressing the seeds under great pressure.

Cottonseed oil is produced by pressing the seeds of the cotton plant and is available throughout the country at moderate prices. However, it does contain more than twice as much saturated fat as do corn oil, safflower oil and sunflower oil.

Sesame seed oil is delicious and delicate and in addition has a long shelf life.

Corn oil is obtained from Indian corn (maize) under high pressure. It is generally available in the United States and the price is moderate. During an intensive series of kitchen tests, corn oil performed satisfactorily in all phases of cooking.

THE DAILY DIET OF A PRUDENT PERSON

The average person in the United States consumes about 3,200 calories per day, but wide variations exist among individuals. Our caloric intake is probably too high, since many people are overweight. There is no point in looking at tables for your height, frame or age group; *you* know if you are overweight or not. If you are, reduce your caloric intake promptly. However, this book is not primarily concerned with weight reduction.

On the basis of 3,200 calories per person per day, an average of 40 percent consists of fat, or 1,280 calories. On a reasonable and prudent diet, it is suggested that this amount be cut in half, to about 20 percent or no more than 750 fat calories per day.˙ However, of these fat calories, one-third should be saturated animal fats and two-thirds unsaturated, high linoleic fats. This ratio applied to an average of 750 fat calories would mean that 250 calories should be the maximum of satfat to match the 500 linfat. For those anxious to reduce a high cholesterol level as soon as possible, the ratio might well be reduced to 1 to 3; that is, 185 satfat calories to 565 linfat calories.

There are extremists who might be tempted to consume nothing but unsaturated fats and oils in an effort to lower their cholesterol level as speedily as possible. However, this procedure may be hazardous, and a reasonable diet as suggested above should be followed, including fair proportions of various foods. The basic aim should be (1) cutting down on total fat calories and (2) seeing that of those fat calories, the larger proportion is of the unsaturated type.

HIDDEN AND VISIBLE FATS

As we remarked previously, many foods have obvious, clearly visible fats. Roast beef, for example, is usually trimmed with visible fat. The conscientious dieter carefully cuts away the visible fat and then, with a degree of righteousness, eats the meat, believing it to be pure protein and free of fat. Unfortunately, that is far from true. Even the most meticulously trimmed roast beef or steak, for example, contains 30 to 40 percent invisible fat, as you can verify from the tables at the back of the book. The average hamburger consists of almost 75 percent fat calories, and most cheeses have similar percentages. Egg yolks are high in fat; and so are sweet and sour cream, cream cheese, butter and ordinary margarine, almost all of which are basically saturated fats. Most cakes (even plain Danish pastry), pies, doughnuts and cookies contain about 50 percent fat. So the problem is not simply that of counting the obvious fat calories in butter, ice cream and similar foods. It is not possible to guess. All foods must be checked for their fat content, particularly for the relationship between saturated as opposed to unsaturated fat.

WHAT TO EAT, WHAT NOT TO EAT

Following are the foods that should be eaten with caution because of their high saturated-fat content:

Egg yolks
Meat

Cheese (except skim milk cheese)
Butter and ordinary margarine
Hydrogenated shortenings
Ice cream
Bacon
Coconut
Coconut oil
Lard
Poultry fat
Whole milk
Candy (particularly milk chocolates, caramels, butterscotch)
Cakes and pastries (does not apply to recipes in this book)
Cocoa and chocolate
Popcorn, potato chips and other similar snack foods
Canned luncheon meats
Frankfurters and sausages
Cream soups
Gravies and sauces (except natural meat juices)
Fried foods

Now we'll list foods which contain low amounts of saturated fats:

Fish and shellfish (see note below)
Liquid vegetable oils—corn, safflower, sesame, cottonseed and sunflower
Grains and cereals—oatmeal, barley, cornmeal, farina, rice, wheat flour
Fruits
Vegetables
Nuts (except Brazil nuts and coconuts)
Plain (not creamed) cottage cheese
Farmer cheese and pot cheese
Fruit gelatine desserts

It should be remembered that foods low in saturated fat are not necessarily low in calories. Almost all vegetables are low in fat and low in calories; cereals have no fat but are moderately high in calories. The two lists above have been prepared bearing in mind primarily saturated and unsaturated fats, and the calorie contents vary widely. (Shellfish, although low in saturated fat, has considerable cholesterol.

SOME DEFINITE RECOMMENDATIONS (UNLESS YOUR DOCTOR SUGGESTS A MORE STRINGENT DIET)

Eggs	3 per week (no limit on egg whites).
Fish	5 times a week (including canned tuna, salmon and sardines; be sure to use oil for cooking fish).
Fat meats (beef, lamb, pork)	3-4 times per week (buy the leanest possible meats, trim away all visible fats *before* cooking; a portion of fat meat must be limited to 4 ounces per serving).
Lean meats and poultry (veal, chicken, turkey)	5 times a week.
Organ meats (liver only)	Once a week (other organ meats may be substituted for liver no more than once a month).
Shellfish	Once a week.
Vegetables	Twice a day, raw or cooked; white or sweet potatoes are permitted once daily in addition to green vegetables.
Fruits	Twice a day; try to have some citrus fruit or juice every day.

Milk	2 cups (1 pint) daily of skim milk, or nonfat *dry* skim milk (either mixed as a beverage or used in cooking). Milk companies are now marketing a fortified skim milk which is much more palatable than the ordinary product. Low-fat buttermilk is recommended in place of skim milk, if preferred.
Cheese	Pot cheese, farmer cheese or plain (not creamed) cottage cheese within reason. Cheese made of whole milk or cream (Cheddar, Swiss, cream, Roquefort, Camembert, etc.) only once or twice a week and only 1-ounce servings. Skim milk cheese (such as some Edam, Gouda, mozzarella, ricotta) twice a week.
Cereals and Breads	At any meal, you can have white, brown or wild rice (but not if potatoes are served). At breakfast, hot cereals or prepared cold cereals with skim milk. Four slices of bread daily (white, rye, whole grain); Italian breads particularly recommended; use liquid-oil margarine on bread.
Fats and oils	*Be sure to incorporate at least 1 ounce of a proper liquid oil in the diet every day*—in salad dressings, as a cooking or baking oil. Limit carefully your intake of butter, ordinary margarine and hydrogenated shortenings. Margarine may be regularly used as a table spread, on cereals or vegetables, or in cooking.

A Few Words About Low-Fat Foods

Special Margarine. Be sure the margarine you buy contains *liquid* oil and is polyunsaturated. Some of the liquid-oil margarines now on the market are hydrogenated, so be very careful before buying your margarine to read the label to be certain the margarine is only partially hydrogenated. This means the margarine contains liquid oil. Buy unsalted margarine if available.

Dry *cottage cheese* means uncreamed cottage cheese. If it is unobtainable, rinse creamed cottage cheese under cold running water, then squeeze dry.

Nonfat *evaporated milk* is available in many supermarkets and may be used like any other nonfat milk. It is particularly good in coffee.

Nonfat *dry milk powder*, mixed with only half the water specified on the package, makes a good substitute for cream. In the recipes, if liquid skim milk is called for, you may use nonfat dry milk powder mixed with the amount of water the package directs.

A note about the calorie and fat content of each recipe: All the figures represent the various counts for each individual serving as specified at the end of the recipe. The grams set forth for each portion should be closely followed for the most satisfactory results. Don't be disturbed by the fact that the combination of saturated fat and polyunsaturated fat contents does not always equal the total fat content; this discrepancy, if it occurs, is caused by the presence of other fats not relevant to our problem.

Some Hints for the Husband.

As a rule, you'll be eating breakfast and dinner at home but having your lunch at a restaurant during weekdays. It should be easy to follow your diet pattern from the restaurant's menu. After a little practice, it will become second nature to choose the low-fat items.

To help you get started, here are some suggestions:

Appetizers: Celery and radishes; grapefruit, melon, fresh fruit cup; tomato, grapefruit or sauerkraut juice; sardines or salmon or tuna.

Soups: Clear soups; vegetable soup; clam broth.

Main Courses: Any kind of broiled or baked fish; all lamb dishes; broiled or boiled chicken; roast squab; veal; turkey; minute steak; vegetable plate (no creamed vegetables); sardine, salmon or tuna fish salad; cottage cheese and fruit salad.

Sandwich Lunches: No butter on the bread, but mayonnaise is acceptable. Choice of sliced chicken, sardines, tuna fish, salmon, tomato and lettuce, sliced turkey, lean roast beef.

Vegetables: Boiled or baked potatoes; any kind of vegetable provided it is not prepared with butter, ordinary margarine, or sauces.

Salads: Any kind, but no cream dressings. Olive oil, French dressings and mayonnaise are permitted.

Desserts: Any kind of fruit (melon, grapefruit, etc.); water ices; angel-food cake; baked apple; applesauce; gelatine desserts; stewed fruit, sponge cake.

Beverage: Coffee (no cream) with milk, if desired; tea with milk, if desired.

Some Hints for the Wife

Don't consider this a diet book, to be used temporarily. It is intended to introduce you to a new method of cooking, much like your former procedure but with a few significant changes. This is not a fad diet, or necessarily a weight-reduction diet, but rather a method of cooking which takes advantage of recent important discoveries with respect to fats. There is no reason to wait any longer for additional discoveries or findings in the field of human nutrition. We are not proposing anything that is not completely healthful and absolutely safe. We shall be cooking our customary dishes but merely limiting the intake of saturated fats and of salt.

This book uses liquid oils, rather than the solid shortenings often called for, so that we may incorporate linoleic acid in the diet.

Although there are some small changes and substitutions in this book from usual cooking methods, these are of minor importance and may easily be followed. You'll find that the finished dishes will be delicious and appetizing to your family.

Before each recipe section you'll find some suggestions. These should be closely followed for best results. Once you learn the procedure, it will become second nature, and you'll never want to cook any other way.

Special Oil and Special Margarine

THE RECIPES that follow specify *special oil* and *special margarine* as shortening.

By *special oil* is meant any of the vegetable oils with iodine numbers above 100, described on pages 53 through 55: safflower, sunflower, cottonseed, sesame and corn oils.

By *special margarine* is meant a vegetable margarine containing liquid corn oil, which is polyunsaturated, as described on page 60.

The important linoleic content of cooking oil is best preserved by seeing that it does not become so hot that it smokes or burns. Bring up heat gently, because this will help prevent it from overheating. Do not reuse frying oils that have been overheated or used overly long, for they become rancid and unpleasant to the taste. Reheating oil also has the effect of making it saturated, thereby destroying its benefits.

RECOMMENDED DAILY ALLOWANCE OF FATS:

Total Calories in Diet	Oleic Acid (grams)	Saturated Fatty Acids (grams)	Linoleic Acid (grams)
1,500	12.5	12.5	16.7
2,000	16.7	16.7	22.2
2,500	20.8	20.8	27.8
3,000	25.0	25.0	33.3

Salt-restricted diets

Unless your doctor has placed you on a salt-free 500- or 1,000-milligram sodium diet, you can use the recipes in this book, for they are written with the mild salt-restriction requirement in mind.

THE LOW SALT, LOW CHOLESTEROL COOKBOOK

Appetizers

FOR everyday meals, be sure to have a large bowl of radishes, sliced cucumbers and celery. If you serve any dips or spreads, don't serve potato chips with them, unless you're sure they've been fried in corn oil or other liquid oils.

Avoid egg mixtures or stuffed egg hors d'oeuvres because egg yolks should be eaten only in limited quantities. Although shellfish are not recommended for main courses more often than once a week, they can be used in moderation in appetizers, and you will find a number of shellfish appetizer recipes in the following pages.

POPPY SEED COCKTAIL WAFERS

1/3 cup poppy seeds
1/3 cup boiling water
2 cups sifted flour
1/2 teaspoon salt
1/8 teaspoon cayenne pepper

1 teaspoon baking powder
1/3 cup special oil
1 egg, beaten
1/3 cup minced onions

Soak the poppy seeds in the boiling water until cold. Sift together the flour, salt, cayenne pepper and baking powder. Work in the oil, egg, onions and undrained poppy seeds. Knead lightly until smooth.

Roll out the dough 1/8 inch thick on a lightly floured surface. Cut into 1-1/2-inch rounds. Arrange on a cookie sheet. Sprinkle with additional poppy seeds, if you like. Bake in a 425° oven 15 minutes or until browned. Serve warm or cold.

Makes about 48.

Per wafer
Calories 20
Saturated fat 0.3 gram
Polyunsaturated fat 1.2 grams
Total fat 2.0 grams

STUFFED CELERY PINWHEELS

1 bunch celery
1/2 cup dry cottage cheese
3 tablespoons buttermilk

1/4 teaspoon salt
2 tablespoons minced chives
2 tablespoons minced pimentos

Wash the celery, cut off the leaves and remove outside stalks. Carefully separate the stalks and keep in order, as they will be put together again.

Beat the cheese, buttermilk and salt until smooth. Blend in the chives and pimentos. Spread in the hollows of the celery and rebuild stalk. Wrap firmly in waxed paper or aluminum foil and chill 2 hours. Cut in 1/2-inch slices.

NOTE: If you don't want pinwheels, just fill the stalks.

Makes about 20 pieces.

Per piece
Calories 10
Saturated fat 0.0 gram
Polyunsaturated fat 0.0 gram
Total fat 0.5 gram

STUFFED CUCUMBER SLICES

1 cucumber
1/2 cup tuna fish
1 tablespoon mayonnaise

1 teaspoon grated onion
1/2 teaspoon lemon juice
1/8 teaspoon white pepper

Select a straight long cucumber.

Peel the cucumber and scoop out the center with a vegetable corer. Mash the tuna fish fine; mix with the mayonnaise, onion, lemon juice and pepper. Stuff the hollow and chill. Cut into 1/2-inch slices.

Makes about 10 pieces.

Per piece
Calories 40
Saturated fat 0.4 gram
Polyunsaturated fat 1.1 grams
Total fat 1.8 grams

CHEESE-CARROT BALLS

3/4 cup dry cottage cheese
2 tablespoons buttermilk
1/2 cup grated carrots

1/2 teaspoon salt
3 drops Tabasco
Minced parsley

Beat the cheese and buttermilk until smooth. Blend in the carrots, salt and Tabasco. Chill 30 minutes. Form teaspoons of the mixture into balls and roll in parsley. Chill again. Pierce with cocktail picks.

Makes about 36.

Per ball
Calories 8
Saturated fat 0.0 gram
Polyunsaturated fat 0.0 gram
Total fat 0.0 gram

TUNA CANAPES

1 7-3/4-ounce can tuna fish
1 tablespoon anchovy paste
1/3 cup chopped tomatoes
1/3 cup chopped green peppers

1/8 teaspoon Worcestershire sauce
3 tablespoons Russian dressing
8 slices toast, quartered

Drain and mash the tuna fish. Blend in the anchovy paste, tomatoes, green peppers, Worcestershire sauce and Russian dressing. Heap on the toast.

Makes 32.

Per canapé
Calories 30
Saturated fat 0.4 gram
Polyunsaturated fat 1.0 gram
Total fat 2.0 grams

CRAB MEAT SPREAD

1/2 pound crab meat
1/2 cup dry cottage cheese
2 tablespoons buttermilk

2 tablespoons dry sherry
1/4 teaspoon salt
1/8 teaspoon white pepper

Remove any cartilage from the crab meat; chop fine. Beat the cheese, buttermilk, sherry, salt and pepper until smooth. Blend in the crab meat. Heap in a bowl.

Makes about 1-3/4 cups; allow 2 tablespoons per serving.

Per serving
Calories 30
Saturated fat 0.1 gram
Polyunsaturated fat 0.1 gram
Total fat 0.2 gram

MUSHROOM SPREAD

2 tablespoons special oil
1/4 cup chopped onions
1/2 pound sliced mushrooms
1/2 teaspoon salt

1/4 teaspoon freshly ground
    black pepper
2 tablespoons minced parsley

Heat the oil in a skillet; sauté the onions 5 minutes. Add the mushrooms, salt and pepper; sauté 5 minutes. Stir in the parsley. Chop to a paste and chill.

Makes about 1 cup; allow 2 tablespoons per serving

Per serving
Calories 40
Saturated fat 1.0 gram
Polyunsaturated fat 2.0 grams
Total fat 3.0 grams

EGGPLANT SPREAD

1 medium-sized eggplant
3 tablespoons special oil
3/4 cup minced onions
3/4 cup minced green peppers
1 clove garlic, minced
1-1/2 cups peeled chopped
    tomatoes

3/4 teaspoon salt
1/4 teaspoon freshly ground
    black pepper
1/4 teaspoon oregano

Wash the eggplant and wrap in aluminum foil. Bake in a 425° oven 25 minutes. Peel and dice fine.

Heat the oil in a skillet; sauté the onions and green peppers 10 minutes. Add the garlic and eggplant; sauté 5 minutes. Mix in the tomatoes, salt, pepper and oregano; cook over low heat 25 minutes, stirring frequently. Chill.

Makes about 4 cups; allow 4 tablespoons per serving.

Per serving
Calories 40
Saturated fat 0.3 gram
Polyunsaturated fat 1.4 grams
Total fat 2.7 grams

EGGPLANT CAVIAR

1 medium-sized eggplant
1/2 cup diced onions
3/4 cup peeled diced tomatoes
1/2 slice white bread
3 tablespoons cider vinegar

3 tablespoons special oil
1 teaspoon salt
1/2 teaspoon freshly ground
  black pepper
1/4 teaspoon sugar

Wash the eggplant and wrap in aluminum foil. Bake in a 425° oven 45 minutes or until tender. Open foil after 20 minutes' baking time. Peel the eggplant and cool.

Chop the onion very fine; add the eggplant, tomatoes and the bread soaked with the vinegar. Chop fine, then blend in the oil, salt, pepper and sugar. Chill. Serve with pumpernickel.

Makes about 3 cups; allow 4 tablespoons per serving.

Per serving
Calories 50
Saturated fat 0.4 gram
Polyunsaturated fat 1.9 grams
Total fat 3.5 grams

CHOPPED CHICKEN LIVER SPREAD

1/2 pound chicken livers
1 whole onion
2 tablespoons special
  margarine
3/4 cup chopped onions

3 tablespoons chicken broth
1/2 teaspoon salt
1/4 teaspoon freshly ground
  black pepper
2 teaspoons cognac

Wash the livers, remove any discolored areas and cover with water. Add the whole onion; bring to a boil and cook over low heat 5 minutes. Drain.

Melt the margarine in a skillet; sauté the chopped onions until lightly browned. Add the broth; cook 1 minute. Use a blender for the livers and onions and run machine until smooth or chop the livers and onions very fine; blend in the salt, pepper and cognac. Pack into a mold or bowl and chill.

Makes about 1-1/2 cups; allow 2 tablespoons per serving.

Per serving
Calories 70
Saturated fat 0.7 gram
Polyunsaturated fat 0.9 gram
Total fat 2.8 grams

LIPTAUR CHEESE

1 cup dry cottage cheese
1/4 cup buttermilk
2 tablespoons special oil
2 teaspoons anchovy paste

2 teaspoons grated onion
1/2 teaspoon dry mustard
1 teaspoon paprika
2 tablespoons chopped capers

Beat together until smooth the cottage cheese, buttermilk, oil and anchovy paste. Stir in the onion, mustard, paprika and capers. Heap in a bowl and chill.

Makes about 1-1/4 cups; allow 2 tablespoons per serving.

Per serving
Calories 50
Saturated fat 0.4 gram
Polyunsaturated fat 1.7 grams
Total fat 3.1 grams

SARDINE DIP

3/4 cup dry cottage cheese
3 tablespoons buttermilk
2 3-1/4-ounce cans skinless and
    boneless sardines
3 tablespoons grated onions

1-1/2 teaspoons prepared
    mustard
1/4 teaspoon freshly ground
    black pepper
2 teaspoons lemon juice

Beat the cottage cheese and buttermilk until smooth. Mash the sardines and add with the onions, mustard, pepper and lemon juice. Mix until smooth.

Makes about 2 cups; allow 2 tablespoons per serving.

Per serving
Calories 50
Saturated fat 0.3 gram
Polyunsaturated fat 0.5 gram
Total fat 1.2 grams

SHRIMP-CHEESE DIP

1 cup dry cottage cheese
1/3 cup buttermilk
3 tablespoons chili sauce
1 tablespoon grated onions
1/2 teaspoon lemon juice

1/2 teaspoon Worcestershire sauce
1 cup finely chopped cooked shrimp

Beat the cottage cheese, buttermilk, chili sauce, onions, lemon juice and Worcestershire sauce until smooth and well blended. Mix in the shrimp. Heap in a bowl. Serve with crisp crackers or toast fingers.

Makes 2-1/3 cups; allow 4 tablespoons per serving.

Per serving
Calories 40
Saturated fat 0.1 gram
Polyunsaturated fat 0.2 gram
Total fat 0.3 gram

CLAM-CHEESE DIP

1 7-ounce can minced clams
1 cup dry cottage cheese
2 teaspoons lemon juice

1/8 teaspoon Tabasco
1/8 teaspoon minced garlic
3 tablespoons buttermilk

Drain the clams, reserving 1/4 cup juice. Mix together the cottage cheese, lemon juice, Tabasco, garlic, buttermilk and clam juice. Stir in the clams. Heap in a bowl.

Makes 2 cups; allow 4 tablespoons per serving.

Per serving
Calories 40
Saturated fat 0.1 gram
Polyunsaturated fat 0.2 gram
Total fat 0.3 gram

GUACAMOLE (Avocado Dip)

1 avocado
3 tablespoons minced onions
1/4 cup peeled chopped tomatoes

3/4 teaspoon salt
1-1/2 teaspoons chili powder
2 teaspoons cider vinegar

Cut the avocado in half lengthwise; scoop out the pulp and reserve the shells, if desired. Chop the avocado, onions, tomatoes, salt, chili powder and vinegar until fine and well blended. Heap in the shells or a bowl; if you plan to keep the dip for a while before serving, place the avocado pit in the center to keep the mix from darkening.

Makes about 1-1/4 cups; allow 2 tablespoons per serving.

Per serving
Calories 60
Saturated fat 1.8 grams
unsaturated fat 0.7 gram
Total fat 6.0 grams

AVOCADO-CHEESE DIP

1 cup dry cottage cheese
1/4 cup buttermilk
1 avocado
2 tablespoons lemon juice
1/2 teaspoon salt

1/8 teaspoon Worcestershire sauce
1/4 cup minced scallions (green onions)

Beat the cottage cheese and buttermilk until smooth. Cut the avocado in half lengthwise and scoop out the pulp; mash smooth. Combine with the cottage cheese, lemon juice, salt, Worcestershire sauce and scallions, mixing until well blended.

Makes about 2 cups; allow 2 tablespoons per serving.

Per serving
Calories 60
Saturated fat 1.1 grams
Polyunsaturated fat 0.4 gram
Total fat 3.8 grams

CHEESE DIP

2 cups pot cheese
1 tablespoon Roquefort cheese
1/4 cup buttermilk
1 tablespoon minced parsley

1 tablespoon minced chives or
    scallions (green onions)
1 tablespoon minced capers
1 teaspoon paprika

Combine the pot cheese, Roquefort cheese and buttermilk in a blender or force through a sieve. Blend in the parsley, chives, capers and paprika. Serve with Melba toast or crackers.

Makes about 2 cups; allow 2 tablespoons per serving.

Per serving
Calories 30
Saturated fat 0.3 gram
Polyunsaturated fat 0.0 gram
Total fat 0.6 gram

CAVIAR DIP

1 cup dry cottage cheese
1 cup buttermilk

2 teaspoons grated onion
1/4 cup black or red caviar

Beat the cottage cheese and buttermilk until smooth; chill 1 hour. Mix in the onion and caviar.

Makes about 2 cups; allow 2 tablespoons per serving.

Per serving
Calories 40
Saturated fat 0.4 gram
Polyunsaturated fat 1.3 grams
Total fat 1.7 grams

ITALIAN-STYLE BOILED CHESTNUTS

1 pound chestnuts   1/2 teaspoon salt
4 bay leaves

Cut a crisscross on the top (pointed end) of the chestnuts. Cover with water; add the bay leaves and salt and bring to a boil. Cook over medium heat 20 minutes or until tender. Drain well.

Serve as a cocktail accompaniment, either in the shell or shelled.

Allow 5 chestnuts per serving.

Per serving
Calories 60
Saturated fat 0.2 gram
Polyunsaturated fat 0.3 gram
Total fat 0.8 gram

Soups

SOUPS are satisfying and filling, but it is necessary to be on guard against fats. This is particularly true if the soup has a meat or chicken base because the cooking process releases fats into the soup. As excess animal fats must be particularly avoided, it is necessary to remove these fats by any one of the following methods.

1. The most efficient way is to prepare the soup earlier in the day, then chill for at least four hours in the refrigerator. The fat will congeal on the surface, where it may readily be lifted off. To hasten the process, place the soup in a bowl and put over ice water before placing in the refrigerator.

2. A few lettuce or cabbage leaves placed on the soup will absorb some of the excess fat. Repeat several times with fresh leaves.

3. Place several ice cubes in the warm soup; the fat will adhere to them. Remove and then repeat with more ice cubes.

4. Skim the surface of the soup carefully with a large soup spoon to remove the visible fat.

CHICKEN SOUP

9 cups water
1 4-5-pound fowl
1 onion
3 stalks celery
6 sprigs parsley
2 leeks

1 carrot, quartered
1 turnip, peeled and sliced
1 parsnip
1 teaspoon salt
8 whole peppercorns, gently
   bruised

Have the butcher give you some extra chicken feet and necks. Remove all the visible fat from the chicken; skin the chicken feet. Combine the water, chicken, feet and necks in a saucepan; bring to a boil and carefully skim the top. Add the onion, celery, parsley, leeks, carrot, turnip, parsnip, salt and peppercorns. Cover and cook over low heat 3 hours.

Remove the chicken and use in other dishes. Strain the soup, chill and remove all the fat.

Serves 6.

Per serving
Calories 40
Saturated fat 0.0 gram
Polyunsaturated fat 0.0 gram
Total fat 0.0 gram
(if carefully skimmed)

BEEF BROTH

2 veal knuckles
4 pounds beef (plate, flank,
    brisket, shin, etc.)
4 quarts water
2 onions

2 stalks celery
1 parsnip
6 sprigs parsley
1-1/2 teaspoons salt
4 cracked peppercorns

Have the veal knuckles cracked. Trim excess fat from meat.
Combine the meat, bones and water in a saucepan. Bring to a
boil, cover and cook over low heat 1-1/2 hours. Add the
onions, celery, parsnip, parsley, salt and peppercorns. Recover
and cook 1-1/2 hours longer. Remove meat and bones and
strain soup. Cool and chill. Carefully remove congealed fat.
Reheat and serve as consommé or use as base of other soups.

Makes about 3 quarts; allow 1 cup per serving.

Per serving
Calories 80
Saturated fat 0.0 gram
Polyunsaturated fat 0.0 gram
Total fat 0.0 gram
(if carefully skimmed)

CHICKEN GUMBO

2 tablespoons special oil
1/2 cup chopped onions
1/2 cup chopped green peppers
4 cups chicken broth
1-1/2 cups canned tomatoes
1 bay leaf
1/8 teaspoon powdered thyme

1-1/2 cups sliced fresh or frozen okra
3/4 teaspoon salt
1/4 teaspoon freshly ground black pepper
1/2 cup cooked rice
1 cup diced cooked chicken

Heat the oil in a saucepan; sauté the onions 10 minutes. Add the green peppers, broth, tomatoes, bay leaf and thyme. Bring to a boil, add the okra, salt and pepper, and cook over low heat 15 minutes. Stir in the rice and chicken. Heat and serve.

Serves 6.

Per serving
Calories 135
Saturated fat 0.7 gram
Polyunsaturated fat 2.7 grams
Total fat 5.1 grams

CHINESE CHICKEN GIBLET SOUP

1/2 pound chicken livers
1/4 pound chicken gizzards
2 teaspoons cornstarch
2 tablespoons soy sauce
2 tablespoons special oil
1/2 teaspoon sugar
1/4 teaspoon freshly ground black pepper

6 cups hot chicken broth
1 pound spinach, washed, drained and shredded or
1 package frozen spinach, thawed and chopped
1 teaspoon powdered ginger

Wash the livers, removing any discolored areas; cut in half. Wash and scrape the gizzards; cut away any fat, then cut crosswise in thin slices. Toss the livers and gizzards with the cornstarch and soy sauce.

Heat the oil in a saucepan; add the liver mixture and cook 1 minute. Add the sugar, pepper, broth, spinach and ginger. Cover loosely and cook over low heat 30 minutes.

Serves 6.

Per serving
Calories 150
Saturated fat 1.3 grams
Polyunsaturated fat 3.3 grams
Total fat 6.9 grams

SUBGUM SOUP

2 teaspoons special oil
1/2 cup sliced celery
1/2 cup sliced mushrooms
4 water chestnuts, diced

1/2 cup bean sprouts
1/2 cup diced cooked chicken
6 cups chicken broth
1 egg, beaten

Heat the oil in a saucepan; cook the celery and mushrooms in it 2 minutes. Stir in the water chestnuts, bean sprouts, chicken and chicken broth; cook over low heat 10 minutes. Add the egg gradually, mixing steadily all the while to prevent lumps from forming. The soup will have ribbons of egg in it. Don't overcook; serve promptly.

Serves 6.

Per serving
Calories 125
Saturated fat 0.6 gram
Polyunsaturated fat 1.0 gram
Total fat 2.7 grams

POTAGE SANTE

1 tablespoon special oil
2 cups sliced scallions (green
  onions) or leeks
1 cup sliced onions
2 cups sliced potatoes
1 cup chopped sorrel or
  spinach

1/4 cup chopped parsley
5 cups beef broth
1 cup skim milk
1/4 teaspoon white pepper
1 teaspoon Worcestershire
  sauce

Heat the oil in a saucepan; sauté the scallions and onions 10 minutes but do not let brown. Add the potatoes, spinach, parsley and broth. Bring to a boil and cook over low heat 30 minutes. Purée in an electric blender or force through a sieve. Stir in the milk, pepper and Worcestershire sauce.

Makes about 8 cups.

Per cup
Calories 100
Saturated fat 0.3 gram
Polyunsaturated fat 1.0 gram
Total fat 1.9 grams

ITALIAN SPINACH SOUP

1 package frozen spinach
2 tablespoons special oil
1/4 cup minced onions
1 clove garlic, minced
1 teaspoon salt

1/4 teaspoon white pepper
1/8 teaspoon nutmeg
6 cups water
3 tablespoons cornmeal

Cook the spinach as package directs; drain and purée in an electric blender or force through a sieve.

Heat the oil in a saucepan; sauté the onions and garlic 5 minutes. Blend in the salt, pepper and nutmeg. Add the spinach and water; bring to a rolling boil and stir in the cornmeal. Cook over low heat 30 minutes, stirring frequently.

Serves 6.

Per serving
Calories 50
Saturated fat 0.6 gram
Polyunsaturated fat 2.7 grams
Total fat 4.9 grams

PUREE OF PEA SOUP

1-1/2 cups split peas
6 cups water
1 tablespoon special
  margarine
1/2 cup chopped onions
1 carrot, grated

2 leeks, sliced
1 teaspoon salt
1/4 teaspoon white pepper
1 teaspoon sugar
1 bay leaf

Wash the peas, cover with water, and bring to a boil. Drain, add the 6 cups water, and bring to a boil. Cover and cook over low heat 1-1/2 hours. While the peas are cooking, melt the margarine in a skillet; sauté the onions, carrot and leeks 10 minutes, stirring frequently. Add to the split peas with the salt, pepper, sugar and bay leaf. Cook 30 minutes longer or until peas are very tender. Discard bay leaf and purée in an electric blender or force through a sieve.

Serves 6.

Per serving
Calories 205
Saturated fat 0.4 gram
Polyunsaturated fat 0.6 gram
Total fat 2.1 grams

CREAM OF TOMATO SOUP

2 tablespoons special
  margarine
1/2 cup sliced onions
1/2 cup sliced carrots
1 20-ounce can tomatoes

1 teaspoon salt
2 teaspoons sugar
1/8 teaspoon nutmeg
1 tablespoon flour
1 cup skim milk

Melt the margarine in a skillet; sauté the onions and carrots 5 minutes. In a saucepan, combine the sautéed vegetables, the tomatoes, salt, sugar and nutmeg. Bring to a boil and cook over low heat 30 minutes. Purée in an electric blender or force through a sieve. Return to the saucepan. Mix the flour and milk until smooth. Add to the soup, stirring constantly to the boiling point. Cook over low heat 5 minutes.

Serves 4.

Per serving
Calories 105
Saturated fat 1.2 grams
Polyunsaturated fat 1.6 grams
Total fat 5.5 grams

CREAM OF MUSHROOM SOUP

2 tablespoons special
    margarine
1/2 pound mushrooms, chopped
1/4 cup chopped onions
5 cups chicken broth

2 tablespoons fine barley
1/4 teaspoon white pepper
1/4 cup nonfat dry milk powder
1/4 cup cold water

Melt the margarine in a saucepan; sauté the mushrooms and onions 5 minutes. Add the broth, bring to a boil; stir in the barley and pepper. Cook over low heat 30 minutes or until barley is tender. Mix the dry milk with the water and stir into the soup; cook 2 minutes. For a smooth soup, purée in an electric blender.

Serves 6.

Per serving
Calories 100
Saturated fat 0.8 gram
Polyunsaturated fat 1.1 grams
Total fat 3.7 grams

ONION SOUP

1 tablespoon special oil
5 cups thinly sliced onions
6 cups beef broth
1/4 teaspoon white pepper

2 tablespoons grated
Parmesan cheese or
4 tablespoons grated
sapsago cheese

Heat the oil in a saucepan; sauté the onions over very low heat, until golden brown and soft. Stir frequently. Add the broth and pepper. Cook over low heat 45 minutes. Divide among 6 individual ovenproof tureens or bowls. Sprinkle with the cheese and place in a preheated 425° oven for 5 minutes.

Serves 6.

Per serving
Calories 175
Saturated fat 1.1 grams
Polyunsaturated fat 1.3 grams
Total fat 3.6 grams

TUSCAN BEAN SOUP

2 cups dried white beans
2 quarts water
2 tablespoons special oil
1/2 cup minced onions

2 cloves garlic, minced
1 teaspoon salt
1/2 teaspoon white pepper
3 tablespoons minced parsley

Wash the beans, cover with water and bring to a boil; let soak 1 hour. Drain and combine with the 2 quarts water. Bring to a boil and cook over low heat 3 hours. Purée half the beans in an electric blender or force through a sieve. Return to the saucepan.

Heat the oil in a skillet; sauté the onions and garlic 5 minutes. Add to the soup with the salt, pepper and parsley. Cook 5 minutes.

Serves 8.

Per serving
Calories 195
Saturated fat 0.5 gram
Polyunsaturated fat 2.0 grams
Total fat 3.7 grams

MINESTRA

1/2 cup chopped onions
1/2 cup coarsely grated carrots
2 stalks celery, sliced
2 leeks, sliced
2 tablespoons special oil
6 cups boiling water
1 teaspoon salt
1 cup green beans, sliced

2 cups diced cabbage
1 bay leaf
1/8 teaspoon oregano
1 cup diced potatoes
1 tomato, peeled and diced
2 tablespoons minced parsley
1 clove garlic, minced

Sauté the onions, carrots, celery and leeks in the oil until lightly browned. Add the water, salt, beans, cabbage, bay leaf and oregano. Bring to a boil, cover and cook over low heat 30 minutes. Add the potatoes and tomato; cook 20 minutes. Stir in the parsley and garlic; cook 10 minutes longer. Serve with grated sapsago cheese if desired.

Serves 4.

Per serving
Calories 95
Saturated fat 0.8 gram
Polyunsaturated fat 4.0 grams
Total fat 6.9 grams

PUREE OF LENTIL SOUP

2 cups lentils
2-1/2 quarts water
1 onion
2 tablespoons special oil

3/4 cup chopped onions
1 teaspoon salt
2 teaspoons curry powder
1/2 cup skim milk

Wash the lentils thoroughly. Combine in a saucepan with the water and onion; bring to a boil, cover loosely, and cook over low heat 2 hours. While the lentils are cooking, heat the oil in a skillet; sauté the onions 10 minutes. Add to the lentils with the salt and curry powder; cook 30 minutes longer, or until the lentils are tender. Purée in an electric blender or force through a sieve. Return to the saucepan and stir in the milk. Heat.

Serves 8.

Per serving
Calories 140
Saturated fat 0.6 gram
Polyunsaturated fat 2.2 grams
Total fat 4.2 grams

CHINESE CORN SOUP

2 tablespoons special oil
1/2 cup minced onions
1 clove garlic, minced
6 cups chicken broth
1-1/2 cups corn kernels, fresh,
   frozen or canned
1/2 teaspoon sugar
1/4 teaspoon freshly ground
   black pepper

1 teaspoon powdered ginger
1 tablespoon cornstarch
2 tablespoons soy sauce
2 tablespoons water
2 eggs
2 scallions (green onions),
   thinly sliced

Heat the oil in a saucepan; sauté the onions and garlic 2 minutes. Add the broth, bring to a boil, and mix in the corn kernels, sugar, pepper and ginger. Cover and cook over low heat 15 minutes. Mix the cornstarch, soy sauce and water together; stir into the soup until thickened. Beat the eggs with the scallions; stir into the soup until set. Don't overcook.

Serves 6.

Per serving
Calories 160
Saturated fat 1.2 grams
Polyunsaturated fat 2.8 grams
Total fat 6.5 grams

CHICKEN LIVER, PEA AND NOODLE SOUP

1/4 cup fine egg noodles
1 cup shelled green peas or
  1/2 package frozen

6 chicken livers
1 tablespoon special oil
4 cups chicken broth

Cook the noodles 2 minutes less than package directs. Drain well. Cook the peas in salted water until tender but firm. Wash the livers, removing any discolored spots; dice the livers. Heat the oil in skillet; sauté the livers 3 minutes.

In a saucepan combine the noodles, peas, livers and broth. Heat.

Serves 4.

Per serving
Calories 145
Saturated fat 0.9 gram
Polyunsaturated fat 2.5 grams
Total fat 4.8 grams

CHINESE FISH SOUP

3/4 pound fillet of sole
1-1/2 tablespoons soy sauce
1-1/2 tablespoons dry sherry
2 tablespoons special oil
6 cups chicken broth
1/4 cup raw rice

1/2 cup chopped onions
1/2 cup thinly sliced celery
1/2 cup grated carrots
1/4 teaspoon white pepper
2 scallions (green onions)
  sliced very thin

Wash the fillets and cut crosswise in narrow pieces; toss with the soy sauce, sherry and oil. Let stand in the refrigerator 1 hour before using.

Bring the broth to a boil; stir in the rice. Cover and cook over low heat 20 minutes. Mix in the onions, celery, carrots, white pepper and scallions. Cook 5 minutes. Add the fish; cover and cook 15 minutes.

Serves 6.

Per serving
Calories 210
Saturated fat 0.7 gram
Polyunsaturated fat 3.0 grams
Total fat 5.2 grams

MANHATTAN CLAM CHOWDER

18 clams or 2 cans minced
   clams
2 tablespoons special oil
1 cup chopped onions
1 cup diced celery
1/2 cup grated carrots
1/2 cup chopped green peppers
2 cups boiling water

2 cups bottled clam juice
1 cup canned tomatoes
1 cup diced potatoes
1/4 teaspoon freshly ground
   black pepper
1/2 teaspoon thyme
1 tablespoon cornstarch
1 tablespoon water

If fresh clams are used, scrub and open them. Chop or grind, reserving the juice. If canned clams are used, drain, reserving the juice.

Heat the oil in a saucepan; sauté the onions, celery, carrots and green peppers 10 minutes, stirring frequently. Add the boiling water, bottled and reserved clam juice and the tomatoes; cook over low heat 10 minutes. Add the potatoes, pepper and thyme; cook 20 minutes. Mix in the clams; cook 10 minutes. Mix the cornstarch with the water; stir into the soup until thickened.

Serves 6.

Per serving
Calories 90
Saturated fat 0.7 gram
Polyunsaturated fat 3.1 grams
Total fat 5.3 grams

NEW ENGLAND FISH CHOWDER

2 tablespoons special oil
1/2 cup chopped onions
1 pound cod, halibut or
   similar fish, cubed
3 cups bottled clam juice

1 cup diced potatoes
1/4 teaspoon white pepper
2 cups hot skim milk
1 tablespoon minced parsley

Heat the oil in a saucepan; sauté the onions 10 minutes but do not let brown. Add the fish; cook 1 minute. Add the clam juice, potatoes and pepper. Bring to a boil and cook over low heat 20 minutes. Stir in the milk and parsley; heat but do not let boil.

Serves 6.

Per serving
Calories 150
Saturated fat 1.1 grams
Polyunsaturated fat 4.2 grams
Total fat 6.8 grams

TOMATO MADRILÉNE

1 envelope (tablespoon) gelatin
1-1/4 cups beef broth

3 cups tomato juice
1/4 teaspoon white pepper

Soften the gelatin in 1/2 cup cold broth. Heat the remaining broth and stir in the gelatin until dissolved. Add the tomato juice and pepper. Chill until jellied, about 5 hours.

Serves 4.

Per serving
Calories 35
Saturated fat 0.0 gram
Polyunsaturated fat 0.0 gram
Total fat 0.0 gram

GAZPACHO

2 pounds ripe tomatoes,
   peeled
3/4 cup diced onions
3/4 cup diced green peppers
2 cloves garlic, minced
1/2 cup wine vinegar

1/4 cup special oil
1 teaspoon salt
1/4 teaspoon freshly ground
   black pepper
1-1/2 cups ice water

Purée the tomatoes, onions, green peppers and garlic in an electric blender or force through a food mill. Stir in the vinegar, and then very gradually beat in the oil. Add the salt, pepper and ice water. Chill 2 hours before serving. Arrange small bowls of diced cucumbers, onions, green peppers, tomatoes and croutons to be served as a garnish in the soup.

Serves 6.

Per serving
Calories 135
Saturated fat 1.0 gram
Polyunsaturated fat 5.1 grams
Total fat 9.0 grams

Fish

FORTUNATELY, all varieties of fish are welcome on a low-fat diet. This may be pleasant news to some, but most Americans are accustomed to eating meat in preference to fish. It is my notion that this state of affairs has been brought about by the unimaginative manner of serving fish in this country.

If you live near the ocean, by all means use fresh fish. Frozen fish is satisfactory, but the choice is more limited and in all fairness it must be admitted that frozen fish lacks the delicacy of flavor and texture of fresh fish. In addition, some frozen fish has a higher salt content due to the processing. So wherever possible, use fresh fish. Those who are near a source of supply of fresh fish should make sure to use it as soon as possible after purchasing it. When buying frozen fish, make sure that it is solidly frozen and keep it that way until you are ready to cook it; then thaw and use at once.

Fish, properly prepared, can become a favorite with your family. For those on a low-fat diet, it offers the double benefit of almost always being low in calories at the same time (with the possible exception of some fat fish like salmon, shad and swordfish). Don't overcook fish; it soon loses its flavor and body. Garnish fish preparations attractively with sprigs of parsley, lemon wedges, or watercress.

Until recently shellfish was permitted in unlimited quantities on low-cholesterol diets, for there are only small amounts of saturated fat in shellfish. But there are also moderate amounts of cholesterol naturally present in shellfish. It was formerly thought that the body couldn't use cholesterol, and the system would rid itself of this unwanted substance by excretion. In recent years, researchers have determined that the serum cholesterol level will increase if cholesterol-high foods are eaten. Therefore, although it is not necessary to eliminate shellfish completely from the diet, the quantity consumed and the frequency of consumption should be limited. Once or at most twice a week, in rather small quantities, is acceptable. An alternative, if you wish to eat shellfish, is to eliminate one egg each week and replace it with a small portion of shellfish.

BROILED SALMON WITH FRUITS

1 grapefruit
2 oranges
2 salmon steaks, 1 inch thick
3/4 teaspoon salt

1/2 teaspoon white pepper
1 tablespoon lemon juice
3 tablespoons melted special
margarine

Cut the grapefruit into 4 quarters. Cut the fruit away from the skin; remove the membranes and seeds and divide in sections. Peel the oranges, remove the membranes and seeds and separate in sections. Arrange fruits alternately in the grapefruit skins.

Rinse and dry the salmon. Rub with the salt, pepper and lemon juice. Brush a baking pan with a little of the margarine; arrange the fish in it. Sprinkle with some melted margarine. Broil in a hot broiler about 3 inches from the heat 15 minutes. Carefully turn fish; brush with the remaining margarine. Arrange grapefruit quarters around fish and broil 10 minutes.

Serves 4.

Per serving
Calories 455
Saturated fat 7.7 grams
Polyunsaturated fat 9.0 grams
Total fat 29.1 grams

PAN-FRIED FISH

4 fillets of sole or 4 fish steaks
   (1-1/2 pounds)
1 tablespoon lemon juice
1/4 cup flour

3/4 teaspoon salt
1/4 teaspoon white pepper
3 tablespoons special oil

Wash and dry the fish. Sprinkle with the lemon juice and dip in a mixture of the flour, salt and pepper. Heat the oil in a skillet; sauté the fish until browned on both sides. Serve with tartar sauce if desired.

Serves 4.

Per serving
•Calories 215
Saturated fat   1.4 grams
Polyunsaturated fat   7.0 grams
Total fat 12.0 grams

FILLET OF MACKEREL MIREILLE

4 fillets of mackerel
2 tablespoons flour
1 teaspoon salt
1/2 teaspoon freshly ground
   black pepper
3 tablespoons special
   margarine

1/4 cup chopped mushrooms
1/2 cup chopped onions
1 clove garlic, minced
1 tablespoon wine vinegar
2 tablespoons minced parsley

Wash and dry the fish. Rub with a mixture of the flour, 1/2 teaspoon salt and 1/4 teaspoon pepper. Melt 2 tablespoons margarine in a skillet. Fry the fish until browned and crisp. Prepare the vegetables while the fish is frying.

Melt the remaining margarine in a skillet; sauté the mushrooms, onions and garlic 10 minutes. Add the vinegar and remaining salt and pepper. Cook 1 minute. Arrange the fish on a platter and pour the vegetables over it. Sprinkle with the parsley.

Serves 4.

Per serving
Calories 235
Saturated fat   4.1 grams
Polyunsaturated fat 12.5 grams
Total fat 22.8 grams

FISH, NICOISE STYLE

6 slices sea bass or similar fish
1/4 cup flour
1-1/2 teaspoons salt
1/4 teaspoon freshly ground
    black pepper
3 tablespoons special oil
1/2 cup thinly sliced onions

1 clove garlic, minced
3/4 cup peeled chopped
    tomatoes
1/2 cup dry white wine
6 black olives, sliced
3 anchovies, minced

Wash and dry the fish; dip in a mixture of the flour, salt and pepper. Heat the oil in a skillet; brown the fish on both sides, adding the onion and garlic when turning the fish. Transfer the fish to a platter. Add the tomatoes to the skillet; cook over medium heat 5 minutes. Mix in the wine and olives; bring to a boil and pour over the fish. Sprinkle with the anchovies.

Serves 6.

Per serving
Calories 230
Saturated fat   1.6 grams
Polyunsaturated fat   6.1 grams
Total fat 10.6 grams

FISH IN PAPRIKA SAUCE

6 slices lake trout, whitefish,
    pike, etc. (2 pounds)
3/4 teaspoon salt
1/4 teaspoon freshly ground
    black pepper
2 tablespoons special
    margarine

1-1/2 cups chopped onions
1 tablespoon paprika
1-1/2 cups boiling water
1/2 cup buttermilk
1 tablespoon minced parsley

Wash and dry the fish; season with the salt and pepper. Melt the margarine in a skillet; sauté the onions 10 minutes. Mix in the paprika. Add the fish, cook 1 minute and turn over. Add the water; cover and cook over low heat 45 minutes.

Transfer the fish to a serving dish. Stir the buttermilk into the sauce; heat but do not let boil. Pour over the fish and serve, sprinkled with the parsley. Good hot or cold.

Serves 6.

Per serving
Calories 135
Saturated fat 2.2 grams
Polyunsaturated fat 5.2 grams
Total fat 9.5 grams

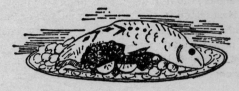

FISH IN PAPER

4 fillets of sole (1 pound)
1 teaspoon salt
1/2 teaspoon freshly ground
black pepper

3 tablespoons special oil
2 tablespoons grated onions
2 tablespoons minced parsley
4 tablespoons dry white wine

Season the fish with the salt and pepper. Cut 4 pieces of aluminum foil large enough to wrap the fillets. Brush one side of the foil with a little oil. Place a fillet in the center of each piece; sprinkle with the onions, parsley, wine and remaining oil. Bring the foil up over the top of the fish and double-fold the edges to make a tight package. Bring the ends up and fold over. Arrange the packages on a baking sheet.

Bake in a preheated 425° oven 25 minutes. Carefully open one package and test fish with a fork; if it flakes easily, it is done. If not, bake it a few more minutes. Serve in the foil.

Serves 4.

Per serving
Calories 195
Saturated fat   1.5 grams
Polyunsaturated fat   7.0 grams
Total fat 12.0 grams

STUFFED FISH EN PAPILLOTE

4-pound striped bass, pike or
    whitefish
1-1/2 teaspoons salt
3/4 teaspoon freshly ground
    black pepper
3 tablespoons special
    margarine
1/2 cup chopped onions

1/4 cup chopped celery
1/4 cup chopped green peppers
1/4 cup chopped mushrooms
1 cup fine bread crumbs
1/2 teaspoon thyme
1/4 cup chopped toasted
    almonds
2 tablespoons dry white wine

Have the fish split and boned. Wash and dry; rub inside and out with 1 teaspoon salt and 1/2 teaspoon pepper.

Melt half the margarine in a skillet; sauté the onions, celery, green peppers and mushrooms 10 minutes. Mix in the bread crumbs, thyme, almonds and the remaining salt and pepper. Stuff the fish; close the opening with skewers or tie with string.

Cut a piece of aluminum foil large enough to cover the fish completely. Melt the remaining margarine and brush the foil with a little of it. Place the fish in the center and bring up the foil. Sprinkle the fish with the wine and the remaining margarine. Overlap the fish with the foil and fold ends. Place on a baking sheet. Bake in a 400° oven 30 minutes. Open the foil and fold it back. Bake 20 minutes longer or until fish flakes easily when tested with a fork. Baste once or twice.

Serves 6.

Per serving (with bass or
    whitefish)
Calories 390
Saturated fat   2.4 grams
Polyunsaturated fat   6.2 grams
Total fat 14.8 grams
Per serving (with pike)
Calories 380
Saturated fat   1.8 grams
Polyunsaturated fat   3.7 grams
Total fat 11.3 grams

BAKED FISH, ARMENIAN STYLE

3 tablespoons special oil
2 cups thinly sliced onions
6 slices (2 pounds) sea bass
1 teaspoon salt
1/2 teaspoon freshly ground
    black pepper
1 tablespoon cider vinegar

1 teaspoon sugar
1/2 cup water
1 cup peeled chopped
    tomatoes
2 lemons, thinly sliced
2 tablespoons minced parsley

Heat 2 tablespoons oil in a large skillet with ovenproof handle; sauté the onions 10 minutes. Arrange the fish over them and season with the salt, pepper, vinegar and sugar. Add the water and cover fish with the tomatoes and lemon slices. Sprinkle with the remaining oil. Cover and bake in a 375° oven 35 minutes or until fish flakes easily. Remove the cover for the last 10 minutes. Sprinkle with the parsley.

Serves 6.

Per serving
Calories 245
Saturated fat 1.2 grams
Polyunsaturated fat 5.9 grams
Total fat 9.7 grams

BAKED STUFFED FISH

2 pounds pike, sea bass,
  whitefish, etc.
1-1/2 teaspoons salt
3/4 teaspoon freshly ground
  black pepper
1 teaspoon paprika
1 slice white bread, trimmed
1/4 cup skim milk

3 tablespoons special oil
3/4 cup chopped onions
1/2 cup chopped celery
1/2 cup chopped mushrooms
1 tablespoon chopped green
  olives
1/4 teaspoon thyme
1/2 cup dry sherry

Have the fish split and boned for stuffing. Season with 1
teaspoon salt, 1/2 teaspoon pepper and the paprika. Soak the
bread in the milk and mash smooth.

Heat 1 tablespoon oil in a skillet; sauté the onions, celery
and mushrooms 10 minutes. Remove from the heat; mix in the
olives, thyme, mashed bread and the remaining salt and pepper. Stuff the fish and close the opening with skewers or by sew-
ing.

Heat the remaining oil in a baking dish. Place the fish in it
and bake in a 350° oven 20 minutes. Pour the sherry over it
and bake 40 minutes longer or until browned and fish flakes
easily when tested with a fork. Baste frequently.

Serves 6.   Per serving
                                            Calories 220
                                      Saturated fat   2.2 grams
                                  Polyunsaturated fat 7.9 grams
                                      Total fat 12.7 grams

SOLE AMANDINE

4 fillets of sole (1 pound)
1/4 cup flour
3/4 teaspoon salt
1/4 teaspoon white pepper
3 tablespoons special
  margarine

1/4 cup blanched sliced almonds
2 tablespoons minced parsley
1 tablespoon lemon juice

Wash and dry the fish; dip in a mixture of the flour, salt and
pepper.

Melt 2 tablespoons margarine in a skillet; sauté the fish until browned on both sides and fish flakes easily. Transfer to a heated serving dish. Melt the remaining margarine in the skillet; stir the almonds into it until lightly browned. Stir in the parsley and lemon juice; pour over the fish.

Serves 4.

Per serving
Calories 235
Saturated fat   2.3 grams
Polyunsaturated fat   4.2 grams
Total fat 14.4 grams

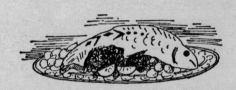

FILLET OF SOLE MEUNIERE

4 fillets of sole (1 pound)
1/4 cup flour
1 teaspoon salt
1/4 teaspoon white pepper

3 tablespoons special
margarine
1 tablespoon minced parsley
2 teaspoons lemon juice

Wash and dry the fillets. Dip in a mixture of the flour, salt and pepper. Melt half the margarine in a skillet; cook the fish in it until browned on both sides. Transfer to a platter and keep hot. Pour off the fat and wipe skillet with a paper towel. Melt the remaining margarine in the skillet until it begins to turn brown. Stir in the parsley and lemon juice. Pour over the fish.

Serves 4.

Per serving
Calories 180
Saturated fat 1.3 grams
Polyunsaturated fat 2.4 grams
Total fat 9.6 grams

FILLET OF SOLE VERONIQUE

4 fillets of sole (1 pound)
1 teaspoon salt
1/4 teaspoon white pepper
2 tablespoons special
 margarine

1/2 cup dry white wine
1 tablespoon lemon juice
1 tablespoon flour
3/4 cup skim milk
1/4 cup seedless green grapes

Wash and dry the fish; season with 1/2 teaspoon salt and the pepper. Melt 1 tablespoon margarine in a glass or pottery baking dish. Arrange the fillets in it. Add the wine and lemon juice. Cover the fish with a piece of aluminum foil. Bake in a 350° oven 15 minutes or until fish flakes easily when tested with a fork.

Melt the remaining margarine in a saucepan. Blend in the flour and remaining salt. Add the milk, stirring steadily to the boiling point. Cook over low heat 5 minutes. Sprinkle the grapes around the fish and pour the sauce over all. Place under the broiler until delicately browned.

Serves 4.

Per serving
Calories 220
Saturated fat 1.3 grams
Polyunsaturated fat 2.4 grams
Total fat 6.5 grams

FILLET OF SOLE WITH MUSHROOM SAUCE

6 fillets of sole (1-1/2 pounds)
1 teaspoon salt
1/4 teaspoon white pepper
2 tablespoons special
 margarine
3/4 cup finely chopped onions

1/2 pound mushrooms, sliced
 thin
1/2 cup dry white wine
1 tablespoon flour
1/2 cup skim milk
1 tablespoon minced parsley

Wash and dry the fillets; season with the salt and pepper. Melt the margarine in a large skillet; sauté the onions 5 minutes. Add half the mushrooms and sauté 2 minutes. Place the fillets in the skillet; cover with the remaining mushrooms and add the wine. Cover and cook over medium heat 15 minutes or until fish flakes easily when tested with a fork. Transfer fillets to a heated serving dish and keep warm.

Mix together the flour and milk; add to the skillet, mixing steadily to the boiling point. Cook over low heat 5 minutes. Pour over the fish and sprinkle with the parsley.

Serves 6.

Per serving
Calories 140
Saturated fat 1.0 gram
Polyunsaturated fat 1.9 grams
Total fat 4.9 grams

BAKED FISH WITH SOY SAUCE

6 slices mackerel, sea bass,
    etc. (2 pounds)
1/2 teaspoon freshly ground
    black pepper

2 cloves garlic, minced
1/4 cup special oil
1/4 cup soy sauce
2 tablespoons lemon juice

Wash and dry the fish; rub with a mixture of the pepper and garlic. Place in an oiled baking dish. Bake in a 375° oven 10 minutes.

Mix together the oil, soy sauce and lemon juice. Pour half the mixture over the fish; bake 10 minutes. Turn fish; add remaining soy mixture and bake 10 minutes longer, basting frequently.

Serves 6.

Per serving (with mackerel)
Calories 225
Saturated fat 4.0 grams
Polyunsaturated fat 17.7 grams
Total fat 27.2 grams
Per serving (with bass)
Calories 225
Saturated fat 1.4 grams
Polyunsaturated fat 7.0 grams
Total fat 13.4 grams

BAKED SPICED FISH

2 tablespoons special oil
4 fillets of sole, flounder
    (1 pound)
1 cup thinly sliced onions
1 cup sliced celery
1 teaspoon salt

1/4 teaspoon freshly ground
    black pepper
1 tablespoon curry powder
1 teaspoon flour
3/4 cup skim milk

Heat 1 tablespoon oil in a baking dish; arrange the fillets in it. Bake in a 350° oven 10 minutes. Prepare the sauce in the meantime.

Heat the remaining oil in a skillet; sauté the onions and celery 10 minutes. Mix in the salt, pepper, curry powder and flour. Add the milk, stirring steadily to the boiling point. Pour over the fish. Bake 25 minutes longer or until fish flakes easily.

Serves 4.

Per serving (with sole)
Calories 145
Saturated fat 1.0 gram
Polyunsaturated fat 4.8 grams
Total fat 5.5 grams
Per serving (with flounder)
Calories 145
Saturated fat 0.9 gram
Polyunsaturated fat 4.4 grams
Total fat 7.7 grams

FISH, PROVENCE STYLE

4 slices sea bass, pike, etc.
1 teaspoon salt
1/2 teaspoon freshly ground
    black pepper
1/4 cup flour
3 tablespoons special oil
3/4 cup thinly sliced onions

1/2 cup peeled chopped
    tomatoes
1/4 cup dry white wine
2 tablespoons sliced black
    olives
2 tablespoons minced parsley

Dip the fish in a mixture of the salt, pepper and flour. Heat the oil in a skillet; sauté the fish with the onions until it browns on both sides and flakes easily when tested with a fork.

Transfer fish (not onions) to a serving dish and keep warm while preparing the sauce.

Add the tomato to the skillet; sauté 5 minutes. Mix in the wine, olives and parsley. Cook 2 minutes, stirring frequently. Pour the sauce over the fish.

Serves 4.

Per serving
Calories 295
Saturated fat   2.0 grams
Polyunsaturated fat   8.1 grams
Total fat 14.2 grams

OVEN-FRIED FISH

4 fillets of fish (sole or
   haddock)
1/2 cup skim milk
1 teaspoon salt

1/2 teaspoon white pepper
1/2 cup fine dry bread crumbs
1/3 cup special oil

Use any white-meat fish you like. Dip in the milk mixed with the salt and pepper, then in the bread crumbs. Heat half the oil in a skillet (with ovenproof handle) or baking pan. Arrange the fillets in it and sprinkle with the remaining oil. Bake in a 475° oven 20 minutes or until browned and fish flakes easily when tested with a fork. Serve with lemon wedges and tartar sauce, if desired.

Serves 4.

Per serving (with sole)
Calories 295
Saturated fat   2.3 grams
Polyunsaturated fat 11.1 grams
Total fat 19.6 grams
Per serving (with haddock)
Calories 295
Saturated fat 2.1 grams
Polyunsaturated fat 10.3 grams
Total fat 18.6 grams

FISH CURRY

4 fillets of sole, sea bass, etc.
    (2 pounds)
3/4 teaspoon salt
4 teaspoons curry powder
3 tablespoons special oil
1 clove garlic, minced

1 cup finely chopped onions
1 tablespoon lemon juice
1 teaspoon sugar
1/4 cup ground blanched
    almonds
1 cup skim milk

Wash and dry the fish; cut into thirds crosswise. Rub the fish with a mixture of the salt and curry powder. Heat the oil in a skillet; sauté the garlic and onions 5 minutes. Add the fish; sauté 1 minute on each side. Mix together the lemon juice, sugar, almonds and milk; add to the skillet. Cover and cook over low heat 15 minutes or until fish flakes easily when tested with a fork.

Serves 6.

Per serving (with sole)
Calories 220
Saturated fat   1.3 grams
Polyunsaturated fat   5.7 grams
Total fat 11.8 grams
Per serving (with bass)
Calories 220
Saturated fat   1.5 grams
Polyunsaturated fat   6.5 grams
Total fat 12.9 grams

FISH AND RICE CASSEROLE

1-1/2 cups canned drained
    tomatoes, chopped
1 cup thinly sliced onions
2 cloves garlic, minced
3/4 cup julienne-cut green
    peppers
1/4 teaspoon saffron
3 tablespoons special oil
6 slices sea bass, perch, etc.
    (about 2 pounds)

1-1/2 teaspoons salt
1/2 teaspoon freshly ground
    black pepper
1 bay leaf
1 cup dry white wine
1/2 cup boiling water
3/4 cup raw rice
2 tablespoons minced parsley

Cook the tomatoes, onions and garlic over low heat 10 minutes. Add the green peppers and saffron. Cook 10 minutes.

Heat the oil in a casserole; brown the fish in it on both sides. Season with the salt and pepper and add the bay leaf, wine, water and tomato mixture. Bring to a boil and add the rice. Cover and cook over low heat 25 minutes or until the rice is tender. Watch carefully and add a little boiling water if necessary. Sprinkle with the parsley. Serve directly from the casserole.

Serves 6.

Per serving (with perch)
Calories 225
Saturated fat 1.0 gram
Polyunsaturated fat 4.9 grams
Total fat 8.3 grams
Per serving (with bass)
Calories 255
Saturated fat 1.2 grams
Polyunsaturated fat 5.9 grams
Total fat 9.7 grams

SALMON AND BROCCOLI CASSEROLE

2 tablespoons special
  margarine
1 tablespoon flour
3/4 teaspoon salt
1/4 teaspoon white pepper
1 cup skim milk
1 cup peeled chopped
  tomatoes

2 packages frozen broccoli,
  half cooked and drained
2 7-3/4-ounce cans salmon,
  drained and flaked
2 tablespoons dry bread
  crumbs

Melt 1 tablespoon margarine in a saucepan; blend in the flour, salt and pepper. Add the milk, stirring steadily to the boiling point. Stir in the tomatoes; cook over low heat 5 minutes.

Spread the broccoli on the bottom of a 2-quart casserole or baking dish. Cover with the salmon and pour the sauce over all. Sprinkle with the bread crumbs and dot with the remaining margarine. Bake in a 375° oven 30 minutes.

Serves 6.

Per serving
Calories 205
Saturated fat 1.6 grams
Polyunsaturated fat 4.6 grams
Total fat 8.9 grams

CREOLE FISH CASSEROLE

2 tablespoons special oil
1-1/2 cups chopped onions
2 tablespoons flour
1-1/2 cups skim milk
2 cups canned drained
    tomatoes
1 cup diced green peppers
3/4 teaspoon salt
1/4 teaspoon thyme
2 tablespoons minced parsley

1-1/2 pounds halibut, cod or
    haddock, cooked and
    flaked
1/4 cup chopped green olives
2 teaspoons Worcestershire
    sauce
1/2 teaspoon freshly ground
    black pepper
2 tablespoons bread crumbs

Heat the oil in a saucepan; sauté the onions 5 minutes. Blend in the flour; add the milk, stirring steadily to the boiling point. Mix in the tomatoes, green peppers, salt and thyme; cook over low heat 15 minutes. Stir in the parsley, fish, olives, Worcestershire sauce and pepper. Turn into a 2-quart casserole; sprinkle with the bread crumbs. Bake in a 375° oven 15 minutes.

Serves 6.

Per serving
Calories 210
Saturated fat 1.1 grams
Polyunsaturated fat 3.9 grams
Total fat 7.7 grams

JELLIED SALMON

4 pounds salmon, in one piece
3 cups dry white wine
3 cups water
2 cloves
1 onion
4 slices lemon
8 peppercorns
1-1/2 teaspoons salt

6 sprigs parsley
1/2 tablespoon gelatin
1/4 cup cold water
1/2 cup mayonnaise
2 tablespoons minced parsley
2 tablespoons minced chives
    or scallions (green onions)
1 tablespoon minced dill

Buy the center cut of the salmon. Wrap the fish in a layer of cheesecloth. In a deep saucepan, combine the wine, water, cloves stuck in the onion, lemon, peppercorns, salt and parsley. Bring to a boil and cook over medium heat 15 minutes. Place the fish in it and cook over low heat 1 hour, or until the part near the bone flakes easily when tested with a fork. Carefully lift out the fish, unwrap and remove skin. Place on a serving dish; continue cooking the stock until reduced to 1 cup. Strain.

Soften the gelatin in the water for 5 minutes. Stir into the hot stock until dissolved. Cook until syrupy, then blend into the mayonnaise. Mix in the parsley, chives and dill. Chill until firm enough to spread, then coat the fish with it. Chill until set. Decorate top with sliced olives, pimentos and green peppers, if desired.

Serves 10.

Per serving
Calories 345
Saturated fat   7.8 grams
Polyunsaturated fat 25.0 grams
Total fat 35.9 grams

FISHBALLS

4 pounds whitefish, pike or
   salmon
Heads and skin of the fish
5 cups water
1-1/2 cups sliced onions
1 carrot, sliced
2 teaspoons salt
1/2 teaspoon freshly ground
   black pepper

1/2 cup diced onions
1 egg yolk
3/4 cup cold water
2 tablespoons cracker meal
1/2 teaspoon white pepper
2 egg whites, stiffly beaten

You may buy a combination of fish if you like. Have it filleted.

In a saucepan, combine the heads and skins, the 5 cups water, sliced onions, carrot, 1 teaspoon salt and the black pepper. Bring to a boil and cook over medium heat while preparing the fish. Grind or chop the fish and diced onions until very fine. (You may use an electric blender, in which case run fish with the egg yolk and water.) Mix in the egg yolk, water, cracker meal, white pepper and remaining salt. Fold in the egg whites. Shape into 18 balls. Carefully place in the boiling liquid. Cover loosely; cook over low heat 1-1/2 hours. Carefully remove fish balls. Strain the stock and pour over the fish. Chill.

Serve 2 balls to each person.

Per serving
Calories 145
Saturated fat   4.3 grams
Polyunsaturated fat 12.0 grams
Total fat 16.6 grams

MOCK SCALLOPS

1-1/2 pounds halibut, cut 1/2 inch thick
2 eggs, beaten
1/2 cup sifted flour
1/2 teaspoon salt
1/4 teaspoon freshly ground black pepper
4 tablespoons special oil

Cut the halibut into 1/2-inch cubes. Dip the cubes in the eggs and then in the flour mixed with the salt and pepper.

Sauté the fish scallops in the oil until browned on all sides. Serve with mustard sauce (see recipe) and lemon wedges.

Serves 8.

Per serving

Calories 205
Saturated fat   3.4 grams
Polyunsaturated fat   6.4 grams
Total fat 14.6 grams

MARINATED FISH, CHILEAN STYLE

6 fillets of snapper, sole, or other white-meat fish
1 cup dry white wine
1 cup lime or lemon juice
1 teaspoon salt
1-1/2 cups thinly sliced onions
1 cup water
1/2 cup cider vinegar
1/2 teaspoon dried ground chili peppers

Wash the fillets, remove any bones, and cut in julienne strips. Marinate in the wine, lime or lemon juice, and 1/2 teaspoon salt for 3 hours.

Soak the onions in the water and remaining salt for 20 minutes. Drain well and squeeze between the hands. Rinse under cold running water and drain again. Soak the onions in the vinegar 1 hour. Drain well and add to the fish with the chili peppers. Chill for 4 hours. Drain and serve on lettuce.

Note: The action of the citrus juice "cooks" the fish.

Serves 8 as an appetizer.

Per serving
Calories 110
Saturated fat 0.9 gram
Polyunsaturated fat 4.4 grams
Total fat 7.7 grams

POACHED FISH, FLORENTINE STYLE

6 fillets of sole (1-1/2 pounds)
2 cups water
1 teaspoon salt
1/4 teaspoon freshly ground
 black pepper
1 onion, sliced
1 bay leaf
1 stalk celery

2 tablespoons special
 margarine
1/4 pound mushrooms, sliced
1 tablespoon flour
1 egg yolk
2 tablespoons dry vermouth
2 cups cooked chopped
 spinach

Wash the fish. In a skillet combine the water, salt, pepper, onion, bay leaf and celery. Bring to a boil and cook over medium heat 10 minutes. Arrange the fish in it; cover and cook over low heat 15 minutes or until fish flakes easily when tested with a fork. Transfer fillets to a serving dish; strain the stock.

Melt the margarine in a saucepan; sauté the mushrooms 5 minutes. Blend in the flour, then add the stock, stirring steadily to the boiling point. Cook over low heat 5 minutes. Beat the egg yolk and vermouth in a bowl; gradually add the mushroom mixture, stirring steadily to prevent curdling.

Cover the fillets with the spinach and pour sauce over all. Place under a hot broiler for 1 minute.

Serves 6.

Per serving
Calories 150
Saturated fat 1.3 grams
Polyunsaturated fat 2.0 grams
Total fat 5.9 grams

SHAD ROE SAUTÉ

Roe of 2 shad
3 cups water
1 onion
1 teaspoon salt
2 tablespoons special
    margarine

1/4 teaspoon white pepper
2 tablespoons minced parsley
1 tablespoon lemon juice

Wash the roe and combine with the water, onion and 1/2 teaspoon salt. Bring to a boil and cook over low heat 15 minutes. Drain and carefully pat dry with paper towels.

Melt the margarine in a skillet; brown the roe on both sides. Sprinkle with the pepper, parsley, lemon juice and remaining salt.

Serves 4.

Per serving
Calories 180
Saturated fat 1.8 grams
Polyunsaturated fat 3.4 grams
Total fat 8.4 grams

TUNA-STUFFED PEPPERS

4 green peppers
1 slice white bread, trimmed
1/4 cup skim milk
1 7-3/4-ounce can tuna fish

4 black olives, chopped
1/4 teaspoon freshly ground
    black pepper
2 tablespoons special oil

Cut a 1/2-inch piece from the stem end of the peppers. Scoop out the seeds and fibers. Soak the bread in the milk and mash smooth. Flake the undrained tuna fish; mix with the bread, olives and black pepper.

Stuff the peppers and arrange in upright positions in an oiled baking dish. Cover and bake in a 350° oven 1 hour. Serve hot or cold.

Serves 4.

Per serving
Calories 235
Saturated fat 2.2 grams
Polyunsaturated fat 6.6 grams
Total fat 12.5 grams

CREAMED TUNA ON TOAST

2 tablespoons special oil
1/2 cup chopped onions
1/2 pound mushrooms, sliced
1 tablespoon flour
3/4 teaspoon salt
1/4 teaspoon freshly ground
   black pepper

1-1/2 cups skim milk
2 7-3/4-ounce cans tuna fish,
   drained and flaked
3 slices toast, trimmed and cut
   in triangles
2 tomatoes, peeled and sliced
2 tablespoons minced parsley

Heat the oil in a skillet; sauté the onions 5 minutes. Add the mushrooms; sauté 5 minutes longer. Blend in the flour, salt and pepper; add the milk, stirring steadily to the boiling point. Cook over low heat 5 minutes. Mix in the tuna.

Arrange the toast on the bottom of a baking dish; place the tomatoes over it. Pour the tuna mixture over all. Bake in a 375° oven 20 minutes. Sprinkle with the parsley.

Serves 6.

Per serving
Calories 270
Saturated fat 1.8 grams
Polyunsaturated fat 3.7 grams
Total fat 6.6 grams

TUNA FISH SALAD

1 7-3/4-ounce can tuna fish
1/2 cup diced cucumbers
1/4 cup chopped scallions
   (green onions)
1/4 cup chopped green peppers
2 teaspoons lemon juice

1/2 teaspoon salt
1/4 teaspoon freshly ground
   black pepper
1/4 cup Special Mayonnaise
   (see recipe)

Drain the tuna fish, then flake. Combine with the remaining ingredients, mixing lightly with a fork. Serve on shredded lettuce and watercress.

Serves 3.

Per serving
Calories 205
Saturated fat 3.6 grams
Polyunsaturated fat 11.7 grams
Total fat 21.3 grams

FISH SALAD

1 pound halibut, haddock or
  cod
1-1/2 cups water
1 whole onion
1 teaspoon salt
6 tablespoons Special
  Mayonnaise (see recipe)

2 teaspoons grated onions
1 teaspoon Worcestershire
  sauce
1/2 cup peeled diced apples
1 cup peeled diced cucumbers
1/2 cup diced celery
2 teaspoons minced parsley

In a saucepan, combine the fish, water, whole onion and
salt. Bring to a boil and cook over medium heat 25 minutes.
Drain, cool and flake.

Mix together the mayonnaise, grated onions and Worcestershire sauce. Combine the apples, cucumbers, celery and fish.
Add the mayonnaise mixture and mix lightly. Serve on shredded lettuce and sprinkle with parsley.

Serves 6.

Per serving

Calories 105
Saturated fat 1.7 grams
Polyunsaturated fat 7.0 grams
Total fat 12.7 grams

BAKED CLAMS

36 cherrystone clams
2 tablespoons special oil
1/4 cup-chopped onions
1/4 cup chopped green peppers

4 tablespoons chopped
  pimento
2 tablespoons dry bread crumbs
1/8 teaspoon Tabasco

Have the clams opened and left on the half shell, but loosen
them. Heat the oil in a skillet; sauté the onions and green peppers 5 minutes. Remove from the heat and mix in the pimento,
bread crumbs and Tabasco. Sprinkle over the clams. Place on a

114

baking pan or 6 individual dishes. Broil 3 inches from the heat
for 5 minutes. Serve at once with lemon wedges.

Serves 6.

Per serving
Calories 145
Saturated fat 0.8 gram
Polyunsaturated fat 3.7 grams
Total fat 6.3 grams

CRAB MEAT RAVIGOTE

1 pound crab meat
1/4 cup tarragon vinegar
1/2 teaspoon salt
1/4 teaspoon white pepper
3/4 cup Special Mayonnaise
(see recipe)

1 teaspoon anchovy paste
2 tablespoons capers, chopped
2 tablespoons chopped onions
2 tablespoons chopped
pimentos

Flake the crab meat, discarding any cartilage. Marinate in
the vinegar 15 minutes, then drain very well. Season with the
salt and pepper. Blend together half the mayonnaise, the anchovy paste, capers, onions and pimentos. Add to the crab
meat and mix lightly. Divide into 6 mounds; place in shells or
lettuce cups. Cover with the remaining mayonnaise and garnish with whole capers, if desired.

Serves 6.

Per serving
Calories 155
Saturated fat   3.3 grams
Polyunsaturated fat 13.8 grams
Total fat 24.8 grams

DEVILED HALIBUT

3/4 pound cooked halibut
2 tablespoons special oil
1/4 cup chopped onions
1/4 cup chopped green pepper
2 tablespoons flour

3/4 teaspoon salt
1/4 teaspoon white pepper
1/4 teaspoon dry mustard
1-1/2 cups skim milk
2 tablespoons dry bread crumbs

Flake the halibut. Heat the oil in a saucepan; sauté the onions and green pepper 10 minutes. Blend in the flour, salt, pepper and mustard. Gradually add the milk, stirring steadily to the boiling point, then cook over low heat 5 minutes. Remove from heat and mix in the halibut. Divide among 4 oiled ramekins or turn into a 1-quart casserole. Sprinkle with the bread crumbs. Bake in a preheated 375° oven 15 minutes for ramekins, 25 minutes for casserole.

Serves 4.

Per serving
Calories 185
Saturated fat 1.1 grams
Polyunsaturated fat 5.2 grams
Total fat 8.9 grams

LOBSTER THERMIDOR

3 tablespoons special
    margarine
2 live lobsters split or
    4 African lobster tails
1/4 cup minced onions
1/2 cup dry white wine
1 tablespoon flour

3/4 cup skim milk
1/2 teaspoon dry mustard
3/4 teaspoon salt
1/2 teaspoon paprika
1/4 teaspoon chervil
1 teaspoon minced parsley
2 tablespoons dry bread crumbs

Melt 1 tablespoon margarine in a skillet; put the lobsters in it flesh side down and sauté 5 minutes. Turn lobsters over; cover and cook over low heat 10 minutes. Cool and remove the meat. Reserve the shells. Slice bodies and dice the claws.

Melt the remaining margarine in a saucepan; sauté the onions 5 minutes. Add the wine; cook over low heat 5 minutes. Mix the flour, milk, mustard, salt and paprika. Add to the wine mixture, stirring steadily to the boiling point. Cook over low heat 5 minutes. Stir the lobster meat into the sauce with the chervil and parsley. Stuff the shells and sprinkle with the bread crumbs. Bake in a 425° oven 10 minutes.

Serves 4.

Per serving
Calories 175
Saturated fat   1.9 grams
Polyunsaturated fat   4.8 grams
Total fat 10.3 grams

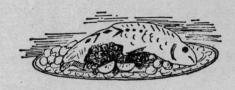

SCALLOPED OYSTERS AND ARTICHOKES

1 package frozen artichoke
   hearts
1 pint undrained oysters
1/2 cup beef broth
2 tablespoons nonfat dry milk
   powder

1/2 teaspoon salt
1/4 teaspoon white pepper
3 tablespoons grated onions
2 tablespoons minced parsley
3/4 cup dry bread crumbs
2 tablespoons special oil

Cook the artichoke hearts 2 minutes less than package directs. Drain. Drain the oysters. Mix the oyster liquor with the broth, dry milk, salt, pepper, onions and parsley. Mix in the oysters and artichokes.

Oil a baking dish and spread half the bread crumbs on the bottom. Turn the oyster mixture into it. Toss the remaining bread crumbs with the oil and sprinkle over the oysters. Bake in a 425° oven 20 minutes or until bubbly and browned.

Serves 6.

Per serving
Calories 105
Saturated fat 1.2 grams
Polyunsaturated fat 3.8 grams
Total fat 6.8 grams

MARINATED BROILED SHRIMP

1/2 cup special oil
1 teaspoon salt
1-1/2 teaspoons chili powder
1/4 teaspoon freshly ground
　　black pepper
2 cloves garlic, minced or 1/2
　　teaspoon garlic powder

3 tablespoons minced parsley
2 tablespoons lemon juice
2 pounds raw shrimp, shelled
　　and deveined

Mix together the oil, salt, chili powder, pepper, garlic, parsley and lemon juice. Marinate the shrimp in the mixture for at least 4 hours (or overnight, if you prefer). Baste and turn occasionally.

Arrange the undrained shrimp in a broiling pan. Broil 4 minutes, turn and broil 4 more minutes.

Serves 6.

Per serving
Calories 165
Saturated fat   2.0 grams
Polyunsaturated fat 10.5 grams
Total fat 14.8 grams.

SHRIMP CURRY

2 cups water
3/4 teaspoon salt
1 stalk celery
1 bay leaf
1-1/2 pounds raw shrimp, shelled
　　and deveined
2 tablespoons special oil

1/2 cup chopped onions
2 tablespoons curry powder
1 tablespoon flour
1 cup beef broth
1/4 cup ground almonds
1 cucumber, peeled and diced
1/4 cup skim milk

In a saucepan, combine and bring to a boil the water, salt, celery and bay leaf; cook over low heat 5 minutes. Add the shrimp; cook over low heat 5 minutes. Drain, strain and reserve 1/2 cup stock.

Heat the oil in a saucepan; sauté the onions 5 minutes. Blend in the curry powder and flour; gradually add the broth, stirring constantly to the boiling point. Mix in the almonds; cook over low heat 10 minutes. Add the reserved stock, shrimp and cucumber; cook 2 minutes. Mix in the milk; heat but do not let boil. Serve with rice.

Serves 6.

Per serving
Calories 230
Saturated fat   1.8 grams
Polyunsaturated fat   7.0 grams
Total fat 18.8 grams

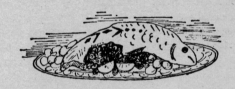

SHRIMP MARINIERE

2 tablespoons special oil
1-1/2 pounds raw shrimp, shelled
*   and deveined*
3/4 cup chopped onions
3/4 teaspoon salt

1/2 teaspoon freshly ground
*   black pepper*
1/4 teaspoon marjoram
1 cup dry white wine
2 tablespoons minced parsley

Heat the oil in a skillet; sauté the shrimp 3 minutes, shaking the pan frequently. Mix in the onions, salt, pepper, marjoram and wine. Cover and cook over low heat 5 minutes. Sprinkle with the parsley.

Serves 6.

Per serving
Calories 145
Saturated fat 0.7 gram
Polyunsaturated fat 3.4 grams
Total fat 5.8 grams

SEAFOOD PILAF

2 tablespoons special oil
3/4 cup chopped onions
1-1/2 cups raw rice
3 cups boiling water
1-1/2 teaspoons salt
1/2 teaspoon white pepper
2 tablespoons special
   margarine

1/4 pound scallops, sliced
1 pound halibut, cooked
   and diced
3 scallions (green onions), sliced
1/2 pound mushrooms, sliced
3/4 cup dry white wine
1/2 cup peeled diced tomatoes
1/4 teaspoon thyme

Heat the oil in a saucepan; sauté the onions 5 minutes. Stir in the rice until coated. Add the water, 1 teaspoon salt and 1/4 teaspoon pepper. Cover and cook over low heat 20 minutes or until tender and dry.

While the rice is cooking, prepare the fish. Melt the margarine in a saucepan; mix in the scallops, halibut, scallions and mushrooms. Cook over high heat 1 minute. Add the wine, tomatoes, thyme and remaining salt and pepper. Cook over medium heat 10 minutes.

Heap the rice on a platter and pour the seafood over it.

Serves 6.

Per serving
Calories 290
Saturated fat 1.3 grams
Polyunsaturated fat 3.9 grams
Total fat 8.8 grams

SEAFOOD SOUFFLÉ

2 tablespoons special
   margarine
2 tablespoons grated onions
1 tablespoon flour
3/4 teaspoon salt
1/4 teaspoon freshly ground
   black pepper

3/4 cup skim milk
1-1/2 cups cooked diced shrimp,
   or flaked cooked halibut
   or crab meat
2 tablespoons dry sherry
1 egg yolk
4 egg whites

Melt the margarine in a saucepan; stir in the onions, flour, salt and pepper. Add the milk, stirring steadily to the boiling point. Cook over low heat 5 minutes. Cool 10 minutes, then fold in the seafood, sherry and egg yolk.

Beat the egg whites until stiff but not dry; fold into the seafood mixture. Turn into a 1-1/2-quart soufflé dish. Bake in a 375° oven 25 minutes. Serve at once.

Serves 4.

Per serving
Calories 170
Saturated fat 2.0 grams
Polyunsaturated fat 2.7 grams
Total fat 8.7 grams

Meats

MOST Americans think of steak and roast beef as everyday items and as normal parts of the diet. Furthermore, we tend to buy fancy cuts of meat, particularly seeking out "choice" or "prime" meats which are heavily marbled with fat. We must educate ourselves to restrict our intake of fatty meats and cut down on our portions. Hungry men think nothing of consuming a one-pound steak or an equivalent quantity of roast beef. This all will have to be changed for a low-fat low-cholesterol diet, and it might well be changed for every adult who wishes to eat a sensible, prudent diet.

Don't buy the fanciest or fattest cuts of meat; it will take only a small adjustment to become accustomed to inferior cuts which are just as flavorsome but not so fatty.

Next, the size of the portions. Allow about 4-6 ounces of uncooked meat per person. It may seem small at first but not after a few meals. *Before* cooking, with a sharp knife carefully trim away all visible fats. Don't serve the fatty types of meat (beef, lamb, pork, tongue, etc.) more than three or four times a week. A leaner meat like veal offers much less of a problem because of its lower fat content, but even this should be eaten with a degree of caution.

When cooking stews or casseroles, prepare them earlier in the day; chill for several hours in the refrigerator. The fat will rise to the surface and congeal, and then may be removed readily. Reheat the stew or casserole and serve.

Never buy ready-ground hamburger because it is full of fat. Buy beef by the pound, trim all visible fat, and grind it yourself, or watch the butcher trim it in your presence and have him grind it.

LONDON BROIL

1-1/2 pounds flank steak
1/2 cup dry red wine
2 tablespoons special oil
1/4 teaspoon thyme
1/2 pound mushrooms, sliced

1 teaspoon cornstarch
1 tablespoon water
1/4 teaspoon salt
1/4 teaspoon freshly ground
   black pepper

Have all the fat trimmed and the meat scored. Marinate the meat in a mixture of the wine, oil and thyme for 2 hours. Drain. Cook the mushrooms in the marinade 5 minutes. Mix the cornstarch with the water, salt and pepper; add the mushroom mixture, stirring steadily to the boiling point. Cook over low heat 5 minutes.

Place the meat on a rack; broil in a hot broiler 3 minutes on each side for rare meat, 4 for medium and 6 for well done. Cut on the diagonal into very thin slices (a board is best for cutting). Serve with the sauce.

Serves 6.

Per serving
Calories 305
Saturated fat 14.2 grams
Unsaturated fat 3.5 grams
Total fat 36.4 grams

GOULASH

1-1/2 pounds bottom round or
    cross rib
2 tablespoons special oil
1 cup chopped onions
3/4 teaspoon salt
1/4 teaspoon freshly ground
    black pepper

1/4 teaspoon minced garlic
1 tablespoon paprika
1/2 cup boiling water
1 8-ounce can tomato sauce

Trim all the fat from the meat; cut meat in 1-1/2-inch cubes. Heat the oil in a heavy saucepan or Dutch oven. Brown the meat in it. Remove meat. In the oil remaining, brown the onions. Return the meat and mix in the salt, pepper, garlic and paprika until meat is coated. Add the water and tomato sauce. Cover and cook over low heat 1-1/2 hours.

Serves 4.

Per serving
Calories 315
Saturated fat 8.9 grams
Polyunsaturated fat 4.4 grams
Total fat 25.8 grams

SAUERBRATEN

3 pounds round or rump of beef
2 cups cider vinegar
1 teaspoon salt
2 teaspoons sugar
3 cloves
8 peppercorns

1 cup chopped onions
1 cup sliced carrots
2 bay leaves
2 tablespoons special oil
1/2 cup boiling water

Trim all the visible fat from the meat. Place in a glass or pottery bowl. Bring to a boil the vinegar, salt, sugar, cloves, peppercorns, onions, carrots and bay leaves. Pour over the meat. Cover and marinate in the refrigerator 2-3 days, turning the meat several times. Drain, reserving all the vegetables and 1 cup liquid. Dry the meat.

Heat the oil in a Dutch oven or heavy saucepan; brown the meat in it. Pour off any fat. Heat the marinade and add to the meat with the water. Cover and cook over low heat 2-1/2 hours or until tender. Thicken the gravy with 2 teaspoons flour mixed with 1 tablespoon water, if necessary.

Serves 10.

Per serving
Calories 265
Saturated fat 11.8 grams
Polyunsaturated fat 2.3 grams
Total fat 29.4 grams

CARBONNADE À LA FLAMANDE (Beef in Beer Sauce)

3 pounds chuck or round of beef
3 tablespoons special oil
2 cups sliced onions
3/4 teaspoon salt
1/2 teaspoon freshly ground black pepper

1/8 teaspoon thyme
1-1/2 cups beer
1 tablespoon sugar
1 tablespoon vinegar

Trim all the fat from the beef; cut into 2-inch cubes. Heat the oil in a Dutch oven or heavy saucepan; brown the onions and beef in it. Add the salt, pepper, thyme, beer, sugar and vinegar. Cover and cook over low heat 1-1/2 hours or until meat is tender. Skim the fat.

Serves 10.

Per serving
Calories 260
Saturated fat 8.4 grams
Polyunsaturated fat 2.9 grams
Total fat 22.7 grams

ITALIAN BEEF A LA MODE

3 pounds rump of beef
1 teaspoon salt
1/2 teaspoon freshly ground
   black pepper
1 clove garlic, minced
1 tablespoon special oil
3/4 cup thinly sliced onions
1 stalk celery, sliced

1 carrot, sliced
1-1/2 cups dry white wine
2 tablespoons wine vinegar
2 cups drained canned chopped
   tomatoes
2 bay leaves
1/2 teaspoon sugar

Rub the meat with a mixture of the salt, pepper and garlic. Heat the oil in a Dutch oven or heavy saucepan; add the meat, onions, celery and carrot. Brown the meat on all sides. Add the wine, vinegar, tomatoes, bay leaves and sugar. Cover and cook over low heat 2-1/2 hours or until tender. Transfer the meat to a heated serving dish. Skim the fat from the gravy and force through a sieve.

Serves 10.

Per serving
Calories 250
Saturated fat 16.5 grams
Polyunsaturated fat 1.9 grams
Total fat 39.5 grams

BEEF STEW, ROMAN STYLE

2 pounds eye or top round
2 tablespoons special oil
1 cup thinly sliced onions
1 clove garlic, minced
1 teaspoon salt
1/2 teaspoon freshly ground
   black pepper

1/4 teaspoon oregano
1 cup dry red wine
1 tablespoon tomato paste
1/2 cup boiling water

Slice the meat 3/8 inch thick. Heat the oil in a Dutch oven or heavy saucepan; sauté the onions and garlic 5 minutes. Add the meat and brown on both sides; season with the salt, pepper, oregano and add the wine, tomato paste and water. Bring to a boil, cover and cook over low heat 1-1/2 hours or until tender. Skim the fat.

Serves 8.

Per serving
Calories 205
Saturated fat   5.8 grams
Polyunsaturated fat   2.3 grams
Total fat 16.0 grams

BEEF ROLLS

6 minute steaks (1-1/2 pounds)
1/2 pound mushrooms, chopped
1/4 cup chopped onions
2 tablespoons chopped parsley
1 clove garlic, minced
1 teaspoon salt

1/2 teaspoon freshly ground
   black pepper
2 tablespoons special oil
1 cup dry red wine
1 tablespoon tomato paste

Have all the visible fat trimmed and the meat pounded very thin. Mix together the mushrooms, onions, parsley, garlic, 1/2 teaspoon salt and 1/4 teaspoon pepper. Spread on each steak and roll up. Tie ends with white thread or secure with toothpicks.

Heat the oil in a skillet; brown the rolls well on all sides. Mix in the wine, tomato paste and remaining salt and pepper; cover and cook over low heat 1 hour.

Serves 6.

Per serving
Calories 320
Saturated fat   8.3 grams
Polyunsaturated fat   3.1 grams
Total fat 22.7 grams

BEEF, CABBAGE AND RICE

2 tablespoons special oil
3 cups cooked rice, chilled
3/4 pound lean top round
1 tablespoon soy sauce
1/2 cup thinly sliced onions
*1/2 cup julienne-cut green
    pepper*

*1-1/2 cups shredded Chinese
    cabbage or sliced celery*
*1/2 teaspoon freshly ground
    black pepper*

Heat 1 tablespoon oil in a skillet; sauté the rice 5 minutes, stirring frequently. Keep warm while preparing the beef. Cut the beef in very narrow strips and toss with the soy sauce.

Heat the remaining oil in a skillet; add the undrained beef; cook over high heat 1 minute, stirring steadily. Add the onions, green pepper, cabbage and pepper. Cook over medium heat 5 minutes. Heap the rice on a platter and cover with the beef mixture.

Serves 4.

Per serving
Calories 360
Saturated fat   4.9 grams
Polyunsaturated fat   4.1 grams
Total fat 16.4 grams

BEEF AND GREEN BEANS, GREEK STYLE

1/4 cup special oil
2 cups chopped onions
1/2 pound lean beef, ground
1 20-ounce can tomatoes
1/2 cup water
3/4 teaspoon salt

*1/2 teaspoon freshly ground
    black pepper*
1 bay leaf
2 tablespoons minced parsley
*1-1/2 pounds green beans, cut, or
    2 packages frozen, thawed*

Heat the oil in saucepan; sauté the onions 5 minutes. Mix in the meat until browned. Add the tomatoes, water, salt, pepper, bay leaf and parsley. Bring to a boil and add the beans; cover and cook over low heat 30 minutes.

Serves 6.

Per serving
Calories 165
Saturated fat 2.9 grams
Polyunsaturated fat 3.1 grams
Total fat 7.8 grams

SUKIYAKI

1 pound fillet of beef or sirloin
    steak
1/4 cup soy sauce
4 teaspoons sugar
3/4 cup beef broth
1 tablespoon dry sherry
2 tablespoons special oil

1 cup thinly sliced onions
1 cup sliced celery
1 cup sliced bamboo shoots
1/2 pound mushrooms, thinly
    sliced
4 scallions (green onions),
    thinly sliced

Trim all the fat and place the meat in the freezer until just firm. (Slightly freezing the meat makes it easier to slice.) Cut in paper-thin slices. Mix together the soy sauce, sugar, broth and sherry.

Heat the oil in a skillet; brown the meat over high heat, then push it to one side. Pour half the soy mixture over it. Put the onions and celery in the skillet; cook over medium heat 3 minutes. Add the bamboo shoots, mushrooms, scallions and remaining soy sauce mixture. Cook 4 minutes. Arrange individual piles on a serving dish, or serve directly from the skillet.

Serves 6.

Per serving
Calories 230
Saturated fat   7.1 grams
Polyunsaturated fat   3.0 grams
Total fat 19.8 grams

BEEF STROGANOFF

1-1/2 pounds sirloin steak,
 1/4 inch thick
2 tablespoons special
 margarine
1/2 cup chopped onions
3/4 pound mushrooms, sliced

3/4 teaspoon salt
1/4 teaspoon freshly ground
 black pepper
2 teaspoons flour
1/2 cup beef broth
3 tablespoons milk

Trim all the visible fat and pound the meat thin with a mallet; cut into strips 2 inches long by 1/4 inch wide.

Melt the margarine in a skillet; sauté the meat and onions 10 minutes. Remove and keep warm. Sauté the mushrooms 5 minutes. Return the meat and onions; sprinkle with the salt, pepper and flour. Add the broth and milk, stirring steadily to the boiling point. Cook 5 minutes longer.

Serves 6.

Per serving
Calories 300
Saturated fat 10.8 grams
Polyunsaturated fat 1.9 grams
Total fat 27.2 grams

SALISBURY STEAK

1-1/2 pounds top round
1 teaspoon salt
1/2 teaspoon freshly ground
 black pepper
1/8 teaspoon thyme
1/4 cup grated onions

1 clove garlic, minced
2 tablespoons minced parsley
2 tablespoons minced green
 pepper
3 tablespoons ice water
1 tablespoon special oil

Trim all the visible fat from the meat before grinding. Mix together the ground meat, salt, pepper, thyme, onions, garlic, parsley, green pepper and ice water. Shape into 6 patties. Oil a broiling pan and place the patties on it.

Broil in a hot broiler (about 2 inches from source of heat) 3 minutes on each side for rare, 4 medium and 6 well done. Serve with heated chili sauce mixed with mustard and Worchestershire sauce, if desired.

Serves 6.

Per serving
Calories 215
Saturated fat   5.7 grams
Polyunsaturated fat   1.7 grams
Total fat 14.9 grams

ITALIAN MEATBALLS

1 pound top round
1 slice white bread, trimmed
1/4 cup skim milk
2 teaspoons finely grated
*   lemon rind*
2 teaspoons minced parsley

1/2 teaspoon salt
1/4 teaspoon freshly ground
*   black pepper*
1 egg white
3 tablespoons flour
2 tablespoons special oil

Be sure all the fat is trimmed from the meat, then have it ground or do it yourself. Soak the bread in the milk, drain and mash smooth. Mix together the meat, bread, lemon rind, parsley, salt, pepper and egg white. Sprinkle the flour onto a board and form round cakes 1/2 inch thick and 1 inch in diameter.

Heat the oil in a skillet and brown the cakes in it 2 minutes on each side.

Serves 6.

Per serving
Calories 205
Saturated fat   4.2 grams
Polyunsaturated fat   2.8 grams
Total fat 13.1 grams

MEAT LOAF

3/4 pound round steak
3/4 pound veal
2 tablespoons special oil
1 egg, beaten
3 tablespoons grated onions
1 clove garlic, minced

3/4 teaspoon salt
1/4 teaspoon freshly ground
   black pepper
1/4 cup dry bread crumbs
1/4 cup chili sauce
1/4 cup water

Have all the visible fat trimmed from the beef and veal; then have it ground once or do it yourself. Mix the meat with all the remaining ingredients. Shape into a loaf and place in a lightly oiled baking pan. Bake in a 375° oven 50 minutes.

Serves 6.

Per serving
Calories 225
Saturated fat 5.8 grams
Polyunsaturated fat 3.1 grams
Total fat 17.1 grams

TEXAS CHILI CON CARNE

1 pound dried pinto (red) beans
1 pound lean boneless beef
4 tablespoons special oil
1 cup chopped onions
2 cloves garlic, minced

1 tablespoon flour
1 16-ounce can tomatoes,
   drained and chopped
3/4 teaspoon salt
3 tablespoons chili powder

Wash the beans, cover with water, bring to a boil, cook 2 minutes, remove from heat, and let soak 1 hour. Drain, add fresh water to cover, and bring to a boil. Cook over low heat 1-1/2 hours, or until beans are almost tender. Drain, reserving 1 cup liquid.

While the beans are cooking, cut the meat into 1/4-inch dice. (Ground beef may be used, but diced beef is more authentic.) Heat the oil in a skillet; sauté the onions and garlic 5 minutes. Add the meat; cook until browned, stirring frequently. Transfer to a casserole or saucepan. Blend in the flour, then add the tomatoes, salt, chili powder and bean water.

Bring to a boil, cover and cook over low heat 1-1/2 hours. Add the beans. Recover and cook 30 minutes longer, stirring frequently.

Serves 8.

Per serving
Calories 240
Saturated fat   4.2 grams
Polyunsaturated fat   2.8 grams
Total fat 12.1 grams

STUFFED PEPPERS

3/4 pound top round
6 large green peppers
1/2 cup grated onions
3 tablespoons raw rice
1 teaspoon salt
1/2 teaspoon freshly ground
    black pepper
1 egg, beaten

2 tablespoons cold water
2 tablespoons special oil
1 cup chopped onions
1 29-ounce can tomatoes,
    drained
2 tablespoons lemon juice
2 tablespoons sugar

Have all the fat trimmed before grinding the meat. Wash the peppers and cut a 1-inch piece from the stem ends. Reserve. Scoop out the seeds and fibers.

Mix together the meat, grated onions, rice, salt, 1/4 teaspoon pepper, the egg and water. Stuff the peppers and replace the tops.

Heat the oil in a heavy saucepan; sauté the chopped onions 10 minutes. Mix in the tomatoes and the remaining pepper. Arrange the peppers in an upright position. Cover and cook over low heat 45 minutes. Add the lemon juice and sugar; cook 30 minutes longer, or until peppers are tender; baste frequently. The gravy should be sweet and sour.

Serves 6.

Per serving
Calories 205
Saturated fat   3.6 grams
Polyunsaturated fat   2.9 grams
Total fat 11.8 grams

LAMB STEW

3 pounds boneless lamb
3 tablespoons special oil
16 small white onions
1 teaspoon salt
1/2 teaspoon freshly ground
    black pepper

Dash ground allspice
1 bay leaf
1-1/2 cups beef broth
2 cups peeled diced potatoes
2 cups shelled green peas or
    1 package frozen, thawed

Cut the lamb into 1-1/2-inch cubes. Heat the oil in a Dutch oven; add the lamb and cook until browned. Add the onions and continue browning. Season with the salt, pepper and allspice; add the bay leaf and broth. Cover and cook over low heat 45 minutes. Add the potatoes and peas, recover, and cook 25 minutes.

Serves 8.

Per serving
Calories 340
Saturated fat 11.6 grams
Polyunsaturated fat 3.5 grams
Total fat 27.4 grams

BREADED LAMB STEAK

o lamb steaks, cut 1/4-inch thick
1 teaspoon salt
1/4 teaspoon freshly ground
    black pepper
1/4 teaspoon thyme

1 egg
1/4 cup cold water
3/4 cup dry bread crumbs
3/4 cup grated sapsago cheese
1/3 cup special oil

Season the steaks with the salt, pepper, and thyme. Beat the egg with the water. Dip the steaks in the egg, then in a mixture of the bread crumbs and cheese, and finally in the egg.

Heat the oil in a heavy skillet; sauté the steaks 5 minutes on each side or to desired degree of rareness.

Serves 6.

Per serving
Calories 295
Saturated fat 12.9 grams
Polyunsaturated fat 3.9 grams
Total fat 27.3 grams

CROWN ROAST OF LAMB

Crown of lamb
1/2 cup minced onions
2 cups fresh bread crumbs
1/2 teaspoon thyme
1-1/2 teaspoons salt
3/4 teaspoon freshly ground
    black pepper

1/2 cup special oil
2 cloves garlic, minced
1-1/2 cups dry sherry
Sautéed mushroom caps

Have the crown trimmed of fat, tied up, rib bones scraped, and the scraped meat ground. Mix the ground lamb with the onions, bread crumbs, thyme, 3/4 teaspoon salt, 1/4 teaspoon pepper and 1/4 cup of the oil.

Rub the crown with the garlic and remaining salt and pepper. Place the lamb in a roasting pan and fill the center with the stuffing. Cover the stuffing with a piece of aluminum foil. Place a potato cube on each bone to keep ends from burning. Roast in a 450° oven 20 minutes. Pour off the fat and add the remaining oil and sherry. Reduce heat to 350° and roast 2 hours longer, or to desired degree of rareness. Baste frequently and remove foil covering for the last 15 minutes of roasting time. Transfer to a heated platter, remove cubes of potato, and replace with a sautéed mushroom cap or paper frill. Skim the fat from the gravy and serve with the roast.

Serves 10.

Per serving

Calories 345
Saturated fat 12.6 grams
Polyunsaturated fat 2.2 grams
Total fat 28.3 grams

135

LAMB WITH YOGURT SAUCE, TURKISH STYLE

1-1/2 pounds lamb steak
1/2 cup grated onion
1/4 cup special oil
1 teaspoon salt
6 peppercorns, crushed

3 slices whole wheat bread,
　　toasted and cut in half
3/4 cup hot beef broth
2 cups yogurt
Paprika

Cut the meat into six pieces and trim off all the fat. Mix together the onion, oil, salt and peppercorns. Marinate the meat in the mixture for 2 hours at room temperature. Drain when ready to broil.

Put the toast in a heat-proof serving dish. Pour the broth over it and keep in a warm oven until all the liquid is absorbed.

Broil the lamb steak to desired degree of rareness and arrange over the toast. While the lamb is broiling, beat the yogurt with a wooden spoon in a saucepan over low heat until warm. Pour over the meat and sprinkle with paprika.

Serves 6.

Per serving
Calories 315
Saturated fat 12.8 grams
Polyunsaturated fat 2.2 grams
Total fat 29.2 grams

BRAISED SHOULDER OF LAMB

4-pound rolled shoulder of lamb,
　　trimmed of all fat
2 cloves garlic, cut in slivers
1-1/2 teaspoons salt
1/2 teaspoon freshly ground
　　black pepper
4 tablespoons special oil

1 cup thinly sliced onions
2 cups canned drained tomatoes
1 cup beef broth
1/2 teaspoon oregano
3 cups cubed eggplant
1/4 cup sliced black olives
2 tablespoons minced parsley

Make a few slits in the lamb and insert the garlic; rub with the salt and pepper. Heat 2 tablespoons of the oil in a Dutch oven; brown the lamb in it on all sides. Add the onions; cook 5 minutes. Pour off the fat. Mix in the tomatoes, broth and oregano; cover and cook over low heat 2 hours. Baste and turn meat frequently.

Heat the remaining oil in a skillet; brown the eggplant in it. Add to the meat; cook 30 minutes or until the meat is tender. Add the olives; cook 5 minutes longer. Remove the meat to a heated serving dish; skim the fat from the gravy; then mix in the parsley. Pour around the lamb.

Serves 10.

Per serving
Calories 310
Saturated fat 12.4 grams
Polyunsaturated fat 2.5 grams
Total fat 28.2 grams

LAMB AND BEANS, SYRIAN STYLE

2 pounds boneless lamb
1 pound dried navy beans
1/2 cup special oil
3/4 cup chopped onions
1 clove garlic, minced
1 teaspoon salt

1/2 teaspoon freshly ground
black pepper
1/2 teaspoon ground coriander
2 8-ounce cans tomato sauce
1/2 cup minced parsley

Cut the lamb into 1-inch cubes. Wash the beans, cover with water, bring to a boil, remove from the heat, and let stand 1 hour. Drain, add fresh water to cover, bring to a boil, and cook over low heat 1 hour.

While the beans are cooking, heat the oil in a Dutch oven; sauté the onions 5 minutes. Add the garlic, lamb, salt, pepper and coriander; cook until meat browns, stirring frequently. Add the tomato sauce; cover and cook over low heat 30 minutes. Drain the beans and add to the meat. Cook 20 minutes longer or until the lamb and beans are tender. Stir in the parsley.

Serves 10.

Per serving
Calories 345
Saturated fat 10.6 grams
Polyunsaturated fat 5.4 grams
Total fat 27.2 grams

SHISH KEBAB

2 pounds boneless lamb
1 cup dry red wine
1 teaspoon salt
1 clove garlic, minced
1/2 teaspoon freshly ground
   black pepper
1/2 teaspoon thyme

1/2 teaspoon oregano
1/2 cup minced parsley
2 green peppers, cut in
   1/2-inch squares
16 mushrooms, cut in half
12 small white onions,
   cut in half

Cut the lamb into 1/2-inch cubes. In a bowl, combine the wine, salt, garlic, pepper, thyme, oregano and parsley. Marinate the lamb in the mixture 12 hours, basting and turning the meat a few times.

When ready to cook, drain the lamb, reserving the marinade. Use 8 skewers, and on them thread the lamb, green pepper, mushrooms and onions, starting and ending with the lamb. Broil in the broiler or over charcoal to desired degree of rareness. Turn frequently and baste with the marinade.

Serves 8.

Per serving

Calories 310
Saturated fat 12.6 grams
Polyunsaturated fat 2.4 grams
Total fat 27.4 grams

BROILED LIVER

1 pound calf's or beef liver
2 tablespoons melted special
   margarine
1/2 teaspoon salt

1/4 teaspoon freshly ground
   black pepper
2 teaspoons minced parsley

Slice the liver about 1/4 inch thick. Have the broiler very hot. Brush a broiling pan with a little of the margarine. Place the liver on the pan and pour remaining margarine over it. Broil 5 inches from the heat, about 2 minutes on each side for rare, 3 minutes medium and 4 for well done. Transfer to a heated serving dish; sprinkle with the salt, pepper and parsley.

Serves 4.

Per serving

Calories 190
Saturated fat 2.9 grams
Polyunsaturated fat 3.7 grams
Total fat 10.8 grams

LIVER AND MUSHROOM SAUTÉ

1 pound calf's liver, sliced
2 tablespoons special oil
1/2 pound mushrooms, sliced
3 tablespoons chopped scallions
    (green onions)
2 teaspoons flour

1/4 cup dry white wine
1/2 teaspoon salt
1/4 teaspoon freshly ground
    black pepper
1 tablespoon minced parsley

Wash and dry the liver. Cut each slice in fourths crosswise. Heat the oil in a skillet; sauté the mushrooms 5 minutes. In the oil remaining, sauté the liver 2 minutes. Return the mushrooms and add the scallions; sauté 2 minutes. Stir in the flour until browned. Add the wine, salt, pepper and parsley. Cover and cook over low heat 3 minutes. Serve on toast, if desired.

Serves 4.

Per serving
Calories 230
Saturated fat 2.8 grams
Polyunsaturated fat 6.1 grams
Total fat 12.6 grams

VEAL ROAST WITH PEAS

3-pound rolled veal roast
1 clove garlic, cut in slivers
1/2 teaspoon rosemary
1 teaspoon salt
1/2 teaspoon freshly ground
    black pepper

1 tablespoon special oil
1 tablespoon tomato paste
1 cup dry white wine
2 cups firm-cooked qeas

Pierce the veal in several places and insert some garlic and rosemary. Rub with the salt and pepper. Heat the oil in a Dutch oven or heavy casserole; brown the meat in it. Mix the tomato paste with the wine and stir it into the pan. Cover and roast in a 300° oven 1-1/2 hours or until tender. Baste occasionally and remove cover for last 15 minutes. Transfer to a heated platter. Skim the fat from the gravy. Add the peas to the gravy and cook over low heat 2 minutes.

Carve the veal and pour the gravy and peas over it.

Serves 10.

Per serving
Calories 320
Saturated fat 4.8 grams
Polyunsaturated fat 1.1 grams
Total fat 12.2 grams

VEAL AND EGGPLANT CASSEROLE

18 veal scallops (1-1/2 pounds)
3 tablespoons special oil
1 eggplant, peeled and sliced
    thin
1 cup thinly sliced onions
2 cups cubed tomatoes

1 cup diced green peppers
1 teaspoon salt
1/2 teaspoon freshly ground
    black pepper
1/2 teaspoon oregano

Trim any visible fat from the meat. Heat 1 tablespoon oil in a skillet; brown the meat in it on both sides. Oil a casserole with 1 teaspoon oil; arrange successive layers of the eggplant, veal, onions, tomatoes and green peppers, seasoning each layer with a mixture of the salt, pepper and oregano. Sprinkle with the remaining oil. Cover and bake in a 350° oven 1 hour and 15 minutes, removing the cover for the last 15 minutes.

Serves 6.

Per serving
Calories 295
Saturated fat   5.3 grams
Polyunsaturated fat   4.1 grams
Total fat 17.2 grams

ITALIAN VEAL STEW

2 tablespoons special oil
1 clove garlic, minced
2 pounds leg of veal, cut in
    2-inch cubes
1 teaspoon salt
1/4 teaspoon freshly ground
    black pepper

1 cup drained Italian-style
    tomatoes
1/2 cup dry white wine
1/2 teaspoon rosemary

Heat the oil in a heavy saucepan; add the garlic and veal. Brown the meat on all sides. Add the salt, pepper, tomatoes, wine and rosemary. Cover and cook over low heat 1-1/2 hours or until tender.

Serves 8.

Per serving
Calories 290
Saturated fat   4.7 grams
Polyunsaturated fat   2.2 grams
Total fat 13.5 grams

HUNGARIAN VEAL GOULASH

2 pounds boneless veal
1/4 cup flour
1/2 teaspoon salt
1/4 teaspoon freshly ground
    black pepper

2 tablespoons special oil
1-1/2 cups thinly sliced onions
2 teaspoons paprika
1 8-ounce can tomato sauce

Trim all the visible fat from the meat; cut meat in 1-inch cubes. Roll in a mixture of the flour, salt and pepper.

Heat the oil in a Dutch oven or heavy skillet; sauté the onions 10 minutes. Sprinkle with the paprika, add the meat, and let brown. Mix in the tomato sauce; cover and cook over low heat 1 hour or until tender. Serve with boiled noodles.

Serves 6.

Per serving
Calories 390
Saturated fat 6.4 grams
Polyunsaturated fat 3.0 grams
Total fat 18.3 grams

VEAL MARENGO

3 pounds boneless veal
4 tablespoons special oil
1 cup chopped onions
1 teaspoon salt
1/2 teaspoon freshly ground
    black pepper
1/3 cup dry white wine

2 cups Italian-style tomatoes
1/4 cup water
1 bay leaf
1/2 teaspoon thyme
3 tablespoons minced parsley
1/2 pound mushrooms, sliced
1/4 cup sliced black olives

Remove all the fat and cut the veal in 1-1/2-inch cubes. Heat 3 tablespoons oil in a Dutch oven or heavy skillet; sauté the onions 10 minutes. Add the veal and let brown. Season with the salt and pepper and add the wine, tomatoes, water, bay leaf, thyme and parsley. Cover and cook over low heat 1-1/4 hours or until tender. While the meat is cooking, sauté the mushrooms in the remaining oil 5 minutes. Add to the meat with the olives. Cook 5 minutes longer.

Serves 10.

Per serving
Calories 265
Saturated fat 6.0 grams
Polyunsaturated fat 3.5 grams
Total fat 18.5 grams

BRAISED MARINATED VEAL

2 pounds shoulder of veal
1/3 cup special oil
2 tablespoons wine vinegar
1-1/2 teaspoons salt
1/4 teaspoon freshly ground
    black pepper
1/2 teaspoon oregano

2 tablespoons minced parsley
1 clove garlic, minced
1-1/2 cups canned tomato sauce
1/2 cup water
2 cups thinly sliced onions
1/4 pound mushrooms, sliced

Have the veal cut 1/2 inch thick and into 2-inch squares.
Remove as much fat as possible. Mix together 3 tablespoons of
the oil, vinegar, salt, pepper, oregano, parsley, garlic, tomato
sauce and water. Marinate the veal in the mixture in the
refrigerator 4 hours or overnight.

Drain, reserving the marinade. Heat the remaining oil in a
skillet; sauté the onions 5 minutes. Add the veal and
mushrooms; brown lightly. Add the marinade; cook over low
heat 30 minutes or until tender. Turn meat occasionally.

Serves 6.   Per serving
                                        Calories 395
                                    Saturated fat   6.7 grams
                               Polyunsaturated fat   7.2 grams
                                    Total fat 24.5 grams

PIQUANT VEAL SCALLOPS

1 cup dry bread crumbs
1 clove garlic, minced
1 teaspoon dry mustard
1 teaspoon salt
2 tablespoons minced parsley
12 veal scallops (1 pound)

3/4 cup dry white wine
2 tablespoons special oil
1/2 teaspoon Worcestershire
    sauce
2 drops Tabasco

Mix together the bread crumbs, garlic, mustard, salt and
parsley. Dip the scallops in the wine (reserve the balance of
wine) and then into the crumb mixture.

Heat the oil in a skillet, sauté the scallops until browned on
both sides and tender. Transfer to a heated serving dish. Stir

the Worcestershire sauce, Tabasco and remaining wine into the skillet, scraping the bottom and sides well. Bring to a boil and pour over the veal.

Serves 4.

Per serving
Calories 405
Saturated fat 5.7 grams
Polyunsaturated fat 4.3 grams
Total fat 18.3 grams

VEAL SCALLOPS WITH CHICKEN LIVERS

8 veal scallops (3/4 pound)
3 tablespoons flour
1 teaspoon salt
1/4 teaspoon white pepper
3 tablespoons special oil
1/4 teaspoon sage

4 chicken livers, diced
3/4 cup peeled chopped
   tomatoes
1/4 teaspoon freshly ground
   black pepper
2 teaspoons minced parsley

Pound or roll the veal very thin. Dip in a mixture of the flour, 1/2 teaspoon salt and the white pepper. Heat the oil in a skillet; add the sage and veal. Sauté until browned on both sides. Remove and keep warm. Sauté the livers for 3 minutes, then mix in the tomatoes, black pepper and remaining salt. Bring to boil and return the veal. Cook over low heat 5 minutes. Sprinkle with parsley and serve with rice.

Serves 4.

Per serving
Calories 235
Saturated fat 4.9 grams
Polyunsaturated fat 6.3 grams
Total fat 18.9 grams

VEAL SMITANE

1/4 cup nonfat dry milk powder
2/3 cup water
1 teaspoon lemon juice
12 veal scallops (1 pound)
1/4 cup flour
1 teaspoon salt

1/4 teaspoon freshly ground
    black pepper
3 tablespoons special oil
3 tablespoons minced scallions
    (green onions)
1 tablespoon tomato paste

Mix together the dry milk, water and lemon juice. Let stand while preparing the meat. Dip the scallops in the flour, mixed with the salt and pepper. Heat the oil in a skillet; sauté the veal until browned on both sides and tender. Transfer to a heated platter and keep warm.

In the oil remaining in the skillet, sauté the scallions 3 minutes. Stir in the tomato paste; cook 1 minute. Blend in the milk mixture. Heat, stirring steadily but do not let boil. Pour over the scallops.

Serves 4.   Per serving

Calories 280
Saturated fat 5.7 grams
Polyunsaturated fat 6.1 grams
Total fat 20.8 grams

VEAL SAUTÉ WITH MUSHROOMS

2 pounds leg of veal
2 tablespoons special oil
3/4 cup thinly sliced onions
1/3 cup dry white wine
2 clove garlic, minced
1 bay leaf
1 teaspoon salt
1/4 teaspoon freshly ground
    black pepper

1/2 teaspoon thyme
2 cups Italian-style tomatoes
1 tablespoon special
    margarine
1/4 pound mushrooms, sliced
2 tablespoons minced parsley

Cut the veal into 1-1/2-inch cubes. Heat the oil in a Dutch oven or heavy casserole; sauté the onions 5 minutes. Add the veal; brown on all sides. Mix in the wine, garlic, bay leaf, salt, pepper, thyme and tomatoes. Cover and cook over low heat 1-1/4 hours or until tender. While the meat is cooking, prepare the mushrooms.

Melt the margarine in a skillet; sauté the mushrooms 5 minutes. Add to the meat; cook 5 minutes. Sprinkle with the parsley and serve.

Serves 6.

Per serving
Calories 315
Saturated fat 6.7 grams
Polyunsaturated fat 3.6 grams
Total fat 20.1 grams

VEAL SCALLOPS IN NICOISE SAUCE

3 tablespoons special oil
1/4 cup chopped onions
1/4 cup chopped green peppers
2/3 cup canned tomato sauce
6 black olives, sliced
12 veal scallops (1 pound)

1/2 cup skim milk
1/3 cup flour
3/4 teaspoon salt
1 clove garlic, minced
1 tablespoon minced parsley

Heat 1 tablespoon oil in a saucepan; sauté the onions and green peppers 10 minutes. Mix in the tomato sauce; bring to a boil and cook over low heat 15 minutes. Stir in the olives.

While the sauce is cooking, prepare the veal. Dip the veal in the milk and then in the flour mixed with the salt, garlic and parsley. Heat the remaining oil in a skillet; sauté the veal until browned on both sides. Add the sauce; cook 2 minutes.

Serves 4.

Per serving
Calories 280
Saturated fat 5.8 grams
Polyunsaturated fat 6.1 grams
Total fat 21.9 grams

VEAL SCALLOPS IN SHERRY

12 veal scallops (1 pound)	1 teaspoon salt
1/2 cup skim milk	1/4 teaspoon white pepper
1/4 cup flour	1/3 cup sweet sherry
2 tablespoons special margarine	1 tablespoon minced parsley

Dip the scallops in the milk and then in the flour. Melt the margarine in a skillet; sauté the scallops until browned on both sides and tender. Transfer to a heated serving dish; sprinkle with the salt and pepper.

Stir the sherry into the skillet, scraping the bottom and sides. Bring to a boil and pour over the scallops. Sprinkle with the parsley.

Serves 4.

Per serving
Calories 295
Saturated fat 5.7 grams
Polyunsaturated fat 2.2 grams
Total fat 16.5 grams

PAPRIKA VEAL IN CREAM SAUCE

12 veal scallops (1 pound)	4 tablespoons nonfat dry milk powder
1/4 cup flour	1/2 cup water
1/2 teaspoon salt	
3 tablespoons paprika	
2 tablespoons special margarine	

Dip the scallops in the flour mixed with the salt and paprika. Melt the margarine in a skillet; sauté the scallops until browned on both sides and tender. Transfer to a heated serving dish.

Mix the dry milk with the water and stir it into the skillet, scraping the bottom and sides. Bring to a boil and pour over the scallops.

Serves 4.

Per serving
Calories 255
Saturated fat 5.7 grams
Polyunsaturated fat 2.1 grams
Total fat 16.5 grams

WIENER SCHNITZEL

12 veal scallops (1 pound)
1/4 cup flour
1 teaspoon salt
1/4 teaspoon freshly ground
 black pepper
1 egg, beaten
1/3 cup dry bread crumbs

3 tablespoons special
 margarine
6 anchovy fillets, cut in half
2 tablespoons capers
1 tablespoon minced parsley
4 lemon wedges

Be sure the veal is pounded very thin. Dip the scallops in the flour mixed with the salt and pepper, then the egg, and finally the bread crumbs. Melt the margarine in a skillet; sauté the veal until browned on both sides and tender. Transfer to a heated serving dish. Place a half anchovy on each and sprinkle with the capers and parsley. Surround with the lemon.

Serves 4.

Per serving
Calories 450
Saturated fat 7.1 grams
Polyunsaturated fat 3.7 grams
Total fat 21.9 grams

PICCATA OF VEAL

12 veal scallops (1 pound)
1/4 cup flour
3/4 teaspoon salt
1/4 teaspoon white pepper

3 tablespoons special oil
3 tablespoons lemon juice
2 tablespoons minced parsley

Have the veal pounded by the butcher as thin as possible, or do it yourself. (Place the veal between two pieces of waxed paper and pound it from the center out until very thin. Use a mallet or cleaver.) Dip the veal in a mixture of the flour, salt and pepper.

Heat the oil in a skillet; sauté the veal until browned on both sides and tender. Remove veal and keep warm. Stir the lemon juice and parsley into the skillet; cook 30 seconds, scraping the pan of any browned particles. Pour over the veal.

Serves 4.

Per serving
Calories 270
Saturated fat   5.7 grams
Polyunsaturated fat   6.1 grams
Total fat 20.8 grams

OSSO BUCO

4 pounds veal shins
3 tablespoons special oil
3/4 cup dry white wine
2 cups chopped tomatoes
1 clove garlic, minced
1/2 lemon, thinly sliced
1 teaspoon salt

1/2 teaspoon freshly ground
    black pepper
3/4 cup boiling water
1/4 cup minced parsley
2 tablespoons grated lemon
    rind

Buy the youngest veal you can, and have the shin bones cut into 2-inch pieces.

Heat the oil in a heavy saucepan or Dutch oven; brown the veal bones in it. Arrange them in an upright position to keep the marrow from falling out. Pour the wine into the pan and cook 10 minutes. Add the tomatoes, garlic, lemon, salt, pepper and water. Cover and cook over low heat 2 hours or until meat is tender. Skim the fat. Sprinkle the parsley and lemon rind over the top.

Serves 6.

Per serving
Calories 160
Saturated fat 13.3 grams
Polyunsaturated fat   6.7 grams
Total fat 38.0 grams

Poultry

CHICKEN is, of course, America's most popular poultry. As a rule, its price is moderate, and birds of various ages are always available. For persons on low-cholesterol low-fat diets, poultry offers an opportunity for fairly large portions, particularly in the younger birds. Don't eat the skin, however.

The youngest (broilers, fryers and squabs) are low in fat content. Roasters contain somewhat more, and mature hens are fat. Broiling and roasting are the preferred methods. If a chicken stew or other cooked dish is to be made, commence its preparation early in the day. Refrigerate it for several hours and remove the congealed fat. Then heat and serve.

The white meat of chicken has less fat than the dark, but even the dark is fairly lean. Turkey also offers a good opportunity for the dieter; remove all visible fat before roasting and do not baste the bird. Game birds, such as pheasant and partridge, are also very low in fat.

Ducks are suitable, but portions must be kept small. Remove visible fat and roast on a rack, allowing all possible fat to drip out.

BROILED CHICKEN

2-1/2-pound broiler,
    quartered
1 teaspoon salt
1/4 teaspoon freshly ground
    black pepper

1/4 teaspoon minced garlic
2 tablespoons special oil
2 tablespoons lemon juice

Wash and dry the chicken; rub with a mixture of the salt, pepper, and garlic, then brush with the oil and lemon juice. Let stand 1 hour.

Place on a rack (skin side down) in a broiling pan and broil in a hot broiler 30 minutes or until tender. Turn skin side up after 15 minutes.

Serves 4.   Per serving
                                            Calories 205
                                    Saturated fat 3.6 grams
                            Polyunsaturated fat 7.0 grams
                                    Total fat 15.2 grams

INDIAN BROILED CHICKEN

2 1-1/4-pound broilers
2 cups buttermilk
2 tablespoons lemon juice
1 teaspoon salt

1/4 teaspoon Tabasco
1 teaspoon ground coriander
1 teaspoon paprika
4 tablespoons special oil

The broilers may be left whole if you wish to prepare them on a rotisserie. For broiling, it is better to split or quarter them. Wash and dry.

Mix together the buttermilk, lemon juice, salt, Tabasco, coriander and paprika. Marinate the chickens in the mixture overnight. Drain very well and brush with the oil. Broil in a hot broiler 15 minutes on each side or until tender; roast whole broilers in a rotisserie 1 hour or until tender.

Serves 4.   Per serving
                                            Calories 275
                                    Saturated fat 4.4 grams
                            Polyunsaturated fat 10.9 grams
                                    Total fat 22.6 grams

SPICED BROILERS

2 1-1/2-pound broilers,
  quartered
1 teaspoon salt
1/2 teaspoon freshly ground
  black pepper

1-1/2 teaspoons powdered ginger
1 clove garlic, minced
2 tablespoons special oil
2 tablespoons water

Wash and dry the chickens; remove any visible fat. Rub with a mixture of the salt, pepper, ginger and garlic.

Heat the oil in a baking pan; arrange the broilers in it skin side down. Bake in a 400° oven 15 minutes. Turn the broilers skin side up, add the water and bake 20 minutes longer or until browned and tender.

Serves 4.

Per serving

Calories 225
Saturated fat 3.6 grams
Polyunsaturated fat 7.0 grams
Total fat 15.6 grams

BARBECUED CHICKEN

2 1-1/4-pound broilers,
  quartered
2 tablespoons special oil
1/2 cup water
1/3 cup cider vinegar
1 teaspoon Worcestershire
  sauce

1/2 teaspoon salt
1/2 teaspoon freshly ground
  black pepper
1 teaspoon chili powder
3 tablespoons catsup
2 teaspoons sugar
1/2 teaspoon dry mustard

Wash the broilers and remove any fat. Heat 1 tablespoon oil in a baking pan and place the broilers in it skin side down. Broil in a hot broiler 15 minutes.

Combine and bring to a boil the water, vinegar, Worcestershire sauce, salt, pepper, chili powder, catsup, sugar, mustard and remaining oil. At the end of the 15 minutes, turn chickens over, pour the sauce over them and broil 20 minutes longer or until tender. Baste frequently.

Serves 4.

Per serving

Calories 255
Saturated fat 3.6 grams
Polyunsaturated fat 7.0 grams
Total fat 15.6 grams

MARINATED BROILED CHICKEN

1/3 cup dry sherry
1/4 cup soy sauce
2 tablespoons sugar
3 tablespoons chopped onions
1 tablespoon prepared
   horseradish

2 teaspoons powdered ginger
2 1-1/2-pound broilers,
   quartered
2 tablespoons special oil

Combine and bring to a boil the sherry, soy sauce, sugar, onions, horseradish and ginger; cook over low heat 2 minutes. Brush the chickens with the mixture thoroughly and let stand 30 minutes.

Oil a broiling pan with 1 tablespoon oil. Arrange the chickens in it skin side down. Broil 15 minutes, then turn skin side up. Brush with the remaining oil. Broil 15 minutes longer or until tender, basting frequently.

Serves 4.

Per serving
Calories 265
Saturated fat   3.6 grams
Polyunsaturated fat   7.0 grams
Total fat 15.7 grams

BROWN FRICASSEE OF CHICKEN

3-1/2-pound fryer, disjointed
1/4 cup flour
1 teaspoon salt
1/2 teaspoon freshly ground
   black pepper

2 tablespoons special oil
1 cup chopped onions
1 clove garlic, minced
3/4 cup boiling water

Wash and dry the chicken; remove as much fat as possible. Roll the pieces in a mixture of the flour, salt and pepper. Heat the oil in a Dutch oven or heavy saucepan; brown the chicken and onions in it. Stir in the garlic. Add the water; cover and cook over low heat 45 minutes or until tender. Add a very little extra water if necessary. Skim the fat.

Serves 4.

Per serving
Calories 290
Saturated fat   2.3 grams
Polyunsaturated fat   4.9 grams
Total fat 11.9 grams

CHICKEN, NEAR EAST STYLE

1/2 pound chestnuts
3-1/2-pound fryer, disjointed
2 tablespoons special oil
1 cup chopped onions
3/4 teaspoon salt

1/4 teaspoon freshly ground
    black pepper
1/2 cup canned tomato sauce
1-1/4 cups boiling water

Cut a crisscross on the top of the chestnuts. Cover with water, bring to a boil and cook over medium heat 10 minutes. Drain; cool slightly and peel. Wash and dry the chicken; remove any visible fat.

Heat the oil in a Dutch oven or casserole; brown the chicken in it. Add the onions; cover and cook over low heat until onions brown. Add the salt, pepper, tomato sauce and half the water. Cover and cook over low heat 30 minutes. Mix in the chestnuts and remaining water; cover and cook over low heat 30 minutes or until chicken and chestnuts are tender.

Serves 4.

Per serving
Calories 285
Saturated fat   2.4 grams
Polyunsaturated fat   5.1 grams
Total fat 12.6 grams

CHICKEN IN RED WINE

3-pound fryer, disjointed
3/4 teaspoon salt
1/4 teaspoon freshly ground
    black pepper
2 tablespoons flour
2 tablespoons special oil

1/2 cup chopped onions
1/4 pound mushrooms, sliced
1-1/2 cups dry red wine
1/4 teaspoon thyme
1 bay leaf

Wash and dry the chicken; rub with a mixture of the salt, pepper and flour. Heat the oil in a Dutch oven or heavy skillet; brown the chicken in it. Remove the chicken. In the fat remaining, sauté the onions 5 minutes. Add the mushrooms; sauté 5 minutes. Pour off any fat. Mix in the wine, thyme and bay leaf; bring to a boil and return the chicken; cover and cook over low heat 45 minutes or until tender.

Serves 4.

Per serving
Calories 305
Saturated fat   2.1 grams
Polyunsaturated fat   4.8 grams
Total fat 11.1 grams

CHICKEN PAPRIKA

3-1/2-pound fryer,
    disjointed
3/4 teaspoon salt
1/4 teaspoon freshly ground
    black pepper
3 tablespoons special oil

1 cup chopped onions
1 tablespoon paprika
3/4 cup boiling water
3 tablespoons nonfat dry milk
    powder
1/4 cup water

Wash and dry the chicken; rub with the salt and pepper. Heat the oil in a deep skillet; brown the chicken in it and remove. In the oil remaining, sauté the onions until browned. Stir in the paprika, then the water. Return the chicken; cover and cook over low heat 45 minutes, or until tender. Mix the dry milk and water; stir into the gravy. Heat.

Serves 4.

Per serving
Calories 325
Saturated fat 2.7 grams
Polyunsaturated fat 6.9 grams
Total fat 15.4 grams

OVEN-FRIED CHICKEN

2 whole chicken breasts
2 tablespoons flour
2 tablespoons crushed
   cornflakes
1 teaspoon salt

1/4 teaspoon freshly ground
   black pepper
1/2 teaspoon paprika
1/4 cup special oil

Cut the whole chicken breasts in half. Wash, dry, and remove any visible fat. Mix together the flour, cornflakes, salt, pepper and paprika; dip the chicken in the mixture until well coated.

Heat the oil in a skillet (with oven-proof handle) or a baking pan. Arrange the chicken in it, skin side down. Bake in a 350° oven 45 minutes or until tender; turn chicken skin side up after 25 minutes.

Serves 4.

Per serving
Calories 235
Saturated fat 1.7 grams
Polyunsaturated fat 7.8 grams
Total fat 14.1 grams

INDIAN CHICKEN STEW

2 tablespoons special oil
1/2 cup finely chopped onions
2 cloves garlic, minced
2 tablespoons curry powder
3/4 teaspoon salt
3-1/2-pound fryer,
    disjointed

1-1/4 cups chicken broth
4 small white onions
2 tablespoons sliced toasted
    almonds

Heat the oil in a skillet or casserole; sauté the chopped onions 5 minutes. Mix in the garlic, curry powder and salt. Add the chicken and let brown. Add the broth and whole onions; cover and cook over low heat 45 minutes or until tender. Sprinkle with the almonds and serve.

Serves 4.

Per serving
Calories 295
Saturated fat   2.6 grams
Polyunsaturated fat   6.2 grams
Total fat 16.6 grams

CHICKEN BREASTS IN SHERRY-TOMATO SAUCE

3 whole chicken breasts
1/2 cup flour
1 teaspoon salt
1/4 teaspoon white pepper
3 tablespoons special oil
1/2 cup chopped onions

3/4 cup peeled chopped
    tomatoes
'4 cup dry sherry
_ cup chicken broth
2 tablespoons minced parsley

Cut the breasts in half, skin and bone them. Dip in a mixture of the flour, salt and pepper. Heat the oil in a skillet; brown the breasts in it on both sides. Remove. Sauté the onions until browned. Stir in the tomatoes, sherry and broth. Return the breasts, cover and cook over low heat 25 minutes or until tender. Sprinkle with the parsley.

Serves 6.

Per serving
Calories 210
Saturated fat 1.0 gram
Polyunsaturated fat 4.2 grams
Total fat 7.6 grams

CHICKEN WITH NUT GRAVY

2 2-1/2-pound broilers,
  disjointed
1/2 cup flour
1 teaspoon salt
4 tablespoons special oil
3 tablespoons cognac

1 cup chopped onions
1-1/2 cups diced green
  peppers
2 teaspoons tomato paste
2 cups chicken broth
1/4 cup chopped walnuts

Wash and dry the chickens; roll in a mixture of the flour and salt. Heat 3 tablespoons oil in a skillet; brown the chicken pieces in it well. Transfer to a casserole or Dutch oven. Heat the cognac, pour it over the chicken, and set aflame.

Add the remaining oil to the skillet; sauté the onions and green peppers 10 minutes. Blend in the tomato paste, broth and walnuts. Cover and bake in 350° oven 45 minutes or until tender. Remove cover for last 10 minutes.

Serves 8.

Per serving
Calories 205
Saturated fat 3.7 grams
Polyunsaturated fat 8.2 grams
Total fat 17.9 grams

BAKED BREAST OF CHICKEN

3 whole chicken breasts
3 tablespoons flour
1 teaspoon salt
1/2 teaspoon freshly ground
  black pepper
3 tablespoons special oil
1 clove garlic, minced

1 cup shelled green peas or
  frozen, thawed
1/2 pound mushrooms, chopped
2 tablespoons minced parsley
1/2 cup sliced celery
1 bay leaf
6 large lettuce leaves

Cut the chicken breasts in half and remove any visible fat. Rub with a mixture of the flour, salt and pepper.

Heat the oil in a deep skillet (with oven-proof handle) or a casserole. Brown the chicken in it. Mix in the garlic; spread the peas, mushrooms, parsley and celery over the chicken. Place the bay leaf in the pan and cover all with the lettuce leaves.

Bake in a 350° oven 35 minutes or until tender.

Serves 6.

Per serving
Calories 155
Saturated fat 1.0 gram
Polyunsaturated fat 4.2 grams
Total fat 7.7 grams

CHICKEN CASSEROLE

2 1-1/4-pound broilers,
  quartered
1 teaspoon salt
1/4 teaspoon white pepper
2 tablespoons special oil
2 cloves
8 small white onions
6 peppercorns

1 bay leaf
1/2 teaspoon thyme
1 tablespoon cornstarch
1 cup chicken broth
2 cups shelled peas or
  1 package frozen, thawed
1/2 teaspoon sugar
1/8 teaspoon nutmeg

Wash and dry the chickens; remove any visible fat. Season with the salt and pepper. Heat the oil in a casserole. Place the chicken in it. Stick the cloves in an onion and add with all the onions, the peppercorns, bay leaf and thyme. Cover and bake in a 350° oven 30 minutes. Skim the fat. Mix the cornstarch with the broth; add to the casserole with the peas, sugar and nutmeg. Recover and bake 35 minutes longer or until chicken is tender.

Serves 4.

Per serving
Calories 385
Saturated fat 3.6 grams
Polyunsaturated fat 7.0 grams
Total fat 15.3 grams

CHICKEN CACCIATORE

3-1/2-pound fryer, disjointed
3 tablespoons flour
1 teaspoon salt
1/2 teaspoon freshly ground
    black pepper
2 tablespoons special oil
3/4 cup chopped onions

2 cups canned Italian-style
    tomatoes
1 green pepper, diced
1/2 cup sliced mushrooms
1/4 teaspoon oregano
1/4 cup dry red wine
2 tablespoons minced parsley

Wash and dry the chicken; remove any visible fat. Toss with a mixture of the flour, salt and pepper. Heat the oil in a deep skillet or casserole; brown the chicken and onions in it. Add the tomatoes, green pepper, mushrooms, oregano and wine. Cover and cook over low heat 50 minutes or until tender. Sprinkle with the parsley.

Serves 4.

Per serving
Calories 305
Saturated fat 2.3 grams
Polyunsaturated fat 4.9 grams
Total fat 11.9 grams

CHICKEN IN BUTTERMILK

2 2-1/2-pound fryers,
  disjointed
1 cup buttermilk
1 teaspoon salt
1/4 teaspoon freshly ground
  black pepper

2 cloves garlic, minced
2 tablespoons special oil
1 cup chopped onions
2 tablespoons curry powder
2 tablespoons ground
  blanched almonds

Wash and dry the chickens; remove any visible fat. Marinate 2 hours in a mixture of the buttermilk, salt, pepper and garlic, turning and basting frequently. Drain chicken well; reserve the marinade.

Heat the oil in a deep skillet or casserole; sauté the onions 10 minutes. Mix in the curry powder; add the chicken and brown lightly. Add the marinade; cover and cook over low heat 1 hour or until tender. Stir in the almonds; cook 2 minutes.

Serves 8.

Per serving
Calories 205
Saturated fat 1.8 grams
Polyunsaturated fat 3.9 grams
Total fat 11.7 grams

CHICKEN WITH TOMATOES

2 whole raw chicken breasts
1 tablespoon dry sherry
2 tablespoons soy sauce
3 tablespoons cornstarch
1/4 cup special oil
1 cup chopped onions

1/2 teaspoon salt
1 teaspoon sugar
1/2 cup chicken broth
2 tomatoes, peeled and cut in
  eighths

Remove the skin and bones of the chicken. Cut each breast into fourths. Rub with the sherry mixed with 1 tablespoon of the soy sauce. Sprinkle with 2 tablespoons of the cornstarch; let stand 15 minutes.

Heat the oil in a skillet; sauté the chicken until browned on both sides, about 10 minutes. Add the onions; sauté 5 minutes. Mix the remaining cornstarch with the remaining soy sauce, the salt, sugar and broth; stir into the skillet until thickened. Add the tomatoes, cover, and cook 3 minutes. Don't overcook.

Serves 4.

Per serving
Calories 220
Saturated fat   1.7 grams
Polyunsaturated fat   7.8 grams
Total fat 14.1 grams

CHICKEN CURRY

3-pound fryer, disjointed
1/2 teaspoon salt
1/4 teaspoon freshly ground
   black pepper
3 tablespoons special oil
1 cup thinly sliced onions

1 tablespoon curry powder
1 cup boiling water
1 tablespoon cornstarch
1/2 cup skim milk
2 tablespoons sesame seeds
   or ground almonds

Wash and dry the chicken; season with the salt and pepper. Heat the oil in a Dutch oven or casserole; brown the chicken and onions in it. Sprinkle with the curry powder and add 1/2 cup of the water. Cover and cook over low heat 15 minutes. Add remaining water; recover and cook 15 minutes longer. Mix together the cornstarch and skim milk; stir into the gravy with the sesame seeds (or ground almonds). Cook 15 minutes longer or until tender.

Serves 4.

Per serving
Calories 285
Saturated fat   3.3 grams
Polyunsaturated fat   9.6 grams
Total fat 23.1 grams

CHICKEN PILAF

1-1/2 cups raw rice
1 3-1/2-pound fryer, disjointed
4 tablespoons special oil
1 cup thinly sliced onions
1-1/2 cups buttermilk

1 teaspoon salt
1/4 teaspoon white pepper
1/2 teaspoon powdered ginger
2 cups hot chicken broth
1 green pepper, sliced thin

Wash the rice, cover with water, and bring to a boil; let stand 15 minutes, then drain well. Wash and dry the chicken; remove any visible fat.

Heat the oil in a casserole or Dutch oven; brown the chicken and onions in it. Add the buttermilk, salt, pepper and ginger;. bring to a boil and cook over low heat 20 minutes. Add the rice and broth and arrange the green peppers on top. Cover and cook over low heat 35 minutes. The pilaf should be fairly dry but not completely so. Watch carefully while cooking and add a little more boiling water if necessary.

Serves 6.

	Per serving
Calories 385	
Saturated fat	2.1 grams
Polyunsaturated fat	5.9 grams
Total fat	12.6 grams

CHICKEN WITH WALNUTS

2 whole raw chicken breasts
1 tablespoon soy sauce
3 tablespoons dry sherry
3/4 teaspoon salt
1 teaspoon sugar
4 tablespoons cornstarch
1 egg, beaten

1/4 cup special oil
1/4 cup blanched walnuts
1 clove garlic, minced
1 teaspoon powdered ginger
1 cup sliced bamboo shoots
    or bean sprouts
1/4 cup boiling water

Remove the skin and bones of the chicken; cut into 1-inch squares. Mix together the soy sauce, sherry, salt and sugar; marinate the chicken in the mixture 30 minutes. Baste and turn the chicken a few times. Drain, reserving the marinade. Dip the chicken in the cornstarch and then in the egg.

Heat the oil in a skillet; brown the walnuts in it and remove.

In the oil remaining, brown the chicken pieces. Add the garlic, ginger, bamboo shoots (or bean sprouts), water and reserved marinade. Cover and cook over low heat 15 minutes. Return the walnuts and cook only 1 minute longer.

Serves 4.

Per serving
Calories 290
Saturated fat   2.4 grams
Polyunsaturated fat 10.5 grams
Total fat 19.6 grams

PINEAPPLE CHICKEN

2 whole raw chicken breasts
3/4 teaspoon salt
1/4 teaspoon white pepper
3 tablespoons cornstarch
1 16-ounce can
     pineapple chunks

3 tablespoons special oil
2 tablespoons soy sauce
2 teaspoons lemon juice

Remove the skin and bones of the chicken; cut meat into 2-inch pieces. Mix together the salt, pepper and 2 tablespoons cornstarch; toss with the chicken pieces. Drain the pineapple, reserving 3/4 cup juice.

Heat the oil in a skillet; sauté the chicken 10 minutes. Add the pineapple; cover and cook over low heat 5 minutes. Mix the remaining cornstarch with the soy sauce, lemon juice and pineapple juice. Add to the skillet, stirring to the boiling point. Cook 3 minutes; don't overcook.

Serves 4.

Per serving
Calories 240
Saturated fat   1.4 grams
Polyunsaturated fat   6.1 grams
Total fat 11.0 grams

CHICKEN AND NOODLES

2 whole raw chicken breasts
4 tablespoons special oil
1 cup thinly sliced onions
2 cups sliced celery
2 cups bean sprouts
3/4 teaspoon salt
1/4 teaspoon freshly ground
    black pepper

2 tablespoons soy sauce
1/2 teaspoon sugar
1 tablespoon cornstarch
3/4 cup chicken broth
1-1/2 cups cooked, drained
    fine noodles

Remove the skin and bones of the chicken; cut into narrow strips. Heat the oil in a deep skillet; sauté the chicken 5 minutes. Mix in the onions, celery, bean sprouts, salt, pepper, soy sauce and sugar. Cover and cook over low heat 8 minutes; don't overcook. Mix together the cornstarch and broth; stir into the skillet until thickened. Add the noodles and stir. Cook 2 minutes only.

Serves 6.

Per serving
Calories 205
Saturated fat   1.5 grams
Polyunsaturated fat   5.4 grams
Total fat 10.2 grams

CHICKEN HASH

2 tablespoons special
    margarine
3/4 cup chopped onions
1-1/2 cups peeled diced
    potatoes
2 cups diced cooked chicken

3/4 teaspoon salt
1/4 teaspoon freshly ground
    black pepper
1/2 cup chicken broth
1 tablespoon minced parsley

Melt the margarine in a skillet; sauté the onions and potatoes 10 minutes. Add the chicken, salt and pepper; cook 1 minute. Mix in the broth and parsley; cook over low heat 10 minutes.

Serves 6.

Per serving
Calories 195
Saturated fat 1.1 grams
Polyunsaturated fat 1.4 grams
Total fat 5.0 grams

CHICKEN À LA KING

2 tablespoons special oil
3/4 cup diced green peppers
1/2 pound mushrooms, sliced
3 cups cubed cooked chicken
3 pimentos, cut julienne

2 tablespoons cornstarch
3 cups chicken broth
1 egg yolk
2 tablespoons dry sherry

Heat the oil in a skillet; sauté the green peppers 5 minutes.
Add the mushrooms; sauté 5 minutes. Mix in the chicken and
pimentos. Keep warm while preparing the sauce.

Mix the cornstarch with the broth until smooth. Cook over
low heat, stirring steadily to the boiling point. Cook 5 minutes
longer. Beat the egg yolk and sherry in a bowl; gradually add
the hot sauce, stirring steadily to prevent curdling. Return to
the saucepan; mix in the chicken mixture. Heat but do not let
boil. Serve on toast.

Serves 6.

Per serving
Calories 230
Saturated fat 1.3 grams
Polyunsaturated fat 3.0 grams
Total fat 6.9 grams

CHICKEN CHOW MEIN

2 tablespoons special oil
1-1/2 cups thinly sliced
onions
2 cups sliced celery
3/4 pound mushrooms, sliced
1-1/2 cups chicken broth

1 cup bean sprouts
1 cup sliced water chestnuts
1 tablespoon cornstarch
3 tablespoons soy sauce
2 cups julienne-cut cooked
chicken

Heat the oil in a deep skillet; sauté the onions 5 minutes.
Add the celery and mushrooms; sauté 5 minutes. Mix in the
broth, bean sprouts and water chestnuts; cook 3 minutes.

Mix the cornstarch and soy sauce together. Stir into the
vegetable mixture until thickened. Add the chicken. Heat and
serve with fine, boiled noodles.

Serves 6.

Per serving
Calories 200
Saturated fat 0.8 gram
Polyunsaturated fat 2.8 grams
Total fat 5.5 grams

CHICKEN PARISIENNE

2 packages frozen broccoli
2 tablespoons special
    margarine
2 tablespoons flour
1/4 teaspoon white pepper

2 cups chicken broth
1/2 cup skim milk
2 tablespoons grated
    Parmesan cheese
18 thin slices cooked chicken

Cook the broccoli 2 minutes less than package suggests; drain well and spread on the bottom of a baking dish.

Melt the margarine in a saucepan; blend in the flour and pepper. Add the broth and milk, stirring steadily to the boiling point. Cook over low heat 5 minutes. Mix in the cheese. Pour half the sauce over the broccoli. Arrange the chicken over it and cover with the remaining sauce. Bake in a 425° oven 10 minutes or until delicately browned.

Serves 6.

Per serving
Calories 210
Saturated fat 2.3 grams
Polyunsaturated fat 1.7 grams
Total fat 7.3 grams

CHICKEN-POTATO PIE

3 cups diced cooked chicken
1 cup cooked peas
1 egg, beaten
1/2 cup chicken broth
2 tablespoons dry bread
    crumbs
2 tablespoons minced parsley

2 cups mashed potatoes
2 tablespoons special
    margarine, melted
1/2 cup hot skim milk
1 teaspoon salt
1/4 teaspoon white pepper
1/8 teaspoon nutmeg

Mix together the chicken, peas, egg, broth, bread crumbs and parsley. Turn into a deep 9-inch pie plate.

Beat until light and fluffy the potatoes, margarine, milk, salt, pepper and nutmeg. Spread over the chicken, covering the edges. Bake in a 375° oven 30 minutes or until browned.

Serves 6.

Per serving
Calories 235
Saturated fat 1.6 grams
Polyunsaturated fat 1.6 grams
Total fat 6.4 grams

BARBECUED SQUABS

4 squabs
1/3 cup dry sherry
1/2 teaspoon salt
1/2 teaspoon freshly ground
    black pepper
1 teaspoon sugar

1/2 teaspoon cinnamon
1 teaspoon powdered ginger
1/8 teaspoon nutmeg
1/2 teaspoon garlic powder
2 tablespoons special oil

Wash and dry the squabs; remove any visible fat. Mix together all the remaining ingredients. Brush the squabs with the mixture inside and out. Roast on a spit in a rotisserie oven for 1 hour or place on a rack in a shallow roasting pan. Roast in a 400° oven 1 hour or until tender. Baste and turn squabs frequently.

Serves 4.

Per serving
Calories 275
Saturated fat   6.4 grams
Polyunsaturated fat   8.0 grams
Total fat 25.8 grams

CHICKEN LIVERS WITH NUT SAUCE

1 pound chicken livers
2 tablespoons special oil
3/4 cup chopped onions
1 clove garlic, minced
3 tablespoons ground pecans

1/2 teaspoon salt
1/4 teaspoon freshly ground
    black pepper
1 teaspoon grated lemon rind
1/2 cup chicken broth

Wash the livers, removing any discolored areas; cut each liver into fourths.

Heat the oil in a skillet; sauté the onions and garlic 10 minutes. Add the livers; sauté until no pink remains. Mix in the pecans, salt, pepper, lemon rind and broth; cook over low heat 10 minutes, stirring frequently.

Serves 4.

Per serving
Calories 240
Saturated fat   2.9 grams
Polyunsaturated fat   7.3 grams
Total fat 19.8 grams

STUFFED SQUAB BROILERS

2 1-1/4-pound squab broilers
1 teaspoon salt
3/4 teaspoon freshly ground
   black pepper
1/2 teaspoon minced garlic
.3 tablespoons special oil

3/4 cup chopped onions
1/2 pound mushrooms, chopped
1 cup cooked fine noodles
1 egg, beaten
2 tablespoons dry sherry
2 tablespoons minced parsley

Have the broilers left whole. Season with 1/2 teaspoon salt, 1/2 teaspoon pepper and the garlic. Heat 2 tablespoons oil in a skillet; sauté the onions 5 minutes. Add the mushrooms and sauté 5 minutes. Remove from the heat; mix in the noodles, egg, sherry, parsley and the remaining salt and pepper. Stuff the chickens, closing the openings with skewers or cover opening with aluminum.

Heat the remaining oil in a baking pan; place the broilers on it. Roast in a 425° oven 15 minutes. Reduce the heat to 350° and roast 35 minutes longer or until browned and tender.

Serves 4.

Per serving
Calories 410
Saturated fat 7.4 grams
Polyunsaturated fat 10.2 grams
Total fat 30.9 grams

CHICKEN LIVER PAPRIKA

1 pound chicken livers
2 tablespoons special oil
1 cup thinly sliced onions
1/2 teaspoon salt

1-1/2 teaspoons paprika
1/4 cup Special Sour Cream
   (see recipe)

Wash the livers; remove any discolored areas and cut in half. Heat the oil in a skillet; sauté the onions until browned. Remove. In the oil remaining, sauté the livers 5 minutes. Return the onions; season with the salt and paprika. Mix in the sour cream; heat but do not let boil. Serve on toast if desired.

Serves 4.

Per serving
Calories 255
Saturated fat 2.6 grams
Polyunsaturated fat 5.8 grams
Total fat 11.8 grams

CHICKEN LIVERS EN BROCHETTE

18 chicken livers
3 tomatoes
24 small mushroom caps
1/2 teaspoon salt

1/2 teaspoon freshly ground
   black pepper
2 tablespoons special oil

Wash the livers, removing any discolored areas. Cut in half.
Cut each tomato into 6 wedges. Use 6 skewers. Arrange the
mushrooms, livers and tomatoes on the skewers, starting and
ending with the mushrooms. Season with the salt and pepper;
brush with the oil.

Place on a rack and broil in a hot broiler about 8 minutes or
until livers are cooked the way you like them. Turn skewers
frequently. Serve with chili sauce, which should be heated.

Serves 6.

Per serving
Calories 140
Saturated fat 1.4 grams
Polyunsaturated fat 3.5 grams
Total fat 6.9 grams

TURKEY AND WILD RICE CASSEROLE

1 cup wild rice
6 tablespoons special oil
1 pound mushrooms, sliced
1/2 cup chopped onions
1 teaspoon salt
1/4 teaspoon freshly ground
   black pepper

3 cups diced cooked turkey
1/4 cup blanched sliced almonds
3 cups chicken broth
1-1/2 cups yogurt

Wash the rice very thoroughly. Cover with water, bring to a
boil, remove from heat, and let soak 1 hour. Drain.

Heat half the oil in a skillet; sauté the mushrooms and
onions 10 minutes. Mix the sautéed vegetables with the
drained wild rice, the salt, pepper, turkey, almonds, broth and
yogurt. Turn into a greased casserole. Cover and bake in a
350° oven 1-1/4 hours. Remove cover, sprinkle with the remaining oil, and bake 20 minutes longer.

Serves 8.

Per serving
Calories 310
Saturated fat   7.9 grams
Polyunsaturated fat   4.3 grams
Total fat 18.3 grams

Vegetables

VEGETABLES may be eaten twice daily in generous servings because with few exceptions they contain little or no fat. When dining out, order boiled or steamed vegetables without butter; this particularly applies to potatoes, which should only be ordered boiled or baked.

The recipes in this section are slightly unusual in many cases. These have been chosen deliberately to pique the interest of the dieter and to remove him from the everyday routine of string beans and green peas. Those who can spare the calories may delight in fried and sautéed potatoes made with special oil; these fortunate people may also douse their plain vegetables liberally with special margarine if they choose.

BRAISED ARTICHOKE HEARTS

2 tablespoons special
  margarine
1/2 cup chopped onions
1/2 cup chicken broth
2 packages frozen artichoke
  hearts

2 tablespoons lemon juice
1/2 teaspoon salt
1/4 teaspoon white pepper

Melt the margarine in a skillet; sauté the onions 10 minutes. Add the broth; bring to a boil. Add the artichoke hearts, lemon juice, salt and pepper; cover and cook over low heat 10 minutes.

Serves 8.

Per serving
Calories 85
Saturated fat 0.6 gram
Polyunsaturated fat 0.8 gram
Total fat 2.8 grams

BRAISED BROCCOLI

1 bunch broccoli or 2
  packages frozen, thawed
3 tablespoons special oil
1/4 cup chopped scallions
  (green onions)

1/2 teaspoon salt
1/4 teaspoon white pepper
3 tablespoons boiling water

If fresh broccoli is used, wash thoroughly and discard the tough ends. Cut lengthwise into 1-inch slices. If frozen broccoli is used, thaw it completely and drain well. Cut each piece in half lengthwise.

Heat the oil in a skillet; sauté the broccoli and scallions 5 minutes (only 3 minutes if frozen broccoli is used). Add the salt, pepper and water; cover and cook over low heat 5 minutes.

Serves 4.

Per serving
Calories 95
Saturated fat 1.7 grams
Polyunsaturated fat 2.4 grams
Total fat 8.1 grams

RED CABBAGE AND APPLES

2 tablespoons special
  margarine
6 cups finely shredded red
  cabbage
1 teaspoon salt
1/4 teaspoon freshly ground
  black pepper

1/2 cup minced onions
3 tablespoons cider vinegar
3 tablespoons water
2 cups peeled diced apples
1 tablespoon sugar

In a heavy saucepan melt the margarine. Add the cabbage, salt, pepper, onions, vinegar and water; cover and cook over very low heat 1 hour. Mix in the apples and sugar; recover and cook 1 hour longer. Watch carefully and add a little water if necessary to keep from burning.

Serves 8.

Per serving
Calories 70
Saturated fat 0.6 gram
Polyunsaturated fat 0.8 gram
Total fat 2.8 grams

SWEET-AND-SOUR CARROTS

10 carrots
1-1/2 cups water
1/2 teaspoon salt
2 tablespoons special
  margarine

2 teaspoons flour
1 tablespoon sugar
1 tablespoon vinegar

Wash, scrape and thinly slice the carrots. Combine in a saucepan with the water and salt; bring to a boil and cook over low heat 10 minutes. Drain, reserving 1/2 cup of the liquid.

Melt the margarine in a saucepan; blend in the flour. Add the liquid, stirring steadily to the boiling point. Mix in the sugar, vinegar and carrots. Cook over low heat 5 minutes.

Serves 4.

Per serving
Calories 110
Saturated fat 1.2 grams
Polyunsaturated fat 1.6 grams
Total fat 5.7 grams

BRAISED CARROTS

3 cups thinly sliced carrots
1/4 cup water
2 tablespoons special
   margarine
1 teaspoon sugar

1/2 teaspoon salt
1 tablespoon minced parsley
1/4 teaspoon freshly ground
   black pepper

In a skillet, combine the carrots, water, margarine, sugar and salt. Cover and cook over low heat 20 minutes or until tender. Shake the pan frequently. The water should have evaporated, and the carrots should be coated with the margarine. Sprinkle with the parsley and pepper.

Serves 4.

Per serving
Calories 85
Saturated fat 1.2 grams
Polyunsaturated fat 1.6 grams
Total fat 5.7 grams

BRAISED CELERY

2 bunches celery
3 tablespoons special oil
1/4 teaspoon salt
1/2 cup chicken broth

1/2 teaspoon Worcestershire
   sauce
1/2 teaspoon sugar

Trim the leaves of the celery. Cut bunches crosswise in 2-inch pieces. Heat the oil in a skillet; add the celery and salt. Sauté 5 minutes, stirring frequently. Add the broth, mixed with the Worcestershire sauce and sugar. Cover and cook over low heat 10 minutes or until tender.

Serves 6.

Per serving
Calories 65
Saturated fat 1.2 grams
Polyunsaturated fat 1.6 grams
Total fat 5.1 grams

STUFFED EGGPLANT

2 small eggplants
3 tablespoons special oil
1-1/2 cups chopped onions
2 cloves garlic, minced
1-1/2 cups chopped peeled
    tomatoes
3/4 teaspoon salt
1/4 teaspoon freshly ground
    black pepper

1/4 teaspoon oregano
1 tablespoon minced parsley
2 tablespoons grated
    Parmesan cheese
4 tablespoons dry bread
    crumbs

Cut the eggplants in half lengthwise; scoop out the pulp and dice it. Reserve the shells.

Heat 2 tablespoons of the oil in a skillet; sauté the onions 5 minutes. Add the garlic and eggplant pulp; sauté 5 minutes. Mix in the tomatoes, salt, pepper and oregano; cook over low heat 10 minutes. Remove from the heat and mix in the parsley and cheese. Stuff the shells; sprinkle with the bread crumbs and remaining oil. Place on a baking sheet; bake in a 375° oven 25 minutes.

Serves 4.

Per serving
Calories 155
Saturated fat 1.7 grams
Polyunsaturated fat 5.9 grams
Total fat 11.1 grams

RATATOUILLE (Mixed Vegetables, Niçoise Style)

3 tablespoons special oil
1 eggplant, peeled and diced
1/2 cup thinly sliced onions
1 zucchini, thinly sliced
1 green pepper, cut julienne
3 tomatoes, thinly sliced

1 teaspoon salt
1/2 teaspoon freshly ground
    black pepper
1 clove garlic, minced
2 tablespoons minced parsley

Heat 1 tablespoon oil in a skillet; sauté the eggplant 10 minutes. Spread in a casserole. Add 2 teaspoons oil to the skillet; sauté the onions and zucchini 10 minutes. Spread over the eggplant. Add 2 teaspoons oil to the skillet; sauté the green pepper 5 minutes. Add to the casserole with the tomatoes, salt, pepper, garlic and parsley. Turn mixture gently with 2 spoons, then sprinkle with the remaining oil. Cover and bake in a 375° oven 1 hour, removing the cover for the last 15 minutes. Serve hot or cold.

Serves 8.

Per serving
Calories 80
Saturated fat 0.6 gram
Polyunsaturated fat 3.0 grams
Total fat 5.1 grams

GREEN BEANS, ITALIAN STYLE

3 tablespoons special oil
1/2 cup chopped onions
1 clove garlic, minced
1 20-ounce can tomatoes,
    drained
1/2 teaspoon salt

1/2 teaspoon freshly ground
    black pepper
1/4 teaspoon oregano
1 bay leaf
2 pounds green beans or
    3 packages frozen

Heat the oil in a saucepan; sauté the onions 10 minutes. Add the garlic, tomatoes, salt, pepper, oregano and bay leaf; bring to a boil and cook over low heat 20 minutes.

If using fresh beans, cut into thirds; add the fresh or frozen beans to the tomato mixture. Cover and cook over low heat 30 minutes.

Serves 8.

Per serving
Calories 75
Saturated fat 0.6 gram
Polyunsaturated fat 3.0 grams
Total fat 5.0 grams

BEAN PANACHÉ

2 tablespoons special oil
1 cup chopped onions
1 pound green beans, cooked
    and drained
1/2 pound wax beans, cooked
    and drained

1 pound lima beans, shelled,
    cooked and drained
1/2 teaspoon salt
1/4 teaspoon freshly ground
    black pepper
2 tablespoons chopped parsley

Heat the oil in a skillet; sauté the onions 10 minutes. Toss
with the green, wax and lima beans. Season with salt and pepper. Sprinkle with the parsley before serving.

Serves 6.   Per serving
                                                    Calories 110
                                           Saturated fat 1.2 grams
                                       Polyunsaturated fat 1.6 grams
                                             Total fat 4.6 grams

INDIAN VEGETABLE CASSEROLE

1 pound green beans or 1 package
    frozen, thawed
1 pound green peas, shelled, or
    1 package frozen, thawed
4 carrots, diced
4 tablespoons special oil
1-1/2 cups thinly sliced onions
1 cup raw rice
1/2 cup yogurt

2 teaspoons ground cumin
1 clove garlic, minced
1/4 teaspoon powdered ginger
2 tablespoons tomato paste
2 cups boiling water
1-1/2 teaspoons salt
1/2 teaspoon freshly ground
    black pepper

In a bowl, combine the beans, peas, carrots and boiling
water to cover. Cover the bowl and let stand 10 minutes; drain.
Heat the oil in a casserole; sauté the onions 10 minutes. Mix
in the rice, yogurt and cumin; cook over low heat 5 minutes.
Add the vegetables; cook over low heat 10 minutes, shaking
the pan frequently. Mix in the garlic, ginger, tomato paste,
water, salt and pepper. Cover and cook over low heat 15
minutes. Watch carefully and add a little more water if
necessary.

Serves 8.   Per serving
                                                    Calories 260
                                           Saturated fat 0.5 gram
                                       Polyunsaturated fat 4.5 grams
                                             Total fat 8.4 grams

GREEN BEANS IN SPICY SAUCE

3 tablespoons special oil
1/2 cup finely chopped onions
1 clove garlic, minced
1 tomato, peeled and chopped
1 teaspoon grated lemon rind
1/2 teaspoon salt

1/8 teaspoon Tabasco
1/2 teaspoon sugar
3/4 cup skim milk
1 pound green beans cut
   French style, or 1
   package frozen, thawed

Heat the oil in a saucepan; sauté the onions, garlic and tomato 3 minutes, stirring frequently. Add the lemon rind, salt, Tabasco, sugar, milk and green beans. Bring to a boil, cover loosely, and cook over low heat 15 minutes or until beans are tender. Don't overcook. Serve hot or cold.

Serves 4.

Per serving
Calories 130
Saturated fat 1.2 grams
Polyunsaturated fat 6.0 grams
Total fat 9.8 grams

GREEN BEANS LYONNAISE

1 pound green beans or 1
   package frozen
2 tablespoons special
   margarine

1/2 cup minced onions
1/2 teaspoon salt
1/8 teaspoon white pepper
1 tablespoon minced parsley

Cook the fresh or frozen beans in salted water until tender but firm. Drain well. Melt the margarine in a skillet; sauté the onions until browned. Mix in the salt, pepper and parsley. Toss with the beans.

Serves 4.

Per serving
Calories 70
Saturated fat 1.2 grams
Polyunsaturated fat 1.6 grams
Total fat 5.6 grams

GLAZED ONIONS

3/4 pound very small white
  onions
2 tablespoons special
  margarine

1 teaspoon sugar
1/2 teaspoon salt

Peel the onions, cover with water, and bring to a boil. Cook over low heat 10 minutes or until barely tender. Drain very well.

Melt the margarine in a skillet. Add the onions, sugar and salt; cover and cook over low heat until onions are glazed, shaking the pan frequently.

Serves 4.

Per serving
Calories 90
Saturated fat 1.2 grams
Polyunsaturated fat 1.6 grams
Total fat 5.3 grams

GREEN PEAS, FRENCH STYLE

1 cup shredded lettuce
2 packages frozen tiny green
  peas, thawed
4 scallions (green onions)
  sliced or 1/3 cup minced
  onions

2 tablespoons special
  margarine
1/2 teaspoon salt
1/2 teaspoon sugar
3 tablespoons water

Combine all the ingredients in a saucepan; cover and cook over low heat 25 minutes. Drain if any liquid remains.

Serves 6.

Per serving
Calories 90
Saturated fat 0.8 gram
Polyunsaturated fat 1.1 grams
Total fat 3.1 grams

BLACK AND WHITE BEANS

2 cups dried black beans
2 cups dried white beans
8 whole cloves garlic
1 teaspoon salt
1/4 cup special oil

1 cup finely chopped onions
2 cloves garlic, minced
1 teaspoon ground cumin
1/2 teaspoon freshly ground
    black pepper

Wash the beans and place in separate saucepans. Cover with water, bring to a boil, and let soak 1 hour. Drain. Add fresh water to cover and 4 cloves garlic to each saucepan. Bring to a boil, cover, and cook over low heat 2 hours or until tender. Drain. Combine the beans and salt in a casserole.

Heat the oil in a skillet; sauté the onions 10 minutes. Stir in the minced garlic for 1 minute, then add to the beans with the cumin and pepper. Mix lightly; cook over low heat 20 minutes.

Serves 12.

Per serving
Calories 160
Saturated fat 1.2 grams
Polyunsaturated fat 1.8 grams
Total fat 5.1 grams

BAKED BEAN CASSEROLE

2 tablespoons special oil
1-1/2 cups thinly sliced onions
1-1/2 cups thinly sliced green peppers
2 1-pound cans vegetarian
    baked beans

2 cups diced tomatoes
1/4 teaspoon salt
1/2 teaspoon freshly ground
    black pepper

Heat the oil in a skillet; sauté the onions and green peppers 10 minutes. In a casserole, arrange successive layers of the beans, tomatoes and sautéed vegetables, sprinkling the vegetables with salt and pepper. Arrange a top layer of tomatoes. Bake in a 350° oven 30 minutes.

Serves 6.

Per serving
Calories 190
Saturated fat 1.1 grams
Polyunsaturated fat 1.7 grams
Total fat 4.9 grams

MACARONI AND KIDNEY BEANS

1 pound dried kidney beans
1/4 cup special oil
1 onion, chopped
2 cloves garlic
1/2 teaspoon salt

1 pound elbow macaroni, half
cooked and drained
2 cups beef broth
1/4 teaspoon dried ground
red peppers

Wash the beans, cover with water, bring to a boil, and let soak 1 hour. Drain.

Heat the oil in a saucepan; sauté the onion and garlic 5 minutes. Add the beans, and water to cover. Cook over medium heat 1-1/2 hours or until beans are tender. Add the salt after 1 hour's cooking time. Drain. Add the macaroni, broth and red peppers. Bring to a boil and cook over medium heat 10 minutes. Serve in deep bowls, with garlic toast and grated sapsago cheese.

Serves 8.

Per serving
Calories 160
Saturated fat 1.2 grams
Polyunsaturated fat 1.6 grams
Total fat 5.6 grams

MUSHROOM-STUFFED CABBAGE

1 head cabbage
3 tablespoons special oil
1/2 pound mushrooms, sliced
1/2 cup chopped onions
1/2 cup raw rice

1 cup boiling water
3/4 teaspoon salt
1/4 teaspoon freshly ground
black pepper
1 cup canned tomato sauce

Cover the cabbage with boiling water and let stand 10 minutes to soften. Carefully remove 16 leaves.

Heat 1 tablespoon of the oil in a skillet; sauté the mushrooms and onions 10 minutes.

Heat 1 tablespoon oil in a saucepan; stir in the rice until it is yellow. Add the boiling water, cover, and cook over low heat until tender and dry. Mix in the sautéed vegetables, salt and pepper. Place a heaping tablespoon of the mixture on each cabbage leaf; turn in the ends and roll up.

Shred half the remaining cabbage and spread in a casserole; arrange the cabbage rolls over it. Add the tomato sauce and remaining oil. Cover and bake in a 350° oven 1 hour, removing the cover for the last 15 minutes.

Serves 4 as a main course.

Per serving
Calories 165
Saturated fat 1.2 grams
Polyunsaturated fat 5.9 grams
Total fat 9.7 grams

POTATO SOUFFLÉ

4 Idaho potatoes
2 tablespoons special
    margarine
3/4 cup skim milk
2 tablespoons nonfat dry milk
    powder

3/4 teaspoon salt
1/4 teaspoon white pepper
1 teaspoon grated orange rind
1 egg yolk
3 egg whites

Bake the potatoes, then scoop out the pulp. Mash smooth or put through a ricer. Beat in the margarine, liquid milk mixed with the dry milk powder, the salt, pepper and orange rind. Beat well, then beat in the egg yolk. Preheat oven to 375°.

Beat the egg whites until stiff but not dry. Fold into the potato mixture. Turn into a 1-1/2-quart soufflé dish. Bake in a 375° oven 20 minutes. Serve at once, or the soufflé will fall.

Serves 6.

Per serving
Calories 160
Saturated fat 1.1 grams
Polyunsaturated fat 1.2 grams
Total fat 4.5 grams

PUMPKIN PANCAKES

2 cups cooked or canned
    pumpkin
1/2 teaspoon salt
1/4 teaspoon powdered ginger
1/4 cup skim milk

1/4 cup fine bread crumbs
1 tablespoon melted special
    margarine
2 tablespoons special oil

Mash the pumpkin very smooth; mix in the salt, ginger, milk, bread crumbs and margarine. Shape into 12 patties.

Heat the oil in a skillet; fry the cakes until browned on both sides.

Serves 6.

Per serving
Calories 90
Saturated fat 1.0 gram
Polyunsaturated fat 3.3 grams
Total fat 6.2 grams

SAUTÉED ZUCCHINI STRIPS

4 small zucchini
3 tablespoons special oil
1/2 teaspoon salt
1/4 teaspoon freshly ground
    black pepper

1/2 teaspoon oregano
1 clove garlic, minced
1 tablespoon minced parsley

Scrub the zucchini but do not peel. Cut into strips 1/4 inch wide by 2 inches long. Heat the oil in a skillet; sauté the zucchini over medium heat until browned on all sides. Add the salt, pepper, oregano, garlic and parsley. Cook over low heat 5 minutes.

Serves 6.

Per serving
Calories 80
Saturated fat 0.8 gram
Polyunsaturated fat 4.0 grams
Total fat 6.4 grams

SPINACH SOUFFLÉ

2 tablespoons special margarine	1/8 teaspoon nutmeg
2 tablespoons grated onions	1-1/4 cups skim milk
2 tablespoons flour	3 cups cooked chopped spinach
3/4 teaspoon salt	1 egg yolk, beaten
1/4 teaspoon white pepper	3 egg whites

Melt the margarine in a saucepan; sauté the onions 3 minutes. Blend in the flour, salt, pepper and nutmeg. Gradually add the milk, stirring steadily to the boiling point. Cook over low heat 5 minutes. Mix in the spinach and egg yolk. Cool 15 minutes.

Beat the egg whites until stiff but not dry; fold into the spinach mixture. Turn into a 1-1/2-quart soufflé dish. Bake in a preheated 375° oven 30 minutes. Serve at once.

Serves 6.

Per serving
Calories 95
Saturated fat 1.1 grams
Polyunsaturated fat 1.2 grams
Total fat 4.6 grams

CREAMED SPINACH

3 pounds fresh spinach or 2 packages frozen	3/4 teaspoon salt
2 tablespoons special margarine	1/8 teaspoon white pepper
1 tablespoon flour	1/8 teaspoon sugar
	1/8 teaspoon nutmeg
	3/4 cup skim milk

Wash the fresh spinach and cook over low heat 5 minutes. Drain well. Or cook the frozen spinach as package suggests. Drain well. Chop the spinach very fine or purée in an electric blender.

Melt the margarine in a saucepan; blend in the flour, salt, pepper, sugar and nutmeg. Add the milk, stirring steadily to the boiling point. Mix in the spinach; cook over low heat 10 minutes.

Serves 6.

Per serving
Calories 60
Saturated fat 0.8 gram
Polyunsaturated fat 1.1 grams
Total fat 3.7 grams

SPINACH CATALAN

3 pounds fresh spinach or
  2 packages frozen
2 tablespoons special oil

1/4 cup pine nuts
2 tablespoons seedless raisins

Cook the fresh spinach without water 3 minutes. Drain and chop. Or cook the frozen spinach 1 minute less than package directs. Drain and chop. Heat the oil in a skillet; lightly brown the nuts in it. Stir in the spinach and raisins.

Serves 6.

Per serving
Calories 115
Saturated fat 0.6 gram
Polyunsaturated fat 3.2 grams
Total fat 5.1 grams

CURRIED TOMATOES

3 pounds firm tomatoes
3 tablespoons special oil
2 cups thinly sliced onions
1 clove garlic, minced

3/4 teaspoon salt
2 teaspoons curry powder
1/4 cup water

Wash, dry and quarter the tomatoes. Heat the oil in a skillet; sauté the onions 5 minutes. Mix in the garlic, salt and curry powder, then add the tomatoes and water. Cover and cook over low heat 15 minutes.

Serves 8.

Per serving
Calories 80
Saturated fat 0.6 gram
Polyunsaturated fat 2.9 grams
Total fat 4.9 grams

BAKED STUFFED TOMATOES

6 tomatoes
2 tablespoons special
    margarine
1/4 cup minced onions
1/2 pound mushrooms, coarsely
    chopped
2 teaspoons chopped capers

2 tablespoons minced parsley
1/2 teaspoon salt
1/4 teaspoon freshly ground
    black pepper
2 tablespoons dry bread
    crumbs
1 clove garlic

Peel the tomatoes. Cut a 1-inch piece off the stem ends, scoop out the pulp, and set tomatoes upside down to drain.

Melt the margarine in a skillet; sauté the onions and mushrooms 5 minutes. Mix in the capers, parsley, salt, pepper, and bread crumbs. Stuff the tomatoes. Rub a baking dish with the garlic; arrange the tomatoes in it. Bake in a 375° oven 20 minutes or until the tomatoes are tender but firm.

Serves 6.

Per serving
Calories 85
Saturated fat 0.8 gram
Polyunsaturated fat 1.1 grams
Total fat 3.8 grams

SAUTEED BANANAS

4 bananas
2 tablespoons cornstarch
1/4 cup sesame seeds

2 tablespoons special
    margarine

Peel the bananas; cut in half lengthwise. Mix together the cornstarch and sesame seeds. Dip the bananas in the mixture. Melt the margarine in a skillet; sauté the bananas in it until browned on both sides.

Serves 4.

Per serving
Calories 160
Saturated fat 1.6 grams
Polyunsaturated fat 3.0 grams
Total fat 8.7 grams

SWEET POTATO AND BANANA CASSEROLE

4 sweet potatoes
3/4 teaspoon salt
3 tablespoons special
   margarine

4 bananas, peeled and sliced
   1/2 inch thick
1/2 cup brown sugar
1/2 cup orange juice

Cook the unpeeled sweet potatoes until tender but firm. Peel and cut in 1/4-inch slices; toss with the salt. Rub a casserole with a little of the margarine. Arrange alternate layers of the sweet potatoes dotted with the margarine and the bananas sprinkled with the brown sugar. End with bananas dotted with margarine. Pour the orange juice over all. Bake in a 350° oven 30 minutes until browned on top.

Serves 8.

Per serving
Calories 235
Saturated fat 0.9 gram
Polyunsaturated fat 1.2 grams
Total fat 3.9 grams

LIMA BEANS AND RICE

1 16-ounce can stewed tomatoes
1/2 cup water
1/2 teaspoon salt
1/4 teaspoon freshly ground
   black pepper

1/8 teaspoon basil
1 pound lima beans or 1 package
   frozen, slightly thawed
1/2 cup raw rice
2 tablespoons butter

Bring the tomatoes and water to a boil. Add the salt, pepper, and basil; cook 5 minutes. Add the lima beans, rice and butter; cover and cook over low heat 20 minutes or until rice and beans are tender. Stir occasionally.

Serves 6.

Per serving
Calories 145
Saturated fat 0.9 gram
Polyunsaturated fat 2.7 grams
Total fat 4.8 grams

FRIED RICE

1-1/2 cups water
3/4 teaspoon salt
1 cup raw rice
2 tablespoons special oil

1/2 cup chopped scallions
(green onions)
1/4 teaspoon minced garlic
2 tablespoons soy sauce

Bring the water and salt to a boil. Stir in the rice, bring to a boil again, cover and cook over low heat 15 minutes or until the rice is tender and dry. Chill.

Heat the oil in a skillet; stir the rice into it until coated. Mix in the scallions and garlic; cook 3 minutes. Blend in the soy sauce.

Serves 6.

Per serving
Calories 145
Saturated fat 0.5 gram
Polyunsaturated fat 2.6 grams
Total fat 4.6 grams

CHINESE FRIED RICE

3 cups cooked drained rice
3 tablespoons special oil
3/4 cup sliced scallions (green onions)
3/4 teaspoon salt
1/4 teaspoon freshly ground black pepper

1-1/2 cups diced cooked shrimp or julienne-cut chicken
1 egg, beaten
3 tablespoons minced parsley
1 tablespoon soy sauce

Be sure the rice is very cold; if you wish, cook it the day before you want to use it.

Heat the oil in a skillet; stir in the rice until browned, pressing out any lumps. Mix in the scallions, salt, pepper and the shrimp or chicken for 1 minute. Make a well in the center of the rice and pour the egg into it, stirring until barely set, then stir into the rice mixture. Add the parsley and soy sauce and stir; cook only 1 minute.

Serves 6.

Per serving
Calories 210
Saturated fat 1.3 grams
Polyunsaturated fat 4.2 grams
Total fat 8.5 grams

SPANISH RICE

2 tablespoons special oil
1/2 cup chopped onions
1-1/2 cups raw rice
2 cups canned chopped
    tomatoes
1 cup boiling water

3/4 teaspoon salt
1/4 teaspoon freshly ground
    black pepper
1/4 teaspoon minced garlic
2 tablespoons minced parsley

Heat the oil in a heavy saucepan; sauté the onions 5 minutes. Mix in the rice until yellow and translucent. Add the tomatoes, water, salt, pepper and garlic; cover and cook over low heat 25 minutes or until tender and dry. Watch carefully and add a little more boiling water if necessary. Mix in the parsley.

Serves 6.

Per serving
Calories 205
Saturated fat 0.5 gram
Polyunsaturated fat 2.6 grams
Total fat 4.7 grams

RISOTTO

3 tablespoons special oil
1/2 cup minced onions
1 cup raw rice

1/2 teaspoon salt
2-1/2 cups hot chicken broth
3 tablespoons minced parsley

Heat the oil in a skillet; sauté the onions 5 minutes. Stir in rice until light brown. Add the salt and broth; cook over low heat 20 minutes or until tender and dry. Add a little water if necessary during cooking time. Stir in the parsley. Serve with grated sapsago cheese, if desired.

Serves 4.

Per serving
Calories 280
Saturated fat 1.2 grams
Polyunsaturated fat 5.9 grams
Total fat 9.9 grams

VEGETABLE GOULASH

2 tablespoons special oil
3/4 cup thinly sliced onions
1 cup diced green peppers
1 20-ounce can tomatoes
1 cup diced potatoes
2 packages frozen mixed
    vegetables, thawed

1 teaspoon salt
1/4 teaspoon freshly ground
    black pepper
1 teaspoon paprika
1 teaspoon sugar
1 tablespoon flour
2 tablespoons water

Heat the oil in a casserole; sauté the onions 5 minutes. Add the green peppers; sauté 5 minutes. Stir in the tomatoes, potatoes, mixed vegetables, salt, pepper, paprika and sugar. Bring to a boil and cook over low heat 20 minutes. Mix together the flour and water; stir into the vegetables until thickened.

Serves 8.

Per serving
Calories 95
Saturated fat 0.7 gram
Polyunsaturated fat 3.0 grams
Total fat 5.2 grams

Salads and Dressings

SALAD greens should be purchased as close to time of serving as possible; from the time they are picked, these delicate leaves soon deteriorate. Wash very carefully to remove sand and dirt by holding under cold running water. If possible, let soak for a half hour in a large bowl of cold water. Drain well. Then wrap loosely in foil or plastic wrap and keep in the hydrator of your refrigerator until needed. *Tear* (do not cut) the lettuce leaves by hand into bite-sized pieces; cutting detracts from the salad.

Almost all salad dressings are suitable except cream dressings. However, those in this section combine both low-fat and gourmet interest so that you may enjoy them freely, in accordance with the calorie count. When dining out order simple salad dressings using olive oil or special oil, but remember to avoid the cream types.

CUCUMBER SALAD

5 cucumbers
3/4 teaspoon salt
1/2 cup special oil
1/4 cup tarragon vinegar

1/4 teaspoon white pepper
1/4 teaspoon sugar
1 tablespoon minced parsley
1 tablespoon minced dill

Peel the cucumbers and score them with a fork. Slice very thin. Place in a glass or pottery bowl; mix with the salt and chill 2 hours. Drain thoroughly.

Mix together the oil, vinegar, pepper, sugar, parsley and dill. Pour over the cucumbers.

Serves 6.

Per serving
Calories 190
Saturated fat   2.0 grams
Polyunsaturated fat   9.8 grams
Total fat 16.2 grams

SALADE NIÇOISE

1 head romaine lettuce
1/2 cup thinly sliced onions
   (red if possible)
1 cucumber, peeled and sliced
1 green pepper, cut julienne
4 anchovies, cut in half
   crosswise
1 7-ounce can tuna fish,
   drained and cut in chunks

3 tablespoons special oil
1 tablespoon wine vinegar
1 teaspoon prepared French
   mustard
1/2 teaspoon salt
1/2 teaspoon freshly ground
   black pepper
1/8 teaspoon minced garlic
4 black olives

Break the lettuce into bite-size pieces and line a bowl with it. Over it arrange the onions, cucumber, green pepper, anchovies and tuna.

Mix together the oil, vinegar, mustard, salt, pepper and garlic. Pour over the salad and turn over gently with a fork and spoon. Garnish with the olives.

Serves 4.

Per serving
Calories 115
Saturated fat   2.7 grams
Polyunsaturated fat   8.7 grams
Total fat   16.1 grams

GREEN BEAN SALAD

1 package frozen green beans,
  cooked and drained
3 tablespoons wine vinegar
3 tablespoons special oil
1/2 teaspoon salt
1/4 teaspoon freshly ground
  black pepper

1 teaspoon sugar
2 tablespoons chopped
  scallions (green onions)
1 tablespoon chopped pimento
1 tablespoon minced parsley

Cool the beans. Beat together the vinegar, oil, salt, pepper and sugar. Toss the beans with the scallions and pimento, then with the dressing. Chill 4 hours. Toss with the parsley and serve on lettuce leaves.

Serves 4.

Per serving
Calories 100
Saturated fat 1.2 grams
Polyunsaturated fat 5.7 grams
Total fat 9.7 grams

CELERY ROOT SALAD

1-1/2 pounds celery root
1/3 cup special oil
3 tablespoons lemon juice
1 tablespoon nonfat dry milk
  powder
1/4 teaspoon dry mustard

1 teaspoon grated onion
1/2 teaspoon salt
1/4 teaspoon freshly ground
  black pepper
2 tablespoons minced parsley

Scrub the celery root and cook in boiling salted water 20 minutes or until tender but firm. Cool, peel and cut into julienne strips.

Beat together the oil, lemon juice, dry milk powder, mustard, onion, salt and pepper. Pour over the celery root and refrigerate for 3 hours before serving. Mix occasionally. Sprinkle with the parsley.

Serves 6.

Per serving
Calories 105
Saturated fat 1.3 grams
Polyunsaturated fat 6.4 grams
Total fat 10.8 grams

PEPPER SALAD

1/3 cup cider vinegar
2 tablespoons special oil
3/4 teaspoon salt
1/4 teaspoon white pepper
1/2 teaspoon mustard seeds
1 teaspoon celery seeds

2 tablespoons brown sugar
4 cups chopped cabbage
4 peppers (green and red),
  chopped
2 tablespoons finely chopped
  onions

Mix together the vinegar, oil, salt, pepper, mustard seeds, celery seeds and brown sugar. Toss together the cabbage, peppers and onions. Add the dressing and mix thoroughly. Chill for 3 hours before serving.

Serves 8.

Per serving
Calories 40
Saturated fat 0.4 gram
Polyunsaturated fat 1.9 grams
Total fat 3.4 grams

COLESLAW WITH BUTTERMILK DRESSING

6 cups shredded cabbage
1/4 cup finely chopped onions
1/4 cup grated carrots
1/4 cup cider vinegar
3 tablespoons special oil

1/2 teaspoon salt
1/4 teaspoon white pepper
1 teaspoon sugar
1/2 cup buttermilk

Cover the shredded cabbage with ice water; let stand 15 minutes. Drain well. Toss with the onions and carrots.

Bring to a boil the vinegar, oil, salt, pepper and sugar. Pour over the cabbage and toss. Let stand 10 minutes, then mix in the buttermilk. Chill.

Serves 6.

Per serving
Calories 95
Saturated fat 0.8 gram
Polyunsaturated fat 4.0 grams
Total 6.1 grams

SPECIAL MAYONNAISE

1/2 teaspoon salt
1/2 teaspoon dry mustard
1/2 teaspoon paprika
Dash cayenne pepper
2/3 cup hot water

2 tablespoons cider vinegar
2 tablespoons lemon juice
1 cup special oil
1/4 cup nonfat dry milk powder

Mix together the salt, mustard, paprika, pepper, water, vinegar and lemon juice.

Use an electric blender or, if you haven't one, a mixer. Beat together the oil and dry milk until well blended. Stop machine and scrape sides after a few seconds. Very gradually add the liquid while machine is running. Beat until thick. Turn into a jar and refrigerate until needed.

Makes about 2-1/2 cups; allow 1 tablespoon per serving.　　**Per serving**
Calories 50
Saturated fat 0.6 gram
Polyunsaturated fat 3.0 grams
Total fat 5.4 grams

REGULAR MAYONNAISE

1 egg yolk
1/4 teaspoon salt
1/8 teaspoon dry mustard

1 cup special oil
1-1/2 tablespoons lemon juice
or cider vinegar

Beat together the egg yolk, salt and mustard with a wire whisk, egg beater or electric mixer. Begin adding the oil drop by drop, beating steadily. When 1/3 the oil is added, beat in half the lemon juice. Now add the oil in a steady stream, still beating steadily. When almost all the oil is added, beat in the remaining lemon juice, then the remaining oil.

Blender Mayonnaise:

Combine the egg yolk, salt and mustard in the blender bowl. Flick machine on and off. Hold cup of oil over the bowl, turn machine on and add oil in a steady slow stream. When half the oil is in, add the lemon juice, then the remaining oil. Turn machine off when all the oil is added and mixture is well blended.

Makes about 1-1/3 cups; allow 1 tablespoon per serving.   Per serving

Calories 100
Saturated fat   1.2 grams
Polyunsaturated fat   5.8 grams
Total fat 10.4 grams

EGG WHITE MAYONNAISE

1/2 teaspoon salt
1/2 teaspoon sugar
1/2 teaspoon dry mustard
1/8 teaspoon paprika

1 egg white
1 cup special oil
4 teaspoons cider vinegar

In a bowl mix the salt, sugar, mustard and paprika. Beat in the egg white until frothy. Add the oil, drop by drop, beating steadily until 1/4 cup is added, then by the teaspoon until 1/2 cup is used up. Beat in 2 teaspoons vinegar, then the remaining oil very gradually, still beating steadily. Beat in remaining vinegar. Spoon into a clean dry jar. Refrigerate until needed.

Makes about 1-1/4 cups; allow 1 tablespoon per serving.   Per serving

Calories 95
Saturated fat   1.2 grams
Polyunsaturated fat   6.1 grams
Total fat 10.7 grams

MUSTARD SAUCE

2 teaspoons cornstarch
1 teaspoon dry mustard
1/2 teaspoon salt
1 teaspoon sugar
Dash cayenne pepper

2 tablespoons special oil
2/3 cup skim milk
1 egg yolk
1 tablespoon cider vinegar

In a saucepan, combine the cornstarch, mustard, salt, sugar and cayenne pepper. Stir in the oil and milk. Cook over low heat, stirring steadily, until the boiling point. Cook 2 minutes longer.

Beat the egg yolk and vinegar in a bowl; gradually add the hot liquid, stirring steadily to prevent curdling. Return to the saucepan; cook over low heat, stirring steadily for 1 minute. Cool. Serve on coleslaw or potato salad.

Makes about 3/4 cup; allow 1 tablespoon per serving.
Per serving
Calories 30
Saturated fat 0.4 gram
Polyunsaturated fat 1.4 grams
Total fat 2.9 grams

FOAMY DRESSING

1 cup special oil
1/4 cup wine vinegar
1 egg white
1/2 teaspoon salt
1/8 teaspoon freshly ground
   black pepper

1/8 teaspoon dry mustard
1/4 teaspoon garlic powder
1 teaspoon sugar
1-1/2 tablespoons catsup

Beat all the ingredients in an electric mixer or with a rotary beater until foamy and well blended. Pour into a covered jar and refrigerate until needed.

Makes about 1-1/2 cups; allow 1 tablespoon per serving.
Per serving
Calories 100
Saturated fat 1.0 gram
Polyunsaturated fat 5.1 grams
Total fat 9.0 grams

CREAMY DRESSING

1 cup dry cottage cheese
1/2 cup special oil
4 tablespoons cider vinegar
1/2 teaspoon salt
1/2 teaspoon freshly ground
    black pepper

1/2 teaspoon dry mustard
1/2 teaspoon paprika
2 tablespoons minced parsley

Use an electric blender or, if you haven't one, an electric mixer or rotary beater. Combine all the ingredients and beat until perfectly smooth. Chill before serving with vegetable or green salads.

Makes about 1-1/2 cups; allow 1 tablespoon per serving.

Per serving
Calories 60
Saturated fat 0.5 gram
Polyunsaturated fat 2.5 grams
Total fat 4.5 grams

OLD-FASHIONED SALAD DRESSING

1/4 cup nonfat dry milk powder
1/2 teaspoon salt
1-1/2 teaspoons dry mustard
2 tablespoons sugar

1/3 cup water
2 cups special oil
1/2 cup cider vinegar

Beat together with a rotary beater the dry milk, salt, mustard, sugar and water. Add 1/4 cup oil at a time, beating until smooth after each addition. Add the vinegar all at once; beat again until smooth and thick.

Makes 1-1/2 pints; allow 1 tablespoon per serving.

Per serving
Calories 40
Saturated fat 1.0 gram
Polyunsaturated fat 5.1 grams
Total fat 9.0 grams

CAPTAIN'S DRESSING

1-1/2 tablespoons nonfat dry
   milk powder
1/2 teaspoon salt
1/4 teaspoon freshly ground
   black pepper
1/2 teaspoon dry mustard

1 tablespoon sugar
3 tablespoons catsup
1/2 cup special oil
1/4 cup water
3 tablespoons cider vinegar

Beat all the ingredients in a blender or with a rotary beater until thick and creamy. Keep refrigerated in a covered jar until needed. Shake well before using.

Makes 1-1/4 cups; allow 1 tablespoon per serving.

Per serving
Calories 100
Saturated fat 0.6 gram
Polyunsaturated fat 3.0 grams
Total fat 5.2 grams

EGG DRESSING

2 eggs
1/2 teaspoon salt
Dash cayenne pepper
1 tablespoon sugar

2 tablespoons special oil
1/3 cup cider vinegar
2 tablespoons water

Beat the eggs, salt, cayenne pepper, sugar and oil in the top of a double boiler. Stir in the vinegar and water; place over hot water and cook, stirring constantly until thickened. Cool. Serve on vegetable or fruit salads. If too thick, thin with skim milk.

Makes about 1 cup; allow 1 tablespoon per serving.

Per serving
Calories 35
Saturated fat 0.5 gram
Polyunsaturated fat 1.1 grams
Total fat 2.5 grams

BOILED DRESSING

2 tablespoons sugar
2 tablespoons cornstarch
1/2 teaspoon salt
1/2 teaspoon dry mustard

3/4 cup cider vinegar
1/4 cup water
2 eggs

In a saucepan, combine the sugar, cornstarch, salt and mustard. Mix in the vinegar and water until smooth. Cook over low heat, stirring constantly to the boiling point. Cook 3 minutes longer.

Beat the eggs in a bowl; gradually add the hot mixture, stirring steadily to prevent curdling. Cool and keep in the refrigerator in an airtight container. If too thick, thin with skim milk or fruit juice, depending on salad served.

Makes about 1-1/2 cups; allow 1 tablespoon per serving.
Per serving
Calories 15
Saturated fat 0.2 gram
Polyunsaturated fat 0.1 gram
Total fat 0.5 gram

FRENCH DRESSING

1/2 cup special oil
3 tablespoons wine vinegar
1/2 teaspoon salt

1/4 teaspoon freshly ground
black pepper
1 clove garlic, minced

Beat all the ingredients in an electric blender or with a rotary beater until creamy. Store in a tightly closed jar in the refrigerator. Shake vigorously before using.

Makes about 3/4 cup; allow 1 tablespoon per serving.
Per serving
Calories 80
Saturated fat 1.0 gram
Polyunsaturated fat 5.1 grams
Total fat 9.0 grams

SPECIAL SOUR CREAM

1/2 cup nonfat dry milk powder   1 tablespoon sour cream
1/2 cup ice water

Beat the dry milk, water and sour cream until foamy and smooth. Cover and let stand overnight; mix 2 or 3 times. Refrigerate until needed. The result will not be as smooth as sour cream, but it makes a delicious substitute.

Makes 1 cup; allow 1 tablespoon per serving.

Per serving
Calories 25
Saturated fat 0.0 gram
Polyunsaturated fat 0.0 gram
Total fat 0.1 gram

VINAIGRETTE SAUCE

3/4 cup French Dressing
  (see recipe)
1/4 teaspoon dry mustard
1 tablespoon minced onion
2 teaspoons minced parsley
2 teaspoons finely chopped
  fresh tarragon or
  1/4 teaspoon dried

2 teaspoons finely chopped
  capers
1 sour pickle, finely chopped
1 hard-cooked egg white,
  chopped

Combine all the ingredients, mixing until well blended.

Makes about 1 cup; allow 1 tablespoon per serving.

Per serving
Calories 80
Saturated fat 0.9 gram
Polyunsaturated fat 3.8 grams
Total fat 7.1 grams

HERB DRESSING

1/2 cup special oil
1/4 cup wine vinegar
1/4 cup tomato juice
1 clove garlic, minced
1/4 teaspoon salt

1/8 teaspoon freshly ground
   black pepper
1/4 cup minced parsley
1/8 teaspoon basil
1/8 teaspoon thyme

Run all the ingredients in an electric blender, or beat with a rotary beater. Delicious with all salads.

Allow 1 tablespoon per serving; makes slightly more than 1 cup.   Per serving
Calories 60
Saturated fat 0.8 gram
Polyunsaturated fat 3.8 grams
Total fat 6.6 grams

LEMON JUICE DRESSING

1/2 cup lemon juice
1/2 cup special oil
1/2 cup water
1/4 teaspoon salt

1/4 teaspoon freshly ground
   black pepper
1/4 teaspoon dry mustard

Beat the lemon juice into the oil, then gradually add the water, beating steadily. Beat in the salt, pepper and mustard. Keep refrigerated in a tightly closed jar until needed. Shake or beat before using.

Allow 2 tablespoons per serving; makes about 1-1/4 cups.   Per serving
Calories 100
Saturated fat 1.2 grams
Polyunsaturated fat 6.1 grams
Total fat 10.8 grams

COTTAGE CHEESE DRESSING

1 cup dry cottage cheese
3 tablespoons special oil
2 tablespoons skim milk
1 tablespoon grated onion
1 teaspoon lemon juice

1/4 teaspoon salt
1/8 teaspoon freshly ground
    black pepper
1/4 cup catsup

Beat all the ingredients in an electric blender, electric mixer, or use a rotary beater. Beat until very smooth. Serve with green or vegetable salads.

Makes about 1-3/4 cups; allow 2 tablespoons per serving.
Per serving
Calories 50
Saturated fat 0.3 gram
Polyunsaturated fat 1.7 grams
Total fat 3.0 grams

HOLLANDAISE SAUCE

2 egg yolks
1/4 teaspoon salt
1/4 cup water

2 tablespoons lemon juice
2 tablespoons special
    margarine

Beat the egg yolks in the top of a double boiler. Add the salt, water and lemon juice very gradually. Break the margarine into small pieces and add. Place over hot water and cook, stirring constantly until thickened. Remove from the heat. Serve on vegetables, particularly asparagus or broccoli.

Allow 1 tablespoon per serving; makes about 2/3 cup.
Per serving
Calories 30
Saturated fat 0.8 gram
Polyunsaturated fat 0.7 gram
Total fat 3.1 grams

PSEUDO HOLLANDAISE SAUCE

1 tablespoon cornstarch
1/4 teaspoon salt
1 cup chicken broth

2 tablespoons lemon juice
2 tablespoons special margarine

Mix the cornstarch and salt with a little broth to a smooth paste. Add the remaining broth, the lemon juice and margarine; cook over low heat, stirring steadily to the boiling point. Cook 3 minutes longer, stirring occasionally. Excellent with all vegetables.

Allow 2 tablespoons per serving; makes about 1 cup.

Per serving
Calories 45
Saturated fat 0.6 gram
Polyunsaturated fat 0.8 gram
Total fat 2.7 grams

WHITE SAUCE (Cream Sauce)

2 tablespoons special oil
4 tablespoons flour
1/2 teaspoon salt

1/8 teaspoon white pepper
2 cups skim milk

In a saucepan mix until smooth the oil, flour, salt and pepper; mix in the milk; cook over low heat, stirring constantly to the boiling point. Cook 5 minutes longer.

Makes 2 cups; allow 2 tablespoons per serving.

Per serving
Calories 35
Saturated fat 0.2 gram
Polyunsaturated fat 1.0 gram
Total fat 1.7 grams

Variation

Cheese Sauce:

Add 1/4 cup grated Cheddar or American cheese and 1 teaspoon dry mustard to the white sauce. Cook over low heat, stirring constantly until cheese melts.

Makes 2 cups; allow 2 tablespoons per serving.

Per serving
Calories 40
Saturated fat 0.5 gram
Polyunsaturated fat 1.0 gram
Total fat 2.2 grams

BÉCHAMEL SAUCE

1 cup skim milk
2 slices onion
1 bay leaf
2 tablespoons special oil or
    melted special
    margarine

4 tablespoons flour
1/2 teaspoon salt
1/8 teaspoon white pepper
1 cup chicken broth

Bring the milk, onion and bay leaf to a boil; let stand 10 minutes, then discard the onion and bay leaf.

In a saucepan, mix together the oil, flour, salt and pepper. Gradually add the milk, then the broth; cook over low heat, stirring steadily to the boiling point. Cook 5 minutes longer.

Makes 2 cups; allow 2 tablespoons per serving.

Per serving (with corn oil)
Calories 30
Saturated fat 0.2 gram
Polyunsaturated fat 1.0 gram
Total fat 1.7 grams
Per serving (with special
    margarine)
Calories 30
Saturated fat 0.3 gram
Polyunsaturated fat 0.4 gram
Total fat 1.5 grams

BROWN SAUCE

2 tablespoons special
    margarine
1/4 cup chopped onions
1/4 cup grated carrots
2 tablespoons flour

1/2 teaspoon salt
1/8 teaspoon freshly ground
    black pepper
3 cups beef broth
1 tablespoon tomato paste

Melt the margarine in a saucepan; sauté the onions and carrots 5 minutes. Blend in the flour until browned. Add the salt,

204

pepper and broth, stirring steadily to the boiling point. Mix in the tomato paste. Cook over low heat 20 minutes. Strain.

Use as a gravy or as a base for other sauces.

Allow 3 tablespoons per serving; makes about 2 cups.

Per serving
Calories 45
Saturated fat 0.4 gram
Polyunsaturated fat 0.6 gram
Total fat 2.0 grams

SPAGHETTI SAUCE

1 tablespoon special oil
1-1/2 cups chopped onions
1/2 cup chopped green peppers
1 clove garlic, minced
1 29-ounce can tomatoes
1 bay leaf

1/2 teaspoon basil
3/4 teaspoon salt
1/2 teaspoon freshly ground
*   black pepper*
1/2 pound mushrooms sliced
2 tablespoons minced parsley

Heat the oil in a saucepan; sauté the onions and green peppers until browned. Add the garlic, tomatoes, bay leaf, basil, salt and pepper. Cover loosely and cook over low heat 2 hours. Mix in the mushrooms and parsley; cook 1/2 hour longer. Discard bay leaf. For a smooth sauce, purée in an electric blender or force through a sieve.

Makes about 3 cups; serves 8.

Per serving
Calories 50
Saturated fat 0.2 gram
Polyunsaturated fat 1.0 gram
Total fat 1.7 grams

RÉMOULADE SAUCE (for seafood)

1 cup Special Mayonnaise
   (see recipe)
1 tablespoon anchovy paste
1/2 teaspoon dry mustard
2 tablespoons cider vinegar
1/2 teaspoon Tabasco
3 tablespoons chopped stuffed
   green olives

3 tablespoons minced sour
   gherkins
1 tablespoon minced parsley
2 teaspoons minced scallions
   (green onions)

Mix until smooth the mayonnaise, anchovy paste, mustard, vinegar and Tabasco. Stir in the olives, gherkins, parsley and scallions. Chill 2 hours before serving.

Serves 6.

Per serving
Calories 140
Saturated fat 1.7 grams
Polyunsaturated fat 8.5 grams
Total fat 14.9 grams

AVOCADO SEAFOOD SAUCE

2 avocados
1/2 cup buttermilk
3 tablespoons grated onions

2 tablespoons prepared
   horseradish
1 teaspoon lemon juice

Peel the avocados and mash smooth or purée in an electric blender. Blend in the buttermilk, onions, horseradish and lemon juice. Serve with all seafood dishes.

Serves 8; makes about 2-1/4 cups.

Per serving
Calories 140
Saturated fat 4.5 grams
Polyunsaturated fat 1.7 grams
Total fat 15.0 grams

CUSTARD SAUCE

3 egg yolks
1/8 teaspoon salt
1/3 cup sugar

2 cups skim milk, scalded
1 teaspoon vanilla extract

Beat the egg yolks, salt and sugar in the top of a double boiler. Gradually add the hot milk, stirring steadily to prevent curdling. Place over hot water and cook, stirring steadily until mixture coats the spoon. Do not let boil. Strain, stir in the vanilla and chill.

Serves 8; makes 2-1/2 cups.

Per serving
Calories 40
Saturated fat 0.8 gram
Polyunsaturated fat 0.3 gram
Total fat 2.3 grams

Breads, Pancakes and Eggs

THE ART of making bread at home has almost been completely forgotten by the typical American housewife, but home-baked breads are worth the effort. No mass-produced bread tastes quite like homemade bread, and any man will agree with you on that point. There are several recipes which are actually not at all difficult to make, and your family's delight will be your reward.

Store-bought bread is reasonably low in fat, particularly the French- or Italian-style breads. When eating out, avoid biscuits and muffins because these are usually made with hydrogenated fats and may hold large amounts of saturated fats. Pancakes, too, should not be ordered in restaurants because they are nearly always prepared with saturated fats. However, they may readily be made at home according to the recipes in this section.

SCONES

1/2 cup sifted flour	2 tablespoons special oil
1/3 cup confectioners' sugar	1 egg
1 teaspoon baking powder	1/4 cup skim milk
1/8 teaspoon salt	1/4 teaspoon grated lemon rind

Sift together the flour, confectioners' sugar, baking powder and salt. Make a well in the center and into it put the oil, egg, milk and lemon rind. Beat with a spoon until smooth; let stand 10 minutes.

Lightly oil a griddle or skillet and heat it. Drop the batter onto it by the tablespoon. Bake until puffed and bubbles cover the tops. Turn and brown other side. Don't turn more than once. Serve with jelly.

Makes about 24 2-inch scones.

Per scone
Calories 40
Saturated fat 0.2 gram
Polyunsaturated fat 0.7 gram
Total fat 1.4 grams

BLINTZES

Pancakes:
1 egg
1 cup skim milk
1/4 teaspoon salt
3/4 cup sifted flour

1 tablespoon special oil
1 tablespoon special margarine

Beat the egg, milk and salt together. Mix in the flour until smooth, then the oil. Chill 30 minutes.

Melt a little of the margarine in a 6- or 7-inch skillet. Pour in just enough batter to coat thinly the bottom of the pan. Fry until the underside is browned. Turn out onto a plate or napkin while preparing the remaining pancakes, stacking them browned side up.

Filling:
1 cup dry cottage cheese
1/4 teaspoon salt
2 teaspoons sugar (optional)
1/2 teaspoon vanilla extract (optional)

1 egg white, stiffly beaten
2 tablespoons special margarine

Force the cottage cheese through a sieve or run in an electric blender until smooth. Mix in the salt and sugar and vanilla, if you like them sweet. Fold in the egg white.

Spread 1 heaping tablespoon of the mixture on each pancake. Turn opposite sides in, then roll up. Melt the margarine in a skillet; brown the blintzes in it. Serve with Special Sour Cream (see recipe).

Makes about 14.

Per blintz
Calories 95
Saturated fat 0.8 gram
Polyunsaturated fat 1.3 grams
Total fat 4.0 grams

NOODLE CHEESE PUDDING

3/4 pound medium noodles
2 egg yolks
3/4 teaspoon salt
2 cups pot cheese or dry
   cottage cheese

2 tablespoons melted special
   margarine
2 tablespoons sugar
   (optional)
2 egg whites, stiffly beaten

Cook the noodles in boiling water 2 minutes less than package directs. Drain and rinse under cold water. Drain well.

Beat the egg yolks and salt; stir in the cheese, margarine and sugar (if you like a sweet pudding). Stir in the noodles. Fold in the egg whites. Turn into a lightly oiled 1-1/2-quart casserole.

Bake in a preheated 375° oven 35 minutes or until browned.

Serves 6.

Per serving
Calories 315
Saturated fat 2.6 grams
Polyunsaturated fat 1.3 grams
Total fat 8.0 grams

HOT CAKES

1 cup sifted flour
1/4 teaspoon salt
1-1/4 teaspoons baking powder

2 teaspoons sugar
3/4 cup skim milk
1 tablespoon special oil

Sift the flour, salt, baking powder and sugar into a bowl. Mix the milk and oil; add to the flour mixture, stirring only until moistened. The batter should be lumpy. Use about 2 tablespoons batter for each pancake; pour onto a lightly oiled hot griddle or skillet. Bake until underside is browned, then turn to brown other side. Don't turn more than once.

Makes 10 pancakes.

Per pancake
Calories 65
Saturated fat 0.2 gram
Polyunsaturated fat 0.8 gram
Total fat 1.5 grams

HERB BREAD

1-1/2 cups skim milk
1/4 cup sugar
1 teaspoon salt
2 cakes or packages yeast
1/2 cup warm water
1 egg, beaten

1 teaspoon nutmeg
1 teaspoon powdered thyme
1 tablespoon caraway or
   poppy seeds
1/4 cup special oil
7 cups sifted flour

Scald the milk, then stir in the sugar and salt; cool to lukewarm. Soften the yeast in the water in a large bowl; stir until dissolved. Stir in the milk mixture, egg, nutmeg, thyme, seeds and oil. Beat in 3 cups of the flour until smooth. Add enough of the remaining flour to make a dough. (It may not be necessary to add all the flour.) Turn out on a lightly floured surface and let stand 15 minutes, then knead until smooth and elastic. Place in a lightly oiled bowl; brush top with oil, cover with a cloth and let rise in a warm place until doubled in bulk.

Punch down and turn out onto a very lightly floured surface. Divide into two equal parts and shape into loaves. Place in two oiled 9-inch loaf pans. Cover and let rise until doubled in bulk. Bake in a preheated 400° oven 40 minutes or until browned and shrunk away from the sides of the pan. Cool on a cake rack 10 minutes before removing from the pan. Continue cooling on the rack.

Makes 36 half-inch slices.

Per slice
Calories 100
Saturated fat 0.3 gram
Polyunsaturated fat 0.9 gram
Total fat 1.8 grams

CORN BREAD

1 cup sifted flour	2 tablespoons sugar
3/4 cup cornmeal	1 egg white
1/2 teaspoon salt	1/4 cup special oil
·2-1/2 teaspoons baking powder	1 cup skim milk

Sift together the flour, cornmeal, salt, baking powder and sugar. Beat together the egg white, oil and milk. Add to the flour mixture, stirring just enough to dampen the dry mixture. Turn into a warm, oiled 8-inch square pan. Bake in a preheated 425° oven 20 minutes or until browned and a cake tester comes out clean.

Cut into 16 squares and serve warm.

Per-square
Calories 80
Saturated fat 0.4 gram
Polyunsaturated fat 2.0 grams
Total fat 3.5 grams

FRENCH BREAD

1 cake or package yeast	3/4 teaspoon salt
1 cup lukewarm water	3-1/2 cups sifted flour
1/2 teaspoon sugar	

Soften the yeast in the water mixed with the sugar and salt. Beat in 2 cups of the flour until very smooth. Add enough of the remaining flour to make a soft dough. Turn out onto a floured surface and knead until smooth and elastic. Place in an oiled bowl, cover, and let rise in a warm place until double in bulk, about 2 hours. Punch down, cover, and let rise again until double in bulk, about 1 hour.

Punch down and roll out into a rectangle, about 10 inches by 18 inches. Roll up from the wide side like a jelly roll. Be sure to roll tightly. Pinch the edges together and place on a baking pan. Cut gashes 3 inches apart and about 1/8 inch

deep. Brush top with cold water and let rise in a warm place
1-1/2 hours. Bake in a preheated 400° oven 40 minutes or until
browned. Brush with cold water every 10 minutes for a crusty
top.

Makes 1 18-inch bread or 36 half-inch slices.

Per slice
Calories 40
Saturated fat 0.0 gram
Polyunsaturated fat 0.0 gram
Total fat 0.0 gram

WHITE BREAD

1 cake or package yeast
1/4 cup lukewarm water
2 cups skim milk, scalded and
   cooled

2 tablespoons sugar
1 teaspoon salt
1 tablespoon special oil
6-1/2 cups sifted flour

Soften the yeast in the water for 5 minutes. Combine the
milk, sugar, salt and oil; add 2 cups flour, mixing until smooth.
Work in the yeast, then add enough of the remaining flour to
make a firm dough. (You may not need all the flour or may require a little more.)

Knead on a lightly floured surface until smooth and shiny.
Place in a lightly oiled bowl and brush the top with a little oil.
Cover and let rise in a warm place until double in bulk, about
1-1/2 hours. Punch down, cover, and let rise again for 45
minutes.

Divide dough in 2 pieces, shape each into a ball. Let stand
10 minutes. Shape into 2 loaves and place in 2 oiled 10-inch
loaf pans. Let rise until double in bulk, about 1 hour. Bake in a
preheated 400° oven 50 minutes or until browned and
slightly shrunk away from the sides of the pan. Cool on a cake
rack.

Makes 20 half-inch slices.

Per slice
Calories 75
Saturated fat 0.2 gram
Polyunsaturated fat 0.5 gram
Total fat 1.0 gram

PARKER HOUSE ROLLS

3/4 cup skim milk
2 tablespoons sugar
1-1/2 teaspoons salt
1 cake or package yeast

3/4 cup lukewarm water
1/4 cup special oil
4 cups sifted flour

Bring the milk to a boil; stir in the sugar and salt and cool to lukewarm. Soften the yeast in the water for 5 minutes; stir in the milk mixture and the oil. Beat in 2 cups flour until smooth. Add enough of the remaining flour to make a soft dough. Knead on a lightly floured surface until smooth. Place in a lightly oiled bowl, brush top with oil, cover, and set in a warm place to rise until double in bulk, about 1-1/2 hours.

Punch dough down on a lightly floured surface and divide in half. Roll each half into a circle 1/2 inch thick. Cut into 2-inch rounds. Crease dough heavily with the dull edge of a knife through the center and brush lightly with oil. Fold over into pocketbook shape. Arrange on an oiled baking sheet, leaving 1 inch between each. Cover and let rise in a warm place 1 hour. Bake in a preheated 400° oven 12 minutes or until browned.

Makes about 24 rolls.

Per roll
Calories 85
Saturated fat 0.3 gram
Polyunsaturated fat 1.3 grams
Total fat 2.4 grams

REFRIGERATOR ROLLS

1 cake or package yeast
1/3 cup sugar
1/2 cup lukewarm water
1 cup skim milk, scalded and
    cooled

1/3 cup special oil
1 teaspoon salt
1 egg, beaten
5-1/2 cups sifted flour

Soften the yeast and 1 teaspoon sugar in the water. Mix in the milk, oil, salt, egg and remaining sugar; beat well. Add just enough of the flour to make a soft dough. It may not be necessary to add all the flour. Knead on a lightly floured surface until smooth and elastic. Place in a lightly oiled bowl and brush top with a little oil. Refrigerate at least 2 hours before using. Shape into 2-inch rolls 2 hours before baking and let rise 2 hours. Bake in a preheated 425° oven 15 minutes or until browned. It is not necessary to bake all the dough at once. Punch down unused dough and cover; keeps 5-7 days in the refrigerator.

Makes about 3 dozen rolls.

Per roll
Calories 90
Saturated fat 0.3 gram
Polyunsaturated fat 1.2 grams
Total fat 2.3 grams

MUFFINS

2 cups sifted flour
1/2 teaspoon salt
3 teaspoons baking powder
2 tablespoons sugar

1 egg, beaten
1-1/4 cups skim milk
1/3 cup special oil

Sift together the flour, salt, baking powder and sugar. Make a well in the center and into it pour the egg, milk and oil. Mix in the flour only until dampened; the batter should be lumpy.

Turn into 18 lightly oiled muffin tins. Bake in a preheated 400° oven 25 minutes or until browned and shrunk away from sides of pan. Serve warm or cold.

Variations:
Cheese Muffins:
Add 1/2 cup grated sapsago cheese to the flour mixture. Proceed as directed.

Blueberry Muffins:
Increase sugar to 1/4 cup and add 1 cup drained, fresh or frozen blueberries to the flour mixture. Proceed as directed.

Nut Muffins:
Add 1/2 cup coarsely chopped pecans or walnuts to the flour mixture. Proceed as directed.

Jam Muffins:

Half fill the muffin tins with batter. Place 1 teaspoon jam in the center and cover with more batter. Proceed as directed.

Per muffin	Plain	Cheese	Blueberry	Nut	Jam
Calories	105	110	120	120	125
Saturated fat (grams)	0.6	0.6	0.6	0.7	0.6
Polyunsaturated fat (grams)	2.3	2.3	2.3	3.4	2.3
Total fat (grams)	3.2	3.2	3.2	4.3	3.2

NUT BREAD

3/4 cup sifted flour
1-1/2 cups whole wheat flour
1/2 teaspoon salt
2-1/2 teaspoons baking powder
1 teaspoon baking soda

3/4 cup (packed) brown sugar
3/4 cup coarsely chopped
walnuts or pecans
1 egg, beaten
1-1/2 cups buttermilk

Sift together the flour, wheat flour, salt, baking powder, baking soda and brown sugar. Mix in the nuts, then the egg and buttermilk until well blended. Turn into an oiled 10-inch loaf pan. Bake in a preheated 325° oven 1 hour or until browned and shrunk away from the sides of the pan. Cool on a cake rack.

Makes 20 half-inch slices

Per slice (with walnuts)
Calories 110
Saturated fat 0.2 gram
Polyunsaturated fat 1.6 grams
Total fat 2.6 grams

Per slice (with pecans)
Calories 110
Saturated fat 0.2 gram
Polyunsaturated fat 0.7 gram
Total fat 3.1 grams

PUFFY OMELET

2 egg whites
1 egg yolk
1/4 cup dry cottage cheese

1/8 teaspoon salt
1 tablespoon special
   margarine

Beat the egg whites until stiff but not dry.

Beat the egg yolk in a bowl, stir in the cottage cheese and salt; fold in the egg whites. Melt the margarine in an 8-inch skillet (with ovenproof handle). Pour the egg mixture into it. Bake in a preheated 400° oven 10 minutes or until puffed and delicately browned.

Serves 1.

Per serving
Calories 290
Saturated fat   4.3 grams
Polyunsaturated fat   4.0 grams
Total fat 17.2 grams

Desserts

FOR the dieter (calories or low-fat or both) the dismal part of the meal is usually the dessert. When he yearns for something sweet to finish his meal, the dieter usually ends up with fruit gelatin or the like. But this need not be so, for this section contains many interesting, flavorsome and comparatively low-calorie low-fat desserts. Also included are recipes which contain high calorie counts but low fats, for those to whom calories are no problem.

For persons who must watch their fat intake, prepared cake mixes are out of the question at the present time, until the manufacturers reduce the contents of saturated fats. All cakes and pies must be prepared strictly according to the recipes given, in order to limit the saturated fat content. Diners out must definitely avoid all commercially prepared cakes, pies and desserts because these items are loaded with saturated fats, perhaps more so than any other food we eat. Don't be careless and order cake or pie in a restaurant, or all your efforts in low-fat dieting will go for nothing. Choose instead simple fruit desserts, compotes or the like. At home, of course, there is a wide variety of recipes to choose from in this section, which has been made especially large.

STRAWBERRY FLUFF

2 cups fresh strawberries or
   2 cups frozen, drained
1 envelope (tablespoon) gelatin
1 cup orange juice

1/4 cup sugar
2 egg whites
Dash salt

Hull, wash, and drain the fresh berries. Purée the berries (reserving 6) in an electric blender or force through a sieve.

Soften the gelatin in the orange juice, then place over hot water until dissolved. Mix in the sugar. Chill until syrupy, about 30 minutes. Add the berry pulp and beat until foamy.

Beat the egg whites and salt until stiff but not dry, then fold into the berry mixture. Turn into a 1-quart mold or individual molds. Arrange the reserved berries on top. Chill until set.

Serves 6.

Per serving
Calories 70
Saturated fat 0.0 gram
Polyunsaturated fat 0.0 gram
Total fat 0.0 gram

BISQUE TORTONI

1 cup cold water
1 cup nonfat dry milk powder
1/4 cup lemon juice
1/4 cup sugar
1 tablespoon sweet sherry

1/2 teaspoon almond extract
1/3 teaspoon vanilla extract
2 tablespoons ground toasted
   almonds

Beat the water and milk powder with an electric mixer or rotary beater until thickened. Beat in the lemon juice until very thick, then add the sugar, beating until the consistency of whipped cream. Fold in the sherry, almond and vanilla extract.

Divide among 8 4-ounce paper cups or other small containers; sprinkle with the ground almonds. Freeze until set.

Serves 8.

Per serving
Calories 85
Saturated fat 0.1 gram
Polyunsaturated fat 0.2 gram
Total fat 1.3 grams

LEMON ICE-CREAM DESSERT

2 tablespoons special margarine
1 tablespoon flour
1/8 teaspoon salt

3-1/2 cups skim milk
1/4 cup sugar
1/2 cup lemon juice
2 teaspoons grated lemon rind

Melt the margarine in a saucepan. Blend in the flour and salt. Gradually add half the milk, stirring steadily to the boiling point. Mix in the sugar, then cook over low heat 5 minutes. Remove from the heat and stir in the remaining milk. Turn into a refrigerator tray and freeze until sides set. Turn into a bowl, add the lemon juice and rind; beat until frothy. Return to the tray and freeze until set.

Serves 6.

Per serving
Calories 125
Saturated fat 0.9 gram
Polyunsaturated fat 1.1 grams
Total fat 3.9 grams

VANILLA FROZEN DESSERT (Ice Cream)

2 tablespoons gelatin
3/4 cup water
1 cup nonfat dry milk powder
1-1/2 cups liquid skim milk, scalded

1/3 cup sugar
2 teaspoons vanilla extract

Soften the gelatin in 1/4 cup of the water. Mix together 1/2 cup of the dry milk powder, the hot liquid milk, the gelatin mixture and 1/4 cup of the sugar. Chill until the consistency of egg whites. Stir in the vanilla.

Beat the remaining dry milk powder and remaining water until it begins to thicken. Add the remaining sugar, beating until the consistency of whipped cream. Fold into the gelatin mixture. Turn into 2 refrigerator trays and freeze in the freezer or refrigerator (set at coldest point) until the edges are firm. Turn into a bowl and beat with an electric mixer or rotary beater until double in bulk. Return to the trays and freeze until set.

Serves 8.

Variation   Strawberry Frozen Dessert
Use 1/2 cup sugar (instead of 1/3) and add 1 cup mashed strawberries to the cooled gelatin mixture. Proceed as directed.

Variation   Banana Frozen Dessert
Add 2 cups mashed bananas to the cooled gelatin mixture. Proceed as directed.

Variation   Coffee Frozen Dessert
Add 1 tablespoon instant coffee to the hot milk. Proceed as directed.

Per serving	Vanilla	Strawberry	Banana	Coffee
Calories	120	135	145	120
Saturated fat (grams)	0.1	0.1	0.1	0.1
Polyunsaturated fat (grams)	0.0	0.0	0.1	0.0
Total fat (grams)	0.2	0.2	0.3	0.2

FRENCH CREAM DESSERT

3 tablespoons cornstarch
3 tablespoons nonfat dry milk
  powder
3 tablespoons sugar
2 cups skim milk

1 egg
1 tablespoon melted special
  margarine
1 tablespoon cognac
1 teaspoon vanilla extract

Mix the cornstarch, dry milk powder and sugar together in the top of a double boiler; gradually add the liquid milk. Place over hot water and cook, stirring steadily until thickened. Cook 15 minutes longer, mixing occasionally.

Beat the egg in a bowl; gradually add the hot liquid, stirring steadily to prevent curdling. Return to the double boiler and cook 2 minutes, stirring constantly, but do not let boil. Remove from the heat and mix in the melted margarine, cognac and vanilla. Cool slightly and spoon into 6 sherbet glasses. Chill. If desired, Lady Fingers or slices of Sponge Cake (see recipes) may be placed in the glasses.

Serves 6.

Per serving
Calories 115
Saturated fat 0.8 gram
Polyunsaturated fat 0.7 gram
Total fat 2.9 grams

LEMON SHERBET

2 cups water
1-1/4 cups sugar
1/2 cup lemon juice

2 teaspoons grated lemon rind
1/3 cup nonfat dry milk powder

Bring 1/2 cup water to a boil; stir in the sugar until dissolved. Add 1-1/2 cups cold water and the lemon juice; stir well. Chill 10 minutes. Sprinkle the rind and dry milk on top. Beat with an electric mixer or rotary beater until slightly thickened. Turn into a freezer tray and freeze until sides are mushy. Turn into a bowl and beat until light and frothy. Return to tray and freeze until set.

Serves 6.

Per serving
Calories 190
Saturated fat 0.0 gram
Polyunsaturated fat 0.0 gram
Total fat 0.0 gram

FROZEN BANANA DESSERT

3 cups mashed bananas
2/3 cup sugar
1/8 teaspoon salt
1/2 cup pineapple juice

1 tablespoon lemon juice
2 tablespoons cognac
1 teaspoon powdered ginger
2 egg whites, beaten stiff

Mix together the bananas, sugar, salt, pineapple juice, lemon juice, cognac and ginger. Fold in the egg whites. Divide among 8 sherbet cups. Place them in freezer section of the refrigerator or home freezer until set.

Serves 8.

Per serving
Calories 135
Saturated fat 0.0 gram
Polyunsaturated fat 0.1 gram
Total fat 0.1 gram

PEACH MERINGUE SURPRISE

3 egg whites
Dash salt
1/4 teaspoon cream of tartar
1/4 cup sugar

1 teaspoon almond extract
2 tablespoons ground almonds
6 canned peach halves, drained

Beat the egg whites, salt and cream of tartar until peaks begin to form. Gradually beat in the sugar until stiff but not dry. Fold in the almond extract and almonds.

Lightly oil a cookie sheet. Using half the meringue, form 6 mounds, leaving 2 inches between each. Place a peach half on each mound, cut side up, and cover with the remaining meringue. Bake in a preheated 325° oven 30 minutes. Remove from the pan with a spatula and cool.

Serves 6.

Per serving
Calories 75
Saturated fat 0.1 gram
Polyunsaturated fat 0.3 gram
Total fat 1.6 grams

FLAKY PIE PASTRY

1-1/2 cups sifted flour
1/2 teaspoon salt

1-1/2 sticks special margarine
4 tablespoons ice water

Sift the flour and salt into a bowl. Cut in the margarine with a pastry blender or two knives until consistency is like coarse cornmeal. Add just enough ice water, tossing with a fork, to form a ball. Chill 20 minutes.

Divide the dough in half and roll out very thin on a lightly floured surface. Fit 1 piece into a 9-inch pie plate. Fill as desired and cover with the second piece; seal the edges with a little water and cut a few gashes in the top. Bake as directed.

Serves 8.

Per serving
Calories 240
Saturated fat   3.5 grams
Polyunsaturated fat   4.9 grams
Total fat 17.0 grams

PASTRY DOUGH

2 cups sifted flour
1/2 teaspoon salt

1/2 cup special oil
5 tablespoons ice water

Sift together the flour and salt. Beat the oil and water together until creamy. Add to the flour all at once; toss with a fork. Shape into 2 balls. Roll out the dough (between two pieces of waxed paper about 12 inches square) into a circle large enough to fit a 9-inch pie plate. Peel off top paper and invert pastry over pie plate. Peel off paper. Fill with desired filling. Roll out remaining pastry and cover the filling, sealing the edges well. Cut a few slits in the top. Bake in a preheated 425° oven 35 minutes or until browned. For pastry shell make half the recipe; flute the edges and prick surface of dough. Bake in a preheated 475° oven 12 minutes or until browned.

Note: Pastry cannot be chilled or kept—bake immediately.

Serves 8. Figure half the calories for a one-crust pie.

Per serving
Saturated fat   1.6 grams
Polyunsaturated fat   7.7 grams
Total fat 13.6 grams

MERINGUE PASTRY SHELL

2 egg whites
Dash salt
1/2 teaspoon vinegar

1/4 teaspoon vanilla extract
2/3 cup sugar

Beat the egg whites, salt, vinegar and vanilla until soft peaks are formed. Gradually beat in the sugar until stiff. Spread over the bottom and sides of a lightly oiled 9-inch pie plate. Bake in a preheated 300° oven 45 minutes or until delicately browned and dry to the touch.

Serves 8.

Per serving
Calories 80
Saturated fat 0.0 gram
Polyunsaturated fat 0.0 gram
Total fat 0.0 gram

APPLE PIE

Pastry for 2-crust pie
5 cups peeled sliced apples
2/3 cup sugar

1 tablespoon lemon juice
1/2 teaspoon cinnamon (optional)
1/4 teaspoon nutmeg (optional)

Line a 9-inch pie plate with half the Flaky Pie pastry (see recipe). Toss together the apples, sugar, lemon juice, cinnamon and nutmeg. Fill the shell and cover with the remaining pastry. Bake in a preheated 400° oven 50 minutes or until browned and apples are tender. Cool on a cake rack.

Serves 8.

Per serving
Calories 365
Saturated fat 3.6 grams
Polyunsaturated fat 5.0 grams
Total fat 17.5 grams

BLUEBERRY PIE

Pastry for 2-crust pie
3 cups fresh blueberries or
drained frozen blueberries

2/3 cup sugar
1 tablespoon cornstarch
1 tablespoon lemon juice

Line a 9-inch pie plate with half the Flaky Pie pastry (see recipe). Toss together the blueberries, sugar, cornstarch and lemon juice. Fill the shell. Cover with the remaining pastry. Bake in a preheated 400° oven 45 minutes or until browned. Cool on a cake rack.

NOTE: If frozen berries are used, thaw them and drain. Reduce sugar to 1/2 cup and increase cornstarch to 2 tablespoons.

Serves 8.

Per serving
Calories 335
Saturated fat   3.6 grams
Polyunsaturated fat   5.0 grams
Total fat 17.5 grams

STRAWBERRY CHIFFON PIE

3 tablespoons water
5 tablespoons sugar
2 egg whites
1 envelope (tablespoon) gelatin
1/4 cup liquid skim milk
1/2 cup nonfat dry milk powder
1 tablespoon lemon juice

1/2 cup ice water
1 tablespoon almond extract
9-inch baked pastry shell (see
recipe for Pastry Dough)
1 cup fresh strawberries, washed
and drained, or whole frozen
strawberries

Boil the 3 tablespoons water and 4 tablespoons of the sugar until a soft ball forms when a drop is placed in cold water. Beat the egg whites until stiff but not dry, then gradually beat in the sugar mixture.

Soften the gelatin in the liquid milk, then place over hot water, stirring until dissolved. Beat into the egg whites. Beat together the dry milk powder, lemon juice and ice water until the consistency of whipped cream. Fold into the egg-white mixture with the almond extract. Turn into the baked pie shell. Arrange the strawberries on top and sprinkle with the remaining sugar. Chill.

Serves 8.

Per serving
Calories 300
Saturated fat   0.8 gram
Polyunsaturated fat   3.9 grams
Total fat 13.0 grams

PUMPKIN PIE

2 eggs
3/4 cup brown sugar
1 cup cooked or canned puréed pumpkin
1/4 teaspoon salt
3/4 teaspoon cinnamon
3/4 teaspoon powdered ginger

1/2 teaspoon nutmeg
3/4 cup skim milk
2 tablespoons melted special margarine
1 tablespoon cognac
9-inch unbaked pastry shell (see recipe for Pastry Dough)

Beat the eggs and brown sugar together until thick. Beat in the pumpkin, salt, cinnamon, ginger and nutmeg until smooth. Beat in the milk, melted margarine and cognac; turn into the pastry shell.

Bake in a preheated 425° oven 15 minutes; reduce the heat to 325° and bake 30 minutes longer, or until a knife inserted in the center comes out clean. Serve warm or cold.

Serves 8.

Per serving
Calories 250
Saturated fat   1.9 grams
Polyunsaturated fat   4.9 grams
Total fat 18.1 grams

LEMON CHIFFON PIE

1 envelope (tablespoon) gelatin
1/4 cup cold water
1/2 cup sugar
1/4 cup boiling water
1/2 cup lemon juice
1 teaspoon grated lemon rind

1/4 teaspoon salt
3 egg whites
1/2 cup light corn syrup
1 baked 9-inch pastry shell (see recipe for Flaky Pastry)

Soften the gelatin in the cold water; mix in the sugar and boiling water until dissolved; stir in the lemon juice and rind. Chill until syrupy but don't let it set, since texture will not be smooth.

Beat the salt and egg whites until stiff but not dry. Gradually add the corn syrup, beating steadily. Fold the lemon mixture into the egg whites. Chill about 20 minutes, stirring occasionally. Mixture should be set enough to be able to heap it. Spoon into the pie shell and chill until set.

Serves 8.

Per serving
Calories 230
Saturated fat 1.8 grams
Polyunsaturated fat 2.4 grams
Total fat 6.1 grams

BOSTON CREAM PIE

Cake:

1-1/3 cups sifted cake flour
1/4 teaspoon salt
2 teaspoons baking powder
3/4 cup sugar
1/3 cup special oil

2 egg yolks
1/3 cup water
1 teaspoon vanilla extract
2 egg whites
1/8 teaspoon cream of tartar

Oil a 9-inch layer cake pan and dust with flour.

Sift the flour, salt, baking powder and sugar into a bowl. Make a well in the center and into it place the oil, egg yolks, water and vanilla. Beat until very smooth.

Beat the egg whites and cream of tartar until stiff. Fold the yolk mixture into the whites carefully but thoroughly. Turn into the prepared pan. Bake in a preheated 350° oven 40 minutes or until top springs back when touched with the finger.

Cool on a cake rack 10 minutes, then loosen cake with a spatula; turn out onto the rack until cold. While cake is baking, prepare the filling.

Filling:

1-1/2 tablespoons cornstarch
1-1/2 tablespoons nonfat dry milk
2 tablespoons sugar

3/4 cup skim milk
1 egg yolk
1 teaspoon orange extract

In the top of a double boiler, mix the cornstarch, dry milk powder and sugar. Gradually add the liquid milk, stirring until smooth. Place over hot water and cook, stirring steadily, until thickened. Cook 5 minutes longer, stirring occasionally.

Beat the egg yolk in a bowl; gradually add the hot liquid, stirring steadily to prevent curdling. Return to top of double boiler and cook 1 minute, stirring steadily. Remove from heat and mix in the orange extract. Cool.

Split the cake and spread with filling. Sprinkle top with confectioners' sugar.

Serves 10.

Per serving
Calories 220
Saturated fat 1.4 grams
Polyunsaturated fat 4.3 grams
Total fat 8.5 grams

229

HONEY SPONGE CAKE

5 eggs
1/4 cup honey
2/3 cup sugar
3/4 cup sifted flour

3/4 teaspoon double-acting baking
    powder
2 teaspoons special oil
Confectioners' sugar

Beat the eggs until light; add the honey and sugar, beating until thick (about 10 minutes). Sift the flour and baking powder onto the mixture; stir only until smooth.

Oil an 8- x 8-inch brownie pan and dust lightly with flour. Turn the batter into it. Bake in a preheated 350° oven 35 minutes or until a cake tester comes out clean. Cool on a cake rack 10 minutes, then turn out onto the rack until completely cool. Turn right side up and sprinkle with the confectioners' sugar. Cut into 2-inch squares.

Makes 16 squares.

Per square
Calories 110
Saturated fat 0.7 gram
Polyunsaturated fat 0.6 gram
Total fat 2.5 grams

POUND CAKE

2-1/4 cups sifted cake flour
1/4 teaspoon salt
1/2 teaspoon baking powder
2 sticks (1 cup) special
    margarine
1 cup sugar

4 egg yolks, beaten
1/4 cup cold water
1 teaspoon vanilla extract
1/2 teaspoon mace
5 egg whites

Oil a 10- x 5-inch loaf pan. Line with waxed paper and lightly oil the paper.

Sift together the cake flour, salt, and baking powder. Cream the margarine; gradually add the sugar, beating well until light and fluffy. Add the egg yolks and water; beat until light. Sift in the flour mixture, a little at a time, mixing until blended. Stir in the vanilla and mace.

Beat the egg whites until stiff but not dry. Fold into the flour mixture carefully. Turn into the prepared pan. Bake in a preheated 300° oven 1-1/4 hours, or until top springs back when pressed with the finger. Cool on a cake rack 15 minutes; run spatula around the edges. Turn out onto the cake rack until cold.

Serves 14.

Per serving
Calories 250
Saturated fat   3.2 grams
Polyunsaturated fat   3.9 grams
Total fat 15.2 grams

CHIFFON CAKE

1-1/8 cups sifted cake flour	2 egg yolks
1/4 teaspoon salt	3/4 teaspoon vanilla extract
1-1/2 teaspoons baking powder	1/4 teaspoon almond extract
3/4 cup sugar	4 egg whites
1/4 cup special oil	1/4 teaspoon cream of tartar
6 tablespoons cold water	

Into a bowl sift the flour, salt, baking powder and sugar. Make a well in the center and into it place the oil, water, egg yolks, vanilla and almond extracts. Beat until smooth.

Beat the egg whites and cream of tartar until stiff. Fold the yolk mixture into the egg whites. Turn into a 9-inch tube pan. Bake in a preheated 325° oven 1 hour, or until top springs back when pressed with the finger.

Invert immediately (if pan doesn't have metal legs to elevate it from table, place tube part over a bottle) until cold. Loosen cake from pan with a spatula and turn out.

Serves 12.

Per serving
Calories 170
Saturated fat 0.9 gram
Polyunsaturated fat 2.7 grams
Total fat 5.5 grams

CUSTARD CHIFFON CAKE

1/2 cup skim milk
3 egg yolks
1-1/2 cups sifted flour
1/4 teaspoon salt
2 teaspoons baking powder
1 cup sugar

1/3 cup special oil
1-1/2 teaspoons vanilla extract
1 teaspoon grated lemon rind
5 egg whites
1/2 teaspoon cream of tartar

Heat the milk to the boiling point. Beat the egg yolks in a bowl; gradually add the hot milk, stirring steadily to prevent curdling. Cool.

Into a bowl sift the flour, salt, baking powder, and sugar. Make a well in the center and into it put the oil, vanilla, rind and egg yolk mixture. Beat until smooth.

Beat the egg whites and cream of tartar until stiff but not dry. Fold the yolk mixture into them. Turn into a 9-inch tube pan. Bake in a preheated 325° oven 1 hour or until top springs back when pressed with the finger.

Invert immediately (if pan doesn't have metal legs to elevate it from table, place tube part over a bottle) until cold. Loosen cake from side of pan with a spatula and turn out.

Serves 12.

Per serving
Calories 180
Saturated fat 1.2 grams
Polyunsaturated fat 3.6 grams
Total 7.8 grams

ANGEL FOOD LOAF

1/2 cup sifted cake flour
Dash salt
3/4 cup sugar

5 egg whites
1/2 teaspoon cream of tartar
1/2 teaspoon vanilla extract

Sift the flour, salt and 1/4 cup sugar 3 times. Beat the egg whites, cream of tartar and vanilla until peaks form. Beat in the remaining sugar 2 tablespoons at a time. Fold in the flour mixture gradually. Turn into a 10-inch loaf pan.

Bake in a preheated 375° oven 25 minutes or until browned and top springs back when pressed with the finger. Invert pan with ends over 2 bowls or bottles to elevate it from table until cold.

Serves 12.

Per serving
Calories 75
Saturated fat 0.0 gram
Polyunsaturated fat 0.0 gram
Total fat 0.0 gram

WHITE CAKE

2-1/2 cups sifted flour
1/2 teaspoon salt
1 tablespoon baking powder
1-1/4 cups sugar

1/2 cup special oil
1 cup skim milk
1 teaspoon vanilla extract
4 egg whites

Oil a 13- x 9-inch loaf pan and dust heavily with flour.

Sift together the flour, salt, baking powder and 1/2 cup sugar. Make a well in the center and in it put the oil, 2/3 cup milk and the vanilla. Beat until smooth, then add remaining milk. Beat again until smooth.

Beat the egg whites until peaks form, then gradually beat in the remaining sugar until stiff. Fold the flour mixture into the egg whites gradually. Turn into the pan. Bake in a preheated 350° oven 35 minutes or until top springs back when pressed with the finger. Cool on a cake rack, then loosen from sides of pan with a spatula. Turn out.

Serves 14.

Per serving
Calories 205
Saturated fat 0.9 gram
Polyunsaturated fat 4.4 grams
Total fat 7.9 grams

STREUSEL CAKE

2 cups sifted flour
1/4 teaspoon salt
2 teaspoons baking powder
1/2 cup sugar
1 egg, beaten

1/2 cup orange juice
1/3 cup special oil
·1/2 cup skim milk
1 tablespoon grated orange rind

Sift the flour, salt, baking powder and sugar into a bowl.
Make a well in the center and into it put the egg, orange juice,
oil, milk and rind. Mix only until flour is dampened; don't
worry if the batter is lumpy. Turn into an oiled 8-inch square
pan. Now prepare the crumbs:

1/4 cup sugar
1/4 cup flour

2 tablespoons special
margarine

Mix together the sugar and flour. Cut in the margarine until
particles adhere. Sprinkle over the top of the batter. Bake in a
preheated 375° oven 35 minutes, or until browned. Cool on
a cake rack. Serve warm or cold.

Serves 16.

Per serving
Calories 160
Saturated fat 0.9 gram
Polyunsaturated fat 3.0 grams
Total fat 6.1 grams

CREÂM LAYER CAKE

1-1/4 cups sifted cake flour
1/4 teaspoon salt
2 teaspoons double-acting
    baking powder
3/4 cup sugar
2 egg yolks

1/4 cup special oil
1/2 cup cold water
1 teaspoon vanilla extract
1/2 teaspoon almond extract
2 egg whites
1/8 teaspoon cream of tartar

Sift the flour, salt, baking powder and sugar into a bowl.
Make a well in the center and into it put the egg yolks, oil,
water, vanilla and almond extracts. Stir the mixture in the well,
then beat in the flour mixture until smooth.

Beat the egg whites and cream of tartar until stiff. Fold the
egg yolk mixture into the whites. Turn into 2 8-inch layer-cake

pans. Bake in a preheated 375° oven 25 minutes or until top springs back when pressed with the finger. Cool on a cake rack, then loosen from sides of pan with a spatula and turn out. Put together with Special "Whipped Cream" and strawberries or with Special Icing (see recipes).

Serves 12. Calorie and fat count is for cake only.

Per serving
Calories 150
Saturated fat 0.9 gram
Polyunsaturated fat 2.7 grams
Total fat 5.4 grams

REFRIGERATOR CHEESECAKE

3 tablespoons special margarine, melted
3/4 cup graham cracker crumbs
3 cups dry cottage cheese
2 envelopes (2 tablespoons) gelatin
3/4 cup water

2 egg yolks
3/4 cup skim milk
1/3 cup sugar
1/4 teaspoon salt
1-1/2 tablespoons vanilla extract
1/2 cup nonfat dry milk powder
2 egg whites

Grease an 8-inch spring-form pan with a little of the margarine. Mix the crumbs with the remaining margarine and press against the bottom and sides of the pan. Chill while preparing the filling.

Force the cheese through a sieve. Soften the gelatin in 1/4 cup water. Beat the egg yolks in the top of a double boiler. Mix in the milk, sugar and salt. Place over hot water and cook, stirring steadily, until thickened. Mix in the gelatin until dissolved; cool 20 minutes. Mix into the cheese with the vanilla.

Beat the remaining water and the dry milk powder until the consistency of whipped cream. Beat the egg whites until stiff but not dry. Fold into the cheese mixture with the whipped milk. Slowly pour into the spring form. Chill until set, about 5 hours.

Serves 10.

Per serving
Calories 195
Saturated fat 1.3 grams
Polyunsaturated fat 1.5 grams
Total fat 5.4 grams

JELLY ROLL

1 cup sifted cake flour
1/4 teaspoon salt
1-1/2 teaspoons baking powder
3/4 cup sugar
2 egg yolks

1/3 cup cold water
3 tablespoons special oil
1 teaspoon vanilla extract
4 egg whites
1/4 teaspoon cream of tartar

Oil a jelly roll pan (11 x 17 inches), line it with waxed paper, and oil again.

Into a bowl sift the flour, salt, baking powder and sugar. Make a well in the center and into it put the egg yolks, water, oil and vanilla. Beat until smooth.

Beat the egg whites and cream of tartar until stiff. Fold the yolk mixture into them. Turn into the prepared pan and spread evenly with a spatula. Bake in a preheated 350° oven 12 minutes or until top springs back when pressed with the finger.

Sprinkle a towel with confectioners' sugar and turn cake out onto it. Carefully peel the paper from it. Roll up the cake the long way in the towel and cool. Unroll cake and spread with jelly or Special "Whipped Cream" (see recipe) and sliced strawberries or crushed drained canned pineapple. Reroll cake and wrap firmly in waxed paper. Chill 1 hour.

Serves 10. Calories and fat count is for cake only.

Per serving
Calories 120
Saturated fat 0.4 gram
Polyunsaturated fat 0.2 gram
Total fat 1.3 grams

LADY FINGERS

2 egg whites
1/8 teaspoon salt
1/4 cup powdered sugar
2 egg yolks

1 teaspoon vanilla extract
1/2 cup sifted cake flour
2 tablespoons granulated sugar

Line a cookie sheet with aluminum foil.

Beat the egg whites and salt together, then beat in the powdered sugar a spoonful at a time until stiff. Beat the egg yolks until thick, then fold into the egg whites with the vanilla.

Sift the flour over the mixture and fold in lightly. Press the mixture through a plain-tipped pastry tube onto the aluminum foil in 2-inch strips, or spread with a spoon into 2-inch strips by about 3/4 inch wide. Leave space between each. Sprinkle with the granulated sugar. Bake in a preheated 350° oven 10 minutes or until delicately browned. Cool 5 minutes, then remove from foil.

Makes about 24.

Per lady finger
Calories 30
Saturated fat 0.2 gram
Polyunsaturated fat 0.1 gram
Total fat 0.5 gram

BUTTERSCOTCH BROWNIES

2/3 cup sifted cake flour
1/4 teaspoon salt
1 teaspoon baking powder
1 cup packed dark-brown sugar
1/4 cup special oil

1 egg
1 teaspoon vanilla extract
1/2 cup chopped walnuts or
    pecans

Sift together the flour, salt and baking powder. Mix until smooth the brown sugar and oil. Beat in the egg and vanilla until light and fluffy. Stir in the nuts, then fold in the flour mixture. Turn into a greased 8-inch square (brownie) pan.

Bake in a preheated 350° oven 35 minutes or until a cake tester comes out clean. Cut into 16 squares.

Per brownie
Calories 120
Saturated fat 0.7 gram
Polyunsaturated fat 3.0 grams
Total fat 8.7 grams

CUPCAKES

1 cup sifted flour
1/4 teaspoon salt
1 teaspoon baking powder
1 egg

1/2 cup sugar
1 teaspoon vanilla extract
1/4 cup skim milk
1/4 cup special oil

Lightly oil 8 cupcake pans and dust with flour.

Sift together the flour, salt and baking powder. Beat the egg, then gradually beat in the sugar until light and fluffy. Mix in the vanilla.

Beat the milk and oil until creamy. Add to the egg mixture alternately with the flour mixture, beating until smooth after each addition. Turn into the prepared pans. Bake in a preheated 350° oven 20 minutes or until browned and a cake tester comes out clean. Cool on a cake rack for 10 minutes, then loosen from sides of pan with a spatula.

Serves 8.

Per serving
Calories 180
Saturated fat 1.0 gram
Polyunsaturated fat 3.2 grams
Total fat 7.7 grams

DATE-BRAN CUPCAKES

1-1/2 cups pitted chopped dates
3/4 teaspoon baking soda
3/4 cup boiling water
1/4 cup special oil
3/4 cup sugar

1/2 teaspoon vanilla extract
1-1/2 cups sifted flour
1/2 cup bran flakes
1/2 cup chopped walnuts or pecans

Toss together the dates and baking soda; mix in the boiling water and let cool. Mix together the oil, sugar and vanilla. Beat in the flour, bran and nuts. Turn into 12 oiled muffin pans.

Bake in a preheated 375° oven 25 minutes or until browned and a cake tester comes out clean. Cool on a cake rack.

Serves 12.

Per serving
Calories 225
Saturated fat 0.8 gram
Polyunsaturated fat 4.0 grams
Total fat 8.0 grams

CAKE SQUARES

2-2/3 cups sifted cake flour
1-1/2 cups sugar
1/2 teaspoon salt
4 teaspoons baking powder
4 egg yolks
2/3 cup special oil

3/4 cup cold water
1 teaspoon vanilla extract
2 teaspoons lemon juice
4 egg whites
1/4 teaspoon cream of tartar

Preheat oven to 350°. Lightly oil a 13- x 9- x 2-inch baking pan and dust with flour.

Sift together the flour, sugar, salt and baking powder into a bowl. Make a well in the center and into it put the egg yolks, oil, water, vanilla and lemon juice. Beat until smooth. Beat the egg whites and cream of tartar until stiff but not dry; fold the flour mixture into them carefully but thoroughly. Turn into the prepared pan. Bake 40 minutes, or until cake springs back when pressed with the finger. Cool on a cake rack for 15 minutes, then loosen cake from pan with a spatula. Turn out onto cake rack until cold. Cut into 24 squares. Sprinkle with confectioners' sugar if desired.

Per square
Calories 160
Saturated fat 1.0 gram
Polyunsaturated fat 3.5 grams
Total fat 7.0 grams

SHORTCAKES

2 cups sifted flour	1 egg
1/2 teaspoon salt	1/3 cup special oil
1 tablespoon baking powder	1/2 cup skim milk
2 tablespoons sugar	

Sift together the flour, salt, baking powder and sugar. Beat the egg and oil in a measuring cup. Add enough of the milk, or more if necessary, to make 1 cup liquid. Add to the flour mixture all at once. Toss with a fork until a dough is formed. Knead lightly on a piece of waxed paper until smooth. Roll out gently to a thickness of 1/2 inch. Cut with a 2-inch cookie cutter. Arrange on a baking sheet. Bake in a preheated 450° oven 12 minutes or until delicately browned. Split with a fork while warm. Spread sliced strawberries, peaches, blueberries or raspberries between the layers and on top. Serve with Special "Whipped Cream" (see recipe), if desired.

Makes 10 shortcakes.

Per serving
Calories 165
Saturated fat 1.0 gram
Polyunsaturated fat 4.2 grams
Total fat 8.1 grams

JAM TORTE

4 egg yolks	2 teaspoons baking powder
3/4 cup berry or apricot jam	1/4 teaspoon salt
1/2 cup special oil	8 egg whites
1 teaspoon vanilla extract	1/4 cup sugar
1-1/2 cups fine dry bread crumbs	

Beat the egg yolks until thick; gradually beat in the jam, then the oil and vanilla. Mix together the bread crumbs, baking powder and salt; stir into the yolk mixture.

Beat the egg whites until frothy, then gradually beat in the sugar until stiff but not dry. Fold the yolk mixture into the whites. Turn into a 9-inch tube pan. Bake in a 325° oven 1 hour or until browned and a cake tester comes out clean.

Invert immediately (if pan doesn't have metal legs to elevate it from table, place tube part over a bottle) until cold. Loosen cake from side of pan with a spatula and turn out.

Serves 14.

Per serving
Calories 195
Saturated fat 1.5 grams
Polyunsaturated fat 4.7 grams
Total fat 9.7 grams

STREUSEL BLUEBERRY TARTS

1-1/2 cups sifted flour
1/4 teaspoon salt
1 teaspoon sugar
1/2 cup special oil

2 tablespoons skim milk
1 pint blueberries, washed and drained

Sift together the flour, salt and sugar. Beat the oil and the milk with a fork until creamy. Pour over the flour mixture, tossing with a fork until blended. Divide among 8 3-inch tart pans or muffin pans. Pat until bottom and sides are covered. Fill with the berries and sprinkle with the following mixture:

3/4 cup sugar
3 tablespoons flour

1/8 teaspoon salt
2 tablespoons special oil

Toss together until crumbly. Bake in a preheated 425° oven 45 minutes or until pastry edges are browned. Cool on a cake rack.

Serves 12.

Per serving
Calories 205
Saturated fat 1.3 grams
Polyunsaturated fat 6.5 grams
Total fat 9.7 grams

Apple Streusel Tarts
Substitute 2-1/2 cups thinly sliced apples mixed with 2 teaspoons lemon juice for the blueberries. Proceed as directed.

Serves 12.

Per serving
Calories 210
Saturated fat 1.3 grams
Polyunsaturated fat 6.5 grams
Total fat 9.7 grams

APRICOT TORTE

Torte Shell:

1-1/2 cups sifted flour
1/2 teaspoon salt
2 tablespoons sugar

1/2 cup special oil
2 tablespoons skim milk
1 egg yolk

Preheat oven to 350°.

Use a 9-inch layer-cake pan. Into it sift the flour, salt and sugar. Beat together until frothy the oil, milk and egg yolk; pour over the flour mixture and mix with a fork until all flour is dampened. Press evenly with the fingers over bottom and sides (to a depth of 2 inches) of the pan.

Filling:

1/2 cup apricot preserves
1-1/3 cups sifted cake flour
1/4 teaspoon salt
1-1/2 teaspoons baking powder
2/3 cup sugar
1/2 cup ground toasted almonds

1/3 cup special oil
2 egg yolks
1/2 cup skim milk
1 teaspoon almond extract
2 egg whites
1/8 teaspoon cream of tartar

Spread the shell with half the preserves.

Sift together the flour, salt, baking powder and sugar into a bowl. Mix in the almonds. Make a well in the center and into it put the oil, egg yolks, milk and almond extract. Beat until smooth. Beat the egg whites and cream of tartar until stiff but not dry; fold into the previous mixture carefully but thoroughly. Turn into the lined pan. Bake 40 minutes or until a cake tester comes out clean. Cool on a cake rack 10 minutes, then carefully turn out. Turn shell side down. When cold, spread remaining preserves on top. Cut into 12 pie-shaped wedges.

Per wedge
Calories 360
Saturated fat   2.5 grams
Polyunsaturated fat   9.3 grams
Total fat 19.2 grams

PINEAPPLE-NUT TORTE

1-1/3 cups sifted cake flour
1/4 teaspoon salt
1-1/2 teaspoons baking powder
2/3 cup sugar
3/4 cup toasted coarsely chopped
   blanched almonds

1/2 cup pineapple juice
1/2 cup special oil
2 egg yolks
2 egg whites
1/8 teaspoon cream of tartar

Into a bowl sift the flour, salt, baking powder and 1/3 cup sugar. Mix in the nuts. Beat together the pineapple juice, oil and egg yolks; beat into the flour mixture until smooth.

Beat the egg whites and cream of tartar until peaks form; gradually beat in the remaining sugar until stiff. Fold into the yolk mixture. Turn into an oiled 9-inch layer-cake pan. Bake in a preheated 350° oven 35 minutes or until top springs back when pressed with the finger. Cool on a cake rack, then loosen from pan with a spatula. Turn out and split in half. Fill and top with the following:

1 #2 can crushed pineapple
1 teaspoon sugar

2 tablespoons cornstarch

Drain the fruit; mix the juice in a saucepan with the sugar and cornstarch. Cook over low heat, stirring constantly to the boiling point. Cook 2 minutes longer. Stir in the pineapple. Cool.

Serves 12.

Per serving

Calories 270
Saturated fat   1.7 grams
Polyunsaturated fat   6.1 grams
Total fat 15.0 grams

CARROT TORTE

2 egg yolks
1/2 cup plus 1 tablespoon sugar
1-1/4 cups blanched ground
almonds

1 cup finely grated carrots
1/8 teaspoon nutmeg
5 egg whites, stiffly beaten

Beat the egg yolks until light, then beat in the sugar until thick. Stir in the almonds, carrots and nutmeg. Fold in the egg whites. Turn into an oiled 9-inch pie plate. Bake in a preheated 275° oven 1 hour and 10 minutes. Cool. The torte is like a moist sponge cake.

Serves 8.

Per serving
Calories 215
Saturated fat 1.4 grams
Polyunsaturated fat 2.5 grams
Total fat 12.7 grams

ANISE CAKES

2-1/2 cups sifted flour
1 tablespoon powdered anise
1/2 teaspoon cinnamon
1/2 cup chopped walnuts

1/4 cup finely chopped candied
orange peel
1-1/2 cups sugar
1-1/2 cups water

Mix together the flour, anise, cinnamon, walnuts and orange peel. Cook the sugar and water until a thread forms when a fork is raised, or a candy thermometer registers 230°. Remove from the heat and beat in the flour mixture until well blended. Turn out onto a board and cool; then knead it very well. If too firm, add a little water. Roll it out 1/4 inch thick; cut into 1-1/2-inch circles.

Oil a baking pan and dust with flour. Arrange the circles on it. Bake in a preheated 275° oven 35 minutes. They should be hard on the outside but slightly soft on the inside, similar to a macaroon.

Makes about 36.

Per cake
Calories 60
Saturated fat 0.1 gram
Polyunsaturated fat 0.6 gram
Total fat 1.0 gram

ITALIAN ANISE CRESCENTS

2-1/2 cups sifted flour
1/4 teaspoon salt
3/4 cup confectioners' sugar
1/4 cup ground almonds

1 tablespoon anise seed
2/3 cup special oil
2 tablespoons cognac
1/2 teaspoon vanilla extract

Sift together the flour, salt and confectioners' sugar. Mix in the nuts and anise. Stir in the oil, cognac and vanilla. Knead lightly until a dough is formed. Break off pieces of the dough and roll between the hands into rolls 2 inches long and about 3/4 inch thick. Arrange on a cookie sheet; bring ends together to form crescents.

Bake in a preheated 350° oven 20 minutes or until lightly browned. Cool on a cake rack.

Makes about 36 crescents.

Per crescent
Calories 80
Saturated fat 0.5 gram
Polyunsaturated fat 2.4 grams
Total fat 4.7 grams

DROP NUT COOKIES

3/4 cup sifted flour
1/4 teaspoon salt
1 egg yolk
2 egg whites

1/2 cup packed dark-brown sugar
1/2 cup chopped walnuts
3 tablespoons special oil
1/2 teaspoon vanilla extract

Sift together the flour and salt. Beat the egg yolk and whites until thick; gradually beat in the brown sugar. Mix in the nuts, oil, vanilla and flour until well blended. Drop by the teaspoonful onto a lightly oiled cookie sheet.

Bake in a preheated 350° oven 12 minutes or until delicately browned.

Makes about 36 cookies.

Per cookie
Calories 40
Saturated fat 0.3 gram
Polyunsaturated fat 1.2 grams
Total fat 2.2 grams

OATMEAL DROPS

1 cup sifted flour
1/4 teaspoon salt
2/3 cup sugar
1/2 teaspoon baking powder
1/4 teaspoon baking soda
1/2 teaspoon cinnamon

1-1/2 cups quick-cooking oatmeal
1/2 cup seedless raisins
1/2 cup special oil
1 egg
1/4 cup skim milk

Sift together the flour, salt, sugar, baking powder, baking soda and cinnamon. Mix in the oatmeal and raisins. Beat in the oil, egg and milk until well mixed.

Drop by the teaspoonful onto a cookie sheet, spacing them 1-1/2 inches apart. Bake in a preheated 400° oven 10 minutes or until delicately browned. Cool on a cake rack.

Makes about 36 cookies.

Per cookie
Calories 75
Saturated fat 0.4 gram
Polyunsaturated fat 1.8 grams
Total fat 3.3 grams

MOLASSES COOKIES

3 cups sifted flour
1/4 teaspoon salt
1-1/2 teaspoons baking soda
1/2 teaspoon cinnamon
1/4 teaspoon ginger
1/4 teaspoon ground cloves

1 egg, beaten
2/3 cup molasses
1/3 cup sugar
2/3 cup special oil
2 tablespoons hot water

Sift together the flour, salt, baking soda, cinnamon, ginger and cloves. Combine the egg, molasses, sugar, oil and hot water in large bowl and mix until well blended. Gradually add the flour mixture and beat until smooth. Drop by the teaspoonful onto lightly oiled cookie sheet. Bake in a 350° oven 12 minutes or until browned.

Makes about 45 cookies.

Per cookie
Calories 85
Saturated fat 0.4 gram
Polyunsaturated fat 1.8 grams
Total fat 3.2 grams

ALMOND DROP COOKIES

1-1/2 cups sifted flour　　　　*6 tablespoons special oil*
3/4 teaspoon baking powder　*2 tablespoons cold water*
1/4 teaspoon baking soda　　*1 egg*
1/4 teaspoon cinnamon　　　*1/2 teaspoon almond extract*
3/4 cup packed dark-brown sugar 1/2 cup coarsely chopped almonds

Sift together the flour, baking powder, baking soda and cinnamon. Make a well in the center, and in it place the brown sugar, oil, water, egg and almond extract. Beat until smooth, then work in the almonds.

Drop by the teaspoonful onto a lightly oiled cookie sheet. Bake in a preheated 350° oven 12 minutes or until delicately browned. Cool on a cake rack.

Makes about 30 cookies.

Per cookie
Calories 75
Saturated fat 0.5 gram
Polyunsaturated fat 1.9 grams
Total fat 4.2 grams

SUGAR BALLS

1-1/4 cups sifted flour
1/4 teaspoon salt
3/4 teaspoon baking powder
1/8 teaspoon mace
1/3 cup special oil

3/4 cup sugar
1 egg
1/2 teaspoon vanilla extract
1/4 cup ground almonds

Sift together the flour, salt, baking powder and mace. Beat together the oil and 1/2 cup sugar. Add the egg and vanilla, beating until light and fluffy. Work in the flour mixture until a ball of dough is formed. Shape teaspoons of the mixture into balls. Mix the almonds with the remaining sugar and dip one side of the balls in the mixture. Place on a lightly oiled cookie sheet, spacing them 2 inches apart. Press down firmly with the tines of a fork.

Bake in a preheated 375° oven 10 minutes or until lightly browned. Remove from pan immediately and let cool on a cake rack.

Makes about 36 cookies.

Per cookie
Calories 60
Saturated fat 0.3 gram
Polyunsaturated fat 1.3 grams
Total fat 2.6 grams

APPLESAUCE COOKIES

2 cups sifted flour
1/4 teaspoon salt
1 tablespoon baking powder
1/4 teaspoon baking soda
1/2 teaspoon cinnamon
1/2 cup special oil
1/2 cup applesauce, fresh or
  canned

1 egg
1 cup brown sugar
1 teaspoon vanilla extract
1/2 cup chopped walnuts or
  pecans

Sift together the flour, salt, baking powder, baking soda and cinnamon. Stir in the oil with a fork until crumbs are formed. Mix in the applesauce. Beat the egg, brown sugar and vanilla

248

until light; mix in the nuts. Gradually add to the flour mixture, beating until smooth after each addition.

Drop by the teaspon onto a cookie sheet, leaving 1-1/2 inches between each. Bake in a preheated 400° oven 10 minutes or until delicately browned. Cool on a cake rack.

Makes about 42 cookies.

Per cookie
Calories 75
Saturated fat 0.4 gram
Polyunsaturated fat 2.0 grams
Total fat 3.8 grams

NUT KISSES

4 egg whites
2/3 cup very fine sugar

1 cup chopped walnuts or almonds
1/4 cup chopped candied fruits

Combine the egg whites and sugar in the top of a double boiler. Place over hot water and beat with a rotary beater until stiff. Remove from the heat and stir in the nuts and fruit.

Oil a baking pan and drop the mixture onto it by the heaping teaspoonful. Bake in a preheated 300° oven 30 minutes.

Makes about 36.

Per kiss
Calories 45
Saturated fat 0.2 gram
Polyunsaturated fat 1.1 grams
Total fat 2.0 grams

SESAME COOKIES

3-1/2 cups sifted flour
1/4 teaspoon salt
1-1/2 teaspoons baking powder
2 egg yolks
2/3 cup sugar
1/2 cup special oil

2 tablespoons orange juice
1 teaspoon vanilla extract
1/4 cup skim milk
2 egg whites, stiffly beaten
1 egg
1/3 cup sesame seeds

Sift together the flour, salt and baking powder. Beat the egg yolks; beat in the sugar until thick and light. Very gradually add the oil alternately with the orange juice and vanilla. Add half the flour mixture alternately with the milk. Fold in the egg whites, then the remaining flour mixture. Knead lightly on a floured surface.

Roll out the dough 1/4 inch thick. Cut into any shape you like. Arrange on a lightly oiled cookie sheet; brush with the egg, beaten with a little water, then sprinkle with the sesame seeds.

Bake in a preheated 350° oven 15 minutes or until delicately browned.

Makes about 60 3-inch cookies.

Per cookie
Calories 55
Saturated fat 0.3 gram
Polyunsaturated fat 1.1 grams
Total fat 2.1 grams

HERMITS

1-3/4 cups sifted flour
1/4 teaspoon salt
1-1/2 teaspoons baking powder
1/8 teaspoon baking soda
1/4 teaspoon ground cloves
1/4 teaspoon nutmeg

1/2 teaspoon cinnamon
1/2 cup seedless raisins
1/3 cup special oil
3/4 cup packed brown sugar
1 egg, beaten
3 tablespoons skim milk

Sift together the flour, salt, baking powder, baking soda, cloves, nutmeg and cinnamon. Stir in the raisins. Beat the oil and brown sugar until well blended, then mix in the egg. Add

250

the flour mixture alternately with the milk. Drop by the table-spoonful onto a lightly oiled cookie sheet.

Bake in a preheated 400° oven 10 minutes or until browned and set. Cool on a cake rack.

Makes about 30 cookies.

Per cookie
Calories 75
Saturated fat 0.3 gram
Polyunsaturated fat 1.4 grams
Total fat 2.7 grams

SPICE BARS

2-3/4 cups sifted flour
1/4 teaspoon salt
1 teaspoon nutmeg
1 teaspoon cinnamon
1 teaspoon ground allspice
1/2 teaspoon mace
1/4 cup molasses

1/4 cup honey
3/4 cup packed dark-brown sugar
1 tablespoon lemon juice
2 teaspoons grated lemon rind
1 egg
1/3 cup chopped candied fruit
1/3 cup chopped almonds

Sift together the flour, salt, nutmeg, cinnamon, allspice and mace. Combine and bring to a boil the molasses and honey. Cool. Beat in the brown sugar, lemon juice, rind and egg. Stir in the flour mixture, then the fruit and nuts. Form into a ball, wrap in foil or waxed paper, and chill overnight.

Break off 1/4 of the dough and roll out on a lightly floured surface 1/2 inch thick. Cut in strips 1-1/2 inches by 2 inches. Arrange on a greased cookie sheet, leaving 1 inch space between them. Repeat with remaining 3/4 of dough. Bake in a preheated 400° oven 10 minutes or until delicately browned and top springs back when touched with the finger. Cool on a cake rack and brush with the following:

3/4 cup sifted confectioners'
sugar

2 tablespoons skim milk
1/2 teaspoon vanilla extract

Mix ingredients until smooth and brush on tops of bars.

Makes about 48.

Per bar
Calories 65
Saturated fat 0.1 gram
Polyunsaturated fat 0.1 gram
Total fat 0.6 gram

FRUIT-NUT BARS

1-1/2 cups sifted flour
1/4 teaspoon salt
1/2 teaspoon baking soda
1/2 teaspoon cinnamon
1/2 teaspoon nutmeg
3/4 cup chopped candied fruit

2 eggs
1/2 cup special oil
3/4 cup brown sugar
1/2 cup marmalade
3/4 cup chopped walnuts

Sift together the flour, salt, baking soda, cinnamon and nutmeg. Stir in the fruits until coated.

Beat together the eggs and oil until frothy, then beat in the brown sugar and marmalade. Stir in the nuts. Add the flour mixture all at once; mix well. Turn into an oiled 9-inch square baking pan. Bake in a preheated 350° oven 40 minutes or until browned and shrunk away from the sides of the pan. Cool on a cake rack, then cut into strips 1 inch by 3 inches.

Makes 24 bars.

Per bar
Calories 150
Saturated fat 0.7 gram
Polyunsaturated fat 3.9 grams
Total fat 7.0 grams

BROWN SUGAR SLICES

1-1/2 cups sifted flour
1/4 teaspoon salt
1/2 teaspoon baking powder
1/3 cup special oil
1/2 cup packed dark-brown sugar

1/2 cup granulated sugar
1 egg
1/2 teaspoon vanilla extract
1/2 cup chopped almonds

Sift together the flour, salt and baking powder. Stir until smooth the oil, brown and granulated sugar. Beat in the egg and vanilla, then stir in the nuts. Add the flour mixture, blending until a ball of dough is formed. Shape into a long roll, 2 inches in diameter. Wrap in foil or waxed paper and chill 3-4 hours or overnight. Cut into very thin slices and arrange on a lightly oiled cookie sheet.

Bake in a preheated 400° oven 10 minutes or until delicately browned.

Makes about 36 cookies.

Per cookie
Calories 70
Saturated fat 0.4 gram
Polyunsaturated fat 1.4 grams
Total fat 3.2 grams

CREAM PUFFS

1/2 cup water
4 tablespoons special
    margarine

1/4 teaspoon salt
1/2 cup sifted flour
2 eggs

Combine the water and margarine; bring to a boil. When the margarine melts, add the salt and flour all at once, beating until the mixture leaves the sides of the pan. Remove from the heat and add 1 egg at a time, beating until smooth and shiny.

Lightly oil a baking pan; divide the mixture into 8 mounds, leaving 2 inches between them. Bake in a preheated 375° oven 40 minutes or until puffed and brown. Split, cool and fill the puffs with Vanilla Frozen Cream Dessert or Special "Whipped Cream" (see recipes).

Serves 8. Count is for cream puffs only.

Per cream puff
Calories 95
Saturated fat 1.4 grams
Polyunsaturated fat 1.8 grams
Total fat 7.1 grams

FRENCH DOUGHNUTS

1 cake or package yeast	*1 cup evaporated skim milk*
1/4 cup lukewarm water	*2 tablespoons special oil*
1/4 teaspoon salt	*2 eggs, beaten*
1/3 cup sugar	*4 cups sifted flour*
1/8 teaspoon nutmeg	*Special oil for deep frying*

Soften the yeast in the water, then mix smooth. In a large bowl, mix the salt, sugar, nutmeg, milk and oil. Stir in the yeast mixture. Beat in the eggs, then the flour, adding just enough to make a soft dough. If necessary, add a little more flour. Knead the dough until smooth and elastic. Place dough in an oiled bowl, brush top with oil, and cover with a cloth. Let rise in a warm place 45 minutes.

Punch down. Divide dough in thirds. Roll out each piece 1/2-inch thick. Cut into triangles about 3/4 inch by 1 inch, then stretch triangles as thin as possible.

Heat the oil to 375°. Fry a few pieces at a time until browned on all sides. Drain. Keep warm while preparing the balance. Sprinkle with confectioners' sugar.

Makes about 48.

> **Per doughnut**
> Calories 75
> Saturated fat 0.9 gram
> Polyunsaturated fat 3.8 grams
> Total fat 6.5 grams

DANISH PASTRY

1 cake or package yeast	*2 eggs*
1/4 cup lukewarm water	*1 teaspoon vanilla extract*
6 tablespoons sugar	*1 teaspoon lemon juice*
1/4 teaspoon salt	*1/4 teaspoon mace*
1-1/4 cups skim milk, scalded	*3-1/2 cups sifted flour (about)*
2 sticks (1/2 pound) special	*1 egg white*
margarine	*1/4 cup chopped walnuts*

Soften the yeast in the water; stir until dissolved. In a large bowl, combine 3 tablespoons sugar, the salt, hot skim milk and 4 tablespoons (1/2 stick) margarine. Mix until margarine melts. Cool, then beat in the eggs. Beat in the yeast, vanilla, lemon juice, mace and 3 cups flour. If too soft, add a little more flour. Knead lightly, then form into a ball. Place in a fresh bowl, cover with a cloth and let rise in a warm place until double in bulk (about 1-1/2 hours). Keep remaining margarine at room temperature.

Punch down the dough and roll out on a lightly floured surface into a large square 1/4-inch thick. Dot with half the margarine; fold dough over into thirds and press the edges together. Roll out again into a square and dot with the remaining margarine. Fold over, press edges together and chill 15 minutes.

Roll out and fold over. Repeat rolling and folding 3 times. Wrap the dough and chill 30 minutes.

Beat the egg white until it begins to stiffen; mix in the walnuts and remaining sugar. Roll out the dough 1/3 inch thick; cut into 2-inch squares. Spread lightly with the walnut mixture; roll up diagonally and turn ends toward each other. Arrange on a baking sheet. Cover and let rise in a warm place 30 minutes.

Bake in a preheated 375° oven 10 minutes or until browned.

Makes about 40.

Per pastry
Calories 100
Saturated fat 1.1 grams
Polyunsaturated fat 1.6 grams
Total fat 5.3 grams

FRUIT BREAD

2 cakes or packages dry yeast
1/4 cup lukewarm water
1 tablespoon nonfat dry milk
  powder
3-1/2 cups sifted flour
1 stick (1/2 cup) special
  margarine
2/3 cup sugar
4 egg whites

1 teaspoon vanilla extract
1/2 teaspoon almond extract
1/4 teaspoon salt
1/3 cup chopped candied fruit
1/3 cup seedless raisins
1/4 cup blanched chopped
  almonds
1 tablespoon special oil

Soften the yeast in the water, then stir in the dry milk. Mix in 1/2 cup flour. Cover and let stand until bubbles form on top.

Cream the margarine; beat in 1/2 cup sugar until fluffy, then the egg whites, one at a time. Beat in the yeast mixture. Work in the vanilla, almond extract, remaining flour, and salt until a soft dough is formed. If too soft to knead, add a little more flour. Divide dough in half. Knead the candied fruit into one half and the raisins and almonds into the other. Form into separate balls; cover and let rise until double in bulk. Punch down and knead each piece until smooth.

On a lightly floured surface, roll each piece into 15-inch-long oblongs. Place one piece over the other and roll up the long way.

Grease a 9-inch tube pan with the oil and sprinkle with the remaining sugar. Fit the roll into it. Cover and let rise until double in bulk.

Bake in a preheated 375° oven 1 hour or until browned and shrunk away from the sides of the pan.

Makes 36 slices.

Per slice
Calories 95
Saturated fat 0.6 gram
Polyunsaturated fat 1.1 grams
Total fat 3.5 grams

DESSERT PILAF

3 tablespoons special
   margarine
1-1/2 cups raw long-grain rice
1/4 teaspoon salt
2 tablespoons sugar

2 teaspoons cinnamon
1/4 teaspoon mace
1/2 teaspoon seedless raisins
2-1/2 cups hot skim milk

Melt the margarine in a heavy saucepan; stir in the rice until transparent. Add the salt, sugar, cinnamon, mace, raisins and hot milk. Cover and cook over low heat 25 minutes or until rice is tender and dry. Serve warm or cold.

Serves 8.

Per serving
Calories 210
Saturated fat 0.6 gram
Polyunsaturated fat 3.0 grams
Total fat 5.2 grams

APPLE BETTY

1 cup crumbled cornflakes
1/2 teaspoon cinnamon
1 teaspoon grated orange rind
2 tablespoons sugar

2 tablespoons special oil
3 cups peeled sliced apples
2 tablespoons brown sugar
2 tablespoons water

Mix together the cornflakes, cinnamon, rind and sugar. Add the oil and toss until well mixed. Spread one-third of the mixture on the bottom of a 1-quart casserole. Toss the apples with the brown sugar; spread half the apples over the cornflake mixture; make another layer of cornflakes, another of apples; add the water; and cover with remaining cornflakes.

Cover and bake in a 375° oven 20 minutes. Remove cover and bake 15 minutes longer or until apples are tender.

Serves 4.

Per serving
Calories 225
Saturated fat 0.8 gram
Polyunsaturated fat 4.0 grams
Total fat 7.0 grams

BROWN SUGAR PUDDING

1/2 cup sifted flour
1/4 teaspoon salt
1 teaspoon double-acting baking
    powder
1/3 cup sugar
1/4 cup skim milk
1 tablespoon special oil

1 teaspoon vanilla extract
1/4 cup slivered almonds
1/2 cup light-brown sugar
3/4 cup water
1 tablespoon special
    margarine

Sift the flour, salt, baking powder and sugar into a bowl. Beat in the milk, oil and vanilla. Stir in the nuts. Turn into an oiled 8-inch square (brownie) pan. The layer will be very thin.

Combine the brown sugar, water and margarine. Bring to a boil, stirring until sugar dissolves. Pour over the batter. Bake in a preheated 350° oven 35 minutes. The syrup will now be on the bottom. Cool 45 minutes before serving.

Serves 8.

Per serving
Calories 190
Saturated fat 0.7 gram
Polyunsaturated fat 1.9 grams
Total fat 5.8 grams

BUTTERMILK PUDDING

1 stick (1/2 cup) special
    margarine
2/3 cup sugar
2 egg yolks
3 egg whites
3 tablespoons cornstarch

1/4 teaspoon salt
2 cups buttermilk
2 teaspoons vanilla extract
1 teaspoon grated lemon rind
Nutmeg

Cream the margarine and sugar until light and fluffy. Beat in the egg yolks, then the whites. Mix in the cornstarch and salt thoroughly. Stir in the buttermilk, vanilla and lemon rind. Turn into a 1-quart baking dish. Sprinkle with nutmeg. Place in a shallow pan of hot water. Bake in a preheated 325°

oven 1 hour or until a knife inserted in the center comes out clean. Serve hot or very cold.

Serves 8.

Per serving
Calories 150
Saturated fat   2.8 grams
Polyunsaturated fat   3.4 grams
Total fat 12.9 grams

SPECIAL CREAM

2 tablespoons nonfat dry milk powder

2-1/2 tablespoons special oil
3/4 cup hot water

Use an electric blender or, if you haven't one, a mixer. Beat the dry milk and oil until well blended. Add 2 tablespoons hot water and beat until foamy. Very gradually add the remaining hot water; beat 2 minutes. Pour into a container and place in ice water until cold. Refrigerate until needed.

Makes 1 cup; allow 2 tablespoons per serving.

Per serving
Calories 50
Saturated fat 0.5 gram
Polyunsaturated fat 2.5 grams
Total fat 4.4 grams

SPECIAL "WHIPPED CREAM"

1/2 cup nonfat dry milk powder
1/2 cup ice water

1 tablespoon lemon juice
1/4 cup sugar

Beat the dry milk and ice water until peaks form. Beat in the lemon juice until stiff. Fold in the sugar. Serve quickly, as the whipped cream does not hold.

Makes about 1 cup; allow 2 tablespoons per serving.

Per serving
Calories 80
Saturated fat 0.0 gram
Polyunsaturated fat 0.0 gram
Total fat 0.0 gram

WHITE FROSTING

1 egg white
3/4 cup sugar
Dash salt

3 tablespoons water
1 teaspoon light corn syrup
3/4 teaspoon vanilla extract

Combine the egg white, sugar, salt, water and corn syrup in the top of a double boiler. Beat with an electric mixer or rotary beater until thoroughly blended and frothy. Place over boiling water and cook, beating steadily, until mixture forms stiff peaks. Remove from heat and beat in the vanilla until stiff enough to spread.

Makes enough to frost a 9-inch layer cake.

Per serving
Calories 85
Saturated fat 0.0 gram
Polyunsaturated fat 0.0 gram
Total fat 0.0 gram

BROWN SUGAR FROSTING

1/4 cup water
1 cup packed dark-brown sugar

2 egg whites

Cook the water and brown sugar until a soft ball is formed when a drop is placed in cold water (or thermometer reaches 236°). Beat the egg whites until stiff and gradually add the sugar mixture, beating until peaks form.

Enough for a 9-inch layer cake.

Per serving
Calories 100
Saturated fat 0.0 gram
Polyunsaturated fat 0.0 gram
Total fat 0.0 gram

GLAZED ALMONDS

2 cups sugar
1/3 cup water
2 tablespoons cognac

1 teaspoon cinnamon
1 pound shelled almonds

Bring the sugar, water, cognac and cinnamon to a boil over low heat, then raise heat. Boil the syrup until a thread forms when a fork is lifted from the syrup. Remove from the heat; stir in the almonds immediately, stirring until well coated. Turn out onto a board until cold.

Per almond
Calories 20
Saturated fat 0.1 gram
Polyunsaturated fat 0.1 gram
Total fat 0.6 gram

ROASTED NUTS

2 cups assorted nuts   *2 tablespoons special oil*

Spread the nuts in a shallow pan. Sprinkle with the oil and toss lightly. Bake in a preheated 350° oven 10 minutes or until lightly browned. Turn out on paper towels and cool.

Per nut
Calories 15
Saturated fat 0.0 gram
Polyunsaturated fat 0.5 gram
Total fat 1.8 grams

FAT CONTENT OF FOOD CHARTS

NUTRITIVE VALUES OF THE EDIBLE PART OF FOODS

Food, approximate measure, and weight (in grams)		Water	Food energy	Protein	Fat (total lipid)	Fatty Acids			Carbohydrate
						Saturated (total)	Unsaturated		
							Oleic	Linoleic	
	Grams	Percent	Calories	Grams	Grams	Grams	Grams	Grams	Grams
MILK, CREAM, CHEESE; RELATED PRODUCTS									
MILK, cow's:									
Fluid, whole .... 1 cup	244..	87	165	9	10	6	3	Trace	12
Fluid, nonfat (skim) .... 1 cup	246..	90	90	9	Trace	....	....	....	13
Buttermilk, cultured, from skim milk .... 1 cup	246..	90	90	9	Trace	....	....	....	13
Evaporated, unsweetened, undiluted .... 1 cup	252..	74	345	18	20	11	7	1	24
Condensed, sweetened, un- diluted .... 1 cup	306..	28	985	25	25	14	8	1	170
Dry, whole .... 1 cup	103..	2	515	27	28	15	9	1	39
Dry, nonfat .... 1 cup	80..	3	290	28	1	....	....	....	42
Milk, goat's: Fluid, whole ---- 1 cup	244..	88	165	8	10	6	2	Trace	11
Cream:									
Half-and-half (milk and cream)................... 1 cup	242..	80	330	8	29	16	10	1	11
1 tablespoon..	15..	80	20	Trace	2	1	1	Trace	1
Light, table or coffee ..... 1 cup	240..	71	525	7	52	29	17	2	10
1 tablespoon..	15..	71	35	Trace	3	2	1	Trace	1
Whipping, unwhipped (volume about double when whipped):									
Medium .... 1 cup	239..	61	745	6	78	43	26	2	8
1 tablespoon..	15..	61	45	Trace	5	3	2	Trace	1
Heavy................ 1 cup	238..	56	860	5	93	51	31	3	7
1 tablespoon..	15..	56	55	Trace	6	3	2	Trace	Trace

MILK, CREAM, CHEESE—Continued

Food, approximate measure, and weight (in grams)		Water	Food energy	Protein	Fat (total lipid)	Fatty Acids			Carbohydrate
						Saturated (total)	Unsaturated Oleic	Unsaturated Linoleic	
	Grams	Percent	Calories	Grams	Grams	Grams	Grams	Grams	Grams
Cheese:									
Blue mold (Roquefort type) 1 ounce	28	40	105	6	9	5	3	Trace	Trace
Cheddar or American:									
Ungrated 1-inch cube	17	36	70	4	6	3	2	Trace	Trace
Grated 1 cup	112	36	455	28	37	20	12	1	2
1 tablespoon	7	36	30	2	2	1	1	Trace	Trace
Cheddar, process 1 ounce	28	39	105	7	9	5	3	Trace	Trace
Cheese foods, Cheddar 1 ounce	28	43	95	6	7	4	2	Trace	2
Cottage cheese, from skim milk:									
Creamed 1 cup	225	78	240	30	11	6	4	Trace	6
1 ounce	28	78	30	4	1	1	Trace	Trace	1
Uncreamed 1 cup	225	79	195	38	1	Trace	Trace	....	6
1 ounce	28	79	25	5	Trace	....	....	....	1
Cream cheese 1 ounce	28	51	105	2	11	6	4	Trace	1
1 tablespoon	15	51	55	1	6	3	2	Trace	Trace
Swiss 1 ounce	28	39	105	7	8	4	3	Trace	1
Milk beverages:									
Cocoa 1 cup	242	79	235	9	11	6	4	Trace	26
Chocolate-flavored milk drink 1 cup	250	83	190	8	6	3	2	Trace	27
Malted milk 1 cup	270	78	280	13	12	7	4	Trace	32
Milk desserts:									
Cornstarch pudding, plain (blanc mange) 1 cup	248	76	275	9	10	6	3	Trace	39
Custard, baked 1 cup	248	77	285	13	14	6	5	1	28

Food, approximate measure, and weight (in grams)		Water	Food energy	Protein	Fat (total lipid)	Saturated (total)	Unsaturated		Carbohydrate
	Grams	Percent	Calories	Grams	Grams	Grams	Oleic Grams	Linoleic Grams	Grams
MILK, CREAM, CHEESE—Continued									
Milk desserts—Continued									
Ice cream, plain, factory packed:									
Slice or cut brick, 1/8 of quart brick... 1 slice or cut brick	71	62	145	3	9	5	3	Trace	15
Container... 3 1/2 fluid ounces	62	62	130	2	8	4	3	Trace	13
Container... 8 fluid oz.	142	62	295	6	18	10	6	1	29
Ice milk... 1 cup	187	67	285	9	10	6	3	Trace	42
Yoghurt, from partially skimmed milk... 1 cup	246	89	120	8	4	2	1	Trace	13
EGGS									
Eggs, large, 24 oz. per dozen:									
Raw:									
Whole, without shell... 1 egg	50	74	80	6	6	2	3	Trace	Trace
White of egg... 1 white	33	88	15	4	Trace	......	......	......	Trace
Yolk of egg... 1 yolk	17	51	60	3	5	2	2	Trace	Trace
Cooked:									
Boiled, shell removed... 2 eggs	100	74	160	13	12	4	5	1	1
Scrambled, with milk and fat... 1 egg	64	72	110	7	8	3	4	1	1
MEAT, POULTRY, FISH, SHELLFISH; RELATED PRODUCTS									
Bacon, broiled or fried crisp. 2 slices	16	8	95	5	8	3	4	1	1

MEAT, POULTRY, FISH—Continued Food, approximate measure, and weight (in grams)	Grams	Water Percent	Food energy Calories	Protein Grams	Fat (total lipid) Grams	Saturated (total) Grams	Unsaturated Oleic Grams	Unsaturated Linoleic Grams	Carbohydrate Grams
Beef, trimmed to retail basis,* cooked:									
Cuts braised, simmered, or pot-roasted:									
Lean and fat .... 3 ounces	85..	53	245	23	16	8	7	Trace	0
Lean only .... 2.5 ounces	72..	62	140	22	5	2	2	Trace	0
Hamburger, broiled:									
Market ground........... 3 ounces	85..	54	245	21	17	8	7	Trace	0
Ground lean .... 3 ounces	85..	60	185	23	10	5	4	Trace	0
Roast, oven-cooked, no liquid added:									
Relatively fat, such as rib:									
Lean and fat .... 3 ounces	85..	38	390	16	36	17	16	1	0
Lean only .... 1.8 ounces	51..	57	120	14	7	3	3	Trace	0
Relatively lean, such as round:									
Lean and fat .... 3 ounces	85..	56	220	23	14	7	6	Trace	0
Lean only .... 2.5 ounces	71..	63	130	21	4	2	2	Trace	0
Steak, broiled:									
Relatively fat, such as sirloin:									
Lean and fat .... 3 ounces	85..	44	330	20	27	13	12	1	0
Lean only .... 2 ounces	56..	59	115	18	4	2	2	Trace	0

*Outer layer of fat on the cut was removed to within approximately 1/2 inch of the lean. Deposits of fat within the cut were not removed.

MEAT, POULTRY, FISH—Continued

Food, approximate measure, and weight (in grams)	Grams	Water Per-cent	Food energy Calo-ries	Pro-tein Grams	Fat (total lipid) Grams	Satu-rated (total) Grams	Unsaturated Oleic Grams	Unsaturated Lino-leic Grams	Carbo-hy-drate Grams
Steak, broiled—Continued									
Relatively lean, such as round:									
Lean and fat .... 3 ounces	85..	55	220	24	13	6	6	Trace	0
Lean only .... 2.4 ounces	69..	61	130	22	4	2	2	Trace	0
Beef, canned:									
Corned beef ...... 3 ounces	85..	59	180	22	10	5	4	Trace	0
Corned beef hash...... 3 ounces	85..	70	120	12	5	2	2	Trace	6
Beef, dried or chipped .... 2 ounces	57..	48	115	19	4	2	2	Trace	0
Beef and vegetable stew ...... 1 cup	235..	82	185	15	10	5	4	Trace	15
Beef potpie, baked:									
Individual pie, 4 1/4-inch diameter, weight before baking about 8 ounces ...... 1 pie	227..	63	460	18	28	10	15	1	32
Chicken, cooked:									
Flesh and skin, broiled .... 3 ounces (without bone).........	85..	61	185	23	9	3	4	2	0
Breast, fried, 1/2 breast:									
With bone .... 3.3 ounces	94..	52	215	24	12	3	6	2	....
Flesh & skin only .... 2.8 ounces	79..	52	215	24	12	3	6	2	....
Leg, fried (high and drumstick):									
With bone .... 4.3 ounces	121..	52	245	27	15	4	7	2	....
Flesh & skin only .... 3.1 ounces	89..	52	245	27	15	4	7	2	....
Chicken, canned, boneless .... 3 ounces	85..	62	170	25	7	2	3	1	0

Food, approximate measure, and weight (in grams)		Water	Food energy	Protein	Fat (total lipid)	Saturated (total)	Fatty Acids Unsaturated Oleic	Fatty Acids Unsaturated Linoleic	Carbohydrate
	Grams	Percent	Calories	Grams	Grams	Grams	Grams	Grams	Grams
MEAT, POULTRY, FISH—Continued									
Chicken, cooked—Continued									
Chicken potpie. *See* Poultry potpie.									
Chile con carne, canned:									
With beans........... 1 cup	250..	72	335	19	15	7	7	Trace	30
Without beans .... 1 cup	255..	67	510	26	38	17	18	1	15
Heart, beef, trimmed of fat, braised....... 3 ounces	85..	61	160	26	5	2	2	Trace	1
Lamb, trimmed to retail basis,* cooked:									
Chop, thick, with bone, 1 chop —									
broiled............ 4.8 ounces	137..	47	405	25	33	18	12	1	0
Lean and fat ...... 4 ounces	112..	47	405	25	33	18	12	1	0
Lean only .... 2.6 ounces	74..	62	140	21	6	3	2	Trace	0
Leg, roasted:									
Lean and fat ...... 3 ounces	85..	54	235	22	16	9	6	Trace	0
Lean only .... 2.5 ounces	71..	62	130	20	5	3	2	Trace	0
Shoulder, roasted:									
Lean and fat ...... 3 ounces	85..	50	285	18	23	13	8	1	0
Lean only .... 2.3 ounces	64..	61	130	17	6	3	2	Trace	0
Liver, beef, fried........ 2 ounces	57..	57	120	13	4	2	2	Trace	6

*Outer layer of fat on the cut was removed to within approximately 1/2 inch of the lean. Deposits of fat within the cut were not removed.

Food, approximate measure, and weight (in grams)		Water	Food energy	Protein	Fat (total lipid)	Fatty Acids			Carbohydrate
						Saturated (total)	Unsaturated		
							Oleic	Linoleic	
	Grams	Percent	Calories	Grams	Grams	Grams	Grams	Grams	Grams
MEAT, POULTRY, FISH—Continued									
Pork, cured, cooked:									
Ham, smoked, lean and fat ...... 3 ounces	85..	48	290	18	24	9	10	2	1
Luncheon meat:									
Cooked ham, sliced...... 2 ounces	57..	48	170	13	13	5	5	1	0
Canned, spiced or unspiced ...... 2 ounces	57..	55	165	8	14	5	6	1	1
Pork, fresh, trimmed to retail basis,* cooked:									
Chop, thick, with bone...... 1 chop — 3.5 ounces	98..	42	260	16	21	8	9	2	0
Lean and fat .... 2.3 ounces	66..	42	260	16	21	8	9	2	0
Lean only .... 1.7 ounces	48..	53	130	15	7	3	3	1	0
Roast, oven-cooked, no liquid added:									
Lean and fat .... 3 ounces	85..	46	310	21	24	9	10	2	0
Lean only .... 2.4 ounces	68..	55	175	20	10	4	4	1	0
Cuts simmered:									
Lean and fat .... 3 ounces	85..	46	320	20	26	9	11	2	0
Lean only .... 2.2 ounces	63..	60	135	18	6	2	3	1	0
Poultry potpie (chicken or turkey): Individual pie, 4 1/4-inch-diameter, about 8 ounces............ 1 pie	227..	60	485	17	28	8	15	3	39

*Outer layer of fat on the cut was removed to within approximately 1/2 inch of the lean. Deposits of fat within the cut were not removed.

MEAT, POULTRY, FISH—Continued

Food, approximate measure, and weight (in grams)		Grams	Water Per- cent	Food en- ergy Calo- ries	Pro- tein Grams	Fat (total lipid) Grams	Satu- rated (total) Grams	Unsaturated Oleic Grams	Lino- leic Grams	Carbo- hy- drate Grams
Sausage:										
Bologna, slice 4.1 by 0.1 inch	8 slices	227	56	690	27	62	26	27	3	2
Frankfurter, cooked	1 frankfurter	51	58	155	6	14	6	6	1	1
Pork, bulk, canned	4 ounces	113	55	340	18	29	10	12	3	0
Tongue, beef, simmered	3 ounces	85	61	205	18	14	7	6	Trace	Trace
Turkey potpie. See Poultry potpie.										
Veal, cooked:										
Cutlet, broiled	3 ounces without bone	85	60	185	23	9	4	4	Trace	0
Roast, medium fat, medium done: Lean and fat	3 ounces	85	55	305	23	14	7	6	Trace	0
Fish and shellfish:										
Bluefish, baked or broiled	3 ounces	85	68	135	22	4	....	....	....	0
Clams:										
Raw, meat only	3 ounces	85	80	70	11	1	....	....	....	3
Canned, solids and liquid	3 ounces	85	87	45	7	1	....	....	....	2
Crabmeat, canned or cooked	3 ounces	85	77	90	14	2	....	....	....	1
Fishsticks, breaded, cooked, frozen; stick, 3.8 by 1.0 by 0.5 inch	10 sticks or 8-ounce package	227	66	400	38	20	5	4	10	15

Food, approximate measure, and weight (in grams)		Water	Food energy	Protein	Fat (total lipid)	Fatty Acids			Carbohydrate
						Saturated (total)	Unsaturated Oleic	Unsaturated Linoleic	
		Percent	Calories	Grams	Grams	Grams	Grams	Grams	Grams
MEAT, POULTRY, FISH—Continued									
Fish and shellfish—Continued									
Haddock, fried.............	3 ounces ...... 85..	67	135	16	5	1	3	Trace	6
Mackerel:									
Broiled, Atlantic	3 ounces ...... 85..	62	200	19	13	....	....	....	0
Canned, Pacific, solids and liquid	3 ounces ...... 85..	66	155	18	9	....	....	....	0
Ocean perch, breaded (egg and breadcrumbs), fried	3 ounces ...... 85..	59	195	16	11	....	....	....	6
Oysters, meat only: Raw, 13-19 medium selects..	1 cup .... 240..	85	160	20	4	....	....	....	8
Oyster stew, 1 part oysters to 3 parts milk by volume, 3-4 oysters.....	1 cup .... 230..	84	200	11	12	....	....	....	11
Salmon, pink, canned........	3 ounces ...... 85..	70	120	17	5	1	1	....	0
Sardines, Atlantic type, canned in oil, drained solids.................	3 ounces ...... 85..	57	180	22	9	2	2	4	1
Shad, baked	3 ounces ...... 85..	64	170	20	10	....	....	....	0
Shrimp, canned, meat only	3 ounces ...... 85..	66	110	23	1	....	....	....	1
Swordfish, broiled with butter or margarine	3 ounces ...... 85..	65	150	24	5	....	....	....	0
Tuna, canned in oil, drained solids	3 ounces ...... 85..	60	170	25	7	2	1	4	0

Food, approximate measure, and weight (in grams)		Water	Food energy	Protein	Fat (total lipid)	Fatty Acids			Carbohydrate
						Saturated (total)	Unsaturated		
							Oleic	Linoleic	
	Grams	Per-cent	Calories	Grams	Grams	Grams	Grams	Grams	Grams
MATURE DRY BEANS AND PEAS, NUTS, PEANUTS; RELATED PRODUCTS									
Almonds, shelled .... 1 cup	142..	5	850	26	77	6	52	15	28
Beans, dry:									
Common varieties, such as Great Northern, navy, and others, canned:									
Red .... 1 cup	256..	76	230	15	1	....	....	....	42
White, with tomato or molasses:									
With pork .... 1 cup	261..	69	330	16	7	3	3	1	54
Without pork .... 1 cup	261..	69	315	16	1	....	....	....	60
Lima, cooked .... 1 cup	192..	64	260	16	1	....	....	....	48
Brazil nuts, broken pieces.... 1 cup	140..	5	905	20	92	18	44	24	15
Cashew nuts, roasted .... 1 cup	135..	5	770	25	65	11	46	5	35
Coconut:									
Fresh, shredded.......... 1 cup	97..	50	330	3	31	27	2	....	13
Dried, shredded, sweetened.......... 1 cup	62..	3	345	2	24	21	2	....	33
Cowpeas or blackeye peas, dry, cooked.......... 1 cup	248..	80	190	13	1	....	....	....	34
Peanuts, roasted, shelled:									
Halves.......... 1 cup	144..	2	840	39	71	16	31	21	28
Chopped.......... 1 tablespoon..	9..	2	50	2	4	1	2	1	2
Peanut butter.......... 1 tablespoon..	16..	2	90	4	8	2	4	2	3
Peas, split, dry, cooked.......... 1 cup	250..	70	290	20	1	....	....	....	52

Food, approximate measure, and weight (in grams)		Water	Food energy	Protein	Fat (total lipid)	Fatty Acids			Carbohydrate
						Saturated (total)	Unsaturated		
							Oleic	Linoleic	
	Grams	Per-cent	Calories	Grams	Grams	Grams	Grams	Grams	Grams
BEANS, PEAS & NUTS—Continued									
Pecans:									
Halves .... 1 cup	108...	3	740	10	77	5	49	15	16
Chopped .... 1 tablespoon..	7.5..	3	50	1	5	Trace	3	1	1
Walnuts, shelled:									
Black or native, chopped .. 1 cup	126..	3	790	26	75	4	26	36	19
English or Persian:									
Halves .... 1 cup	100...	4	650	15	64	4	10	40	16
Chopped .... 1 tablespoon..	8...	4	50	1	5	Trace	1	3	1
VEGETABLES AND VEGETABLE PRODUCTS									
Asparagus:									
Cooked, cut spears........... 1 cup	175..	92	35	4	Trace	....	....	....	6
Canned spears, medium:									
Green.................... 6 spears	96..	92	20	2	Trace	....	....	....	3
Bleached................. 6 spears	96..	92	20	2	Trace	....	....	....	4
Beans:									
Lima, immature, cooked .. 1 cup	160..	75	150	8	1	....	....	....	29
Snap, green:									
Cooked:									
In small amount of water, short time .. 1 cup	125..	92	25	2	Trace	....	....	....	6
In large amount of water, long time.. 1 cup	125..	92	25	2	Trace	....	....	....	6
Canned:									
Solids and liquid...... 1 cup	239..	94	45	2	Trace	....	....	....	10
Strained or chopped. 1 ounce	28...	93	5	Trace	Trace	....	....	....	1
Bean sprouts, *See Sprouts,*									

VEGETABLES—Continued

Food, approximate measure, and weight (in grams)		Water	Food energy	Protein	Fat (total lipid)	Saturated (total)	Unsaturated Oleic	Unsaturated Linoleic	Carbohydrate
	Grams	Percent	Calories	Grams	Grams	Grams	Grams	Grams	Grams
Beets, cooked, diced............ 1 cup	165..	88	70	2	Trace	....	....	....	16
Broccoli spears, cooked....... 1 cup	150..	90	45	5	Trace	....	....	....	8
Brussels sprouts, cooked..... 1 cup	130..	85	60	6	1	....	....	....	12
Cabbage: Raw:									
Finely shredded........... 1 cup	100..	92	25	1	Trace	....	....	....	5
Cole slaw .... 1 cup	120..	84	100	2	7	1	1	4	9
Cooked: In small amount of water, short time .... 1 cup	170..	92	40	2	Trace	....	....	....	9
In large amount of water, long time...... 1 cup	170..	92	40	2	Trace	....	....	....	9
Cabbage, celery or Chinese: Raw, leaves and stem, 1-inch pieces.............. 1 cup	100..	95	15	1	Trace	....	....	....	2
Cooked.................... 1 cup	190..	95	25	2	1	....	....	....	5
Carrots: Raw: Whole, 5 1/2 by 1 inch (25 thin strips)........ 1 carrot	50..	88	20	1	Trace	....	....	....	5
Grated................... 1 cup	110..	88	45	1	Trace	....	....	....	10
Cooked, diced .... 1 cup	145..	92	45	1	1	....	....	....	9
Canned, strained or chopped .... 1 ounce.........	28..	92	5	Trace	0	....	....	....	2
Cauliflower, cooked, flower— buds........... 1 cup	120..	92	30	3	Trace	....	....	....	6

Food, approximate measure, and weight (in grams)		Grams	Water Per-cent	Food energy Calo-ries	Pro-tein Grams	Fat (total lipid) Grams	Satu-rated (total) Grams	Oleic Grams	Lino-leic Grams	Carbo-hy-drate Grams
VEGETABLES—Continued										
Celery, raw:										
Stalk, large outer, 8 by about 1 1/2 inches at root end	1 stalk	40	94	5	1	Trace				1
Pieces, diced	1 cup	100	94	20	1	Trace				4
Collards, cooked	1 cup	190	87	75	7	1				14
Corn, sweet:										
Cooked, ear 5 by 1 3/4 inches	1 ear	140	76	65	2	1				16
Canned, solids and liquid	1 cup	256	80	170	5	1				41
Cowpeas, cooked, immature seeds	1 cup	160	75	150	11	1				25
Cucumbers 10-ounce; 7 1/2 by about 2 inches:										
Raw, pared	1 cucumber	207	96	25	1	Trace				6
Raw, pared, center slice 1/8-inch thick	6 slices	50	96	5	Trace	Trace				1
Dandelion greens, cooked	1 cup	180	86	80	5	1				16
Endive, curly (including escarole)	2 ounces	57	93	10	1	Trace				2
Kale, cooked	1 cup	110	87	45	4	1				8
Lettuce, headed, raw:										
Head, looseleaf, 4-inch diameter	1 head	220	95	30	3	Trace				6
Head, compact, 4 3/4-inch-diameter, 1 pound	1 head	454	95	70	5	1				13
Leaves	2 large or 4 small	50	95	5	1	Trace				1

Food, approximate measure, and weight (in grams)		Water	Food energy	Protein	Fat (total lipid)	Fatty Acids			Carbohydrate
						Saturated (total)	Unsaturated		
							Oleic	Linoleic	
	Grams	Percent	Calories	Grams	Grams	Grams	Grams	Grams	Grams
VEGETABLES—Continued									
Mushrooms, canned, solids and liquid	1 cup 244..	93	30	3	Trace	....	....	....	9
Mustard greens, cooked	1 cup 140..	92	30	3	Trace	....	....	....	6
Okra, cooked, pod 3 by 5/8 inch	1 pod 85..	90	30	2	Trace	....	....	....	6
Onions:									
Mature:									
Raw, onion 2 1/2-inch diameter	1 onion 110..	88	50	2	Trace	....	....	....	11
Cooked	1 cup 210..	90	80	2	Trace	....	....	....	18
Young green, small, without tops	6 onions 50..	88	25	Trace	Trace	....	....	....	5
Parsley, raw, chopped	1 tablespoon 3.5..	84	1	Trace	Trace	....	....	....	Trace
Parsnips, cooked	1 cup 155..	84	95	2	1	....	....	....	22
Peas, green:									
Cooked	1 cup 160..	82	110	8	1	....	....	....	19
Canned, solids and liquid	1 cup 249..	82	170	8	1	....	....	....	32
Canned, strained	1 ounce 28..	86	10	1	Trace	....	....	....	2
Peppers, hot, red, without seeds, dried; ground chili powder	1 tablespoon 15..	13	50	2	1	....	....	....	9
Peppers, sweet:									
Raw, medium, about 6 per pound:									
Green pod without stem and seeds	1 pod 62..	93	15	1	Trace	....	....	....	3

Food, approximate measure, and weight (in grams)		Water	Food energy	Protein	Fat (total lipid)	Fatty Acids			Carbohydrate
						Saturated (total)	Unsaturated		
							Oleic	Linoleic	
	Grams	Per-cent	Calo-ries	Grams	Grams	Grams	Grams	Grams	Grams
VEGETABLES—Continued									
Sweet Peppers—Continued									
Red pod without stem and seeds .... 1 pod	60..	91	20	1	Trace	....	....	....	4
Canned, pimientos, medium .... 1 pod	38..	92	10	Trace	Trace	....	....	....	2
Potatoes, medium, about 3 per pound:									
Baked, peeled after baking.......... 1 potato.........	99..	75	90	3	Trace	....	....	....	21
Boiled:									
Peeled after boiling..... 1 potato.........	136..	80	105	3	Trace	....	....	....	23
Peeled before boiling... 1 potato.........	122..	80	90	3	Trace	....	....	....	21
French-fried, piece 2 by 1/2 by 1/2 inch:									
Cooked in deep fat, ready to eat......... 10 pieces	57..	45	155	2	7	2	1	4	20
Frozen, ready to heat for serving .... 10 pieces	57..	64	95	2	4	1	1	2	15
Mashed:									
Milk added .... 1 cup	195..	80	145	4	1	....	....	Trace	30
Milk and butter added... 1 cup	195..	76	230	4	12	7	4	Trace	28
Potato chips, medium, 2-inch diameter............. 10 chips	20..	3	110	1	7	2	2	4	10
Pumpkin, canned......... 1 cup	228..	90	75	2	1	....	....	....	18
Radishes, raw, small, without tops .... 4 radishes	40..	94	10	Trace	Trace	....	....	....	2

279

Food, approximate measure, and weight (in grams)		Water	Food energy	Protein	Fat (total lipid)	Fatty Acids			Carbohydrate
						Saturated (total)	Unsaturated Oleic	Unsaturated Linoleic	
	Grams	Percent	Calories	Grams	Grams	Grams	Grams	Grams	Grams
VEGETABLES—Continued									
Sauerkraut, canned, drained solids .... 1 cup	150..	91	30	2	Trace	....	....	....	7
Spinach:									
Cooked .... 1 cup	180..	91	45	6	1	....	....	....	6
Canned, drained solids..... 1 cup	180..	91	45	6	1	....	....	....	6
Canned, strained and creamed .... 1 ounce.........	28..	90	10	1	Trace	....	....	....	2
Sprouts, raw:									
Mung bean.......... 1 cup	90..	92	20	3	Trace	....	....	....	4
Soybean............. 1 cup	107..	86	50	7	1	....	....	....	6
Squash:									
Cooked:									
Summer, diced............ 1 cup	210..	95	35	1	Trace	....	....	....	8
Winter, baked, mashed. 1 cup	205..	86	95	4	1	....	....	....	23
Canned, winter, strained or chopped .... 1 ounce	28..	92	10	Trace	Trace	....	....	....	2
Sweet potatoes:									
Cooked, medium, 5 by 2 inches, weight raw about 6 ounces:									
Baked, peeled after baking .... 1 sweet potato	110..	64	155	2	1	....	....	....	36
Boiled, peeled after boiling .... 1 sweet potato	147..	71	170	2	1	....	....	....	39
Candied, 3 1/2 by 2 1/4 inches......... 1 sweet potato	175..	60	295	2	6	2	3	1	60

Food, approximate measure, and weight (in grams)		Water	Food energy	Protein	Fat (total lipid)	Fatty Acids			Carbohydrate
						Saturated (total)	Unsaturated		
							Oleic	Linoleic	
	Grams	Percent	Calories	Grams	Grams	Grams	Grams	Grams	Grams
VEGETABLES—Continued									
Sweet potatoes—Continued									
Canned, vacuum or solid pack .... 1 cup	218..	72	235	4	Trace	....	....	....	54
Tomatoes:									
Raw, medium, 2 by 2 1/2 inches, about 3 per pound .... 1 tomato	150..	94	30	2	Trace	....	....	....	6
Canned or cooked .... 1 cup	242..	94	45	2	Trace	....	....	....	9
Tomato juice, canned .... 1 cup	242..	94	50	2	Trace	....	....	....	10
Tomato catsup .... 1 tablespoon..	17..	70	15	Trace	Trace	....	....	....	4
Turnips, cooked, diced .... 1 cup	155..	92	40	1	Trace	....	....	....	9
Turnip greens:									
Cooked:									
In small amount of water, short time ..... 1 cup	145..	90	45	4	1	....	....	....	8
In large amount of water, long time ..... 1 cup	145..	90	45	4	1	....	....	....	8
Canned, solids and liquid... 1 cup	232..	94	40	3	1	....	....	....	7
FRUITS AND FRUIT PRODUCTS									
Apples, raw, medium, 2 1/2-inch-diameter, about 3 per pound .... 1 apple	150..	85	70	Trace	Trace	....	....	....	18
Apple brown betty .... 1 cup	230..	64	350	4	8	4	3	Trace	69
Applejuice, fresh or canned .. 1 cup	249..	86	125	Trace	0	....	....	....	34

Food, approximate measure, and weight (in grams)		Water	Food energy	Protein	Fat (total lipid)	Fatty Acids			Carbohydrate
						Saturated (total)	Unsaturated		
							Oleic	Linoleic	
	Grams	Per-cent	Calo-ries	Grams	Grams	Grams	Grams	Grams	Grams

FRUITS AND FRUIT PRODUCTS—Continued

Food, approximate measure, and weight (in grams)		Water	Food energy	Protein	Fat (total lipid)	Saturated (total)	Oleic	Linoleic	Carbohydrate
Apples—Continued									
Applesauce, canned:									
Sweetened.................... 1 cup	254..	80	185	Trace	Trace	....	....	....	50
Unsweetened............... 1 cup	239..	88	100	Trace	Trace	....	....	....	26
Apricots:									
Raw, about 12 per pound... 3 apricots	114..	85	55	1	Trace	....	....	....	14
Canned in heavy sirup:									
Halves and sirup .... 1 cup	259..	77	220	2	Trace	....	....	....	57
Halves, medium, and sirup .... 4 halves; 2 tablespoons sirup	122..	77	105	1	Trace	....	....	....	27
Dried:									
Uncooked, 40 halves, small................. 1 cup	150..	25	390	8	1	....	....	....	100
Cooked, unsweetened, fruit and liquid .... 1 cup	285..	76	240	5	1	....	....	....	62
Apricots and applesauce, canned (strained or chopped)........... 1 ounce..........	28..	80	20	Trace	Trace	....	....	....	5
Apricot nectar .... 1 cup	250..	85	140	1	Trace	....	....	....	36
Avocados, raw: California varieties, mainly Fuerte:									
10-ounce avocado, about 3 1/3 by 4 1/4 inches, peeled, pitted ....1/2 avocado	108..	74	185	2	18	4	8	2	6
.... 1 cup	152..	74	260	3	26	5	12	3	9

FRUITS AND FRUIT PRODUCTS—Continued

Food, approximate measure, and weight (in grams)		Water	Food energy	Protein	Fat (total lipid)	Fatty Acids			Carbohydrate
						Saturated (total)	Unsaturated		
							Oleic	Linoleic	
	Grams	Percent	Calories	Grams	Grams	Grams	Grams	Grams	Grams
Avocados—Continued									
Florida varieties:									
13-ounce avocado, about 4 by 3 inches, peeled, pitted............1/2 avocado	123..	78	160	2	14	3	6	2	11
1/2-inch cubes............ 1 cup	152..	78	195	2	17	3	8	2	13
Bananas, raw, 6 by 1 1/2 inches, about 3 per pound.... 1 banana	150..	76	85	1	Trace	....	....	....	23
Blackberries, raw .... 1 cup	144..	85	85	2	1	....	....	....	19
Blueberries, raw .... 1 cup	140..	83	85	1	1	....	....	....	21
Cantaloups, raw, medium, 5-inch-diameter, about 1 2/3 pounds ....1/2 melon	385..	94	40	1	Trace	....	....	....	9
Cherries:									
Raw, sour, sweet, hybrid... 1 cup	114..	83	65	1	1	....	....	....	15
Canned, red, sour, pitted.... 1 cup	247..	88	105	2	1	....	....	....	26
Cranberry juice cocktail, canned .... 1 cup	250..	85	140	Trace	Trace	....	....	....	36
Cranberry sauce, sweetened, canned or cooked .... 1 cup	277..	48	550	Trace	1	....	....	....	142
Dates, "fresh" and dried, pitted, cut.................. 1 cup	178..	20	505	4	1	....	....	....	134
Figs:									
Raw, small, 1 1/2-inch-diameter, about 12 per pound .... 3 figs	114..	78	90	2	Trace	....	....	....	22
Dried, large, 2 by 1 inch..... 1 fig	21..	23	60	1	Trace	....	....	....	15

FRUITS AND FRUIT PRODUCTS—Continued

Food, approximate measure, and weight (in grams)	Grams	Water Percent	Food energy Calories	Protein Grams	Fat (total lipid) Grams	Saturated (total) Grams	Unsaturated Oleic Grams	Linoleic Grams	Carbohydrate Grams
Fruit cocktail, canned in heavy sirup, solids and liquid ... 1 cup	256..	80	195	1	1	....	....	....	50
Grapefruit:									
Raw, medium, 4 1/4-inch diameter, size 64:									
White ... 1/2 grapefruit	285..	89	50	1	Trace	....	....	....	14
Pink or red ... 1/2 grapefruit	285..	89	55	1	Trace	....	....	....	14
Raw sections, white ... 1 cup	194..	89	75	1	Trace	....	....	....	20
Canned:									
Sirup pack, solids and liquid ... 1 cup	249..	81	170	1	Trace	....	....	....	44
Water pack, solids and liquid ... 1 cup	240..	91	70	1	Trace	....	....	....	18
Grapefruit juice:									
Fresh ... 1 cup	246..	90	95	1	Trace	....	....	....	23
Canned:									
Unsweetened ... 1 cup	247..	89	100	1	Trace	....	....	....	24
Sweetened ... 1 cup	250..	86	130	1	Trace	....	....	....	32
Frozen, concentrate, unsweetened:									
Undiluted, can, 6 fluid ounces ... 1 can	207..	62	300	4	1	....	....	....	72
Water added ... 1 cup	247..	89	100	1	Trace	....	....	....	24

Food, approximate measure, and weight (in grams)		Water	Food energy	Pro-tein	Fat (total lipid)	Fatty Acids			Carbo-hy-drate
						Satu-rated (total)	Unsaturated Oleic	Unsaturated Lino-leic	
	Grams	Per-cent	Calo-ries	Grams	Grams	Grams	Grams	Grams	Grams
FRUITS AND FRUIT PRODUCTS—Continued									
Grapefruit juice—Continued									
Frozen, concentrate, sweetened:									
Undiluted, can, 6 fluid ounces......... 1 can	211..	57	350	3	1	....	....	....	85
Water added............ 1 cup	249..	88	115	1	Trace	....	....	....	28
Dehydrated:									
Crystals, can, net weight 4 ounces......... 1 can	114..	1	430	5	1	....	....	....	103
Water added............ 1 cup	247..	90	100	1	Trace	....	....	....	24
Grapes, raw:									
American type (slip skin), such as Concord, Delaware, Niagara, and Scuppernong .... 1 cup	153..	82	70	1	1	....	....	....	16
European type (adherent skin), such as Malaga, Muscat, Sultanina (Thompson Seedless), and Flame Tokay .... 1 cup	160..	81	100	1	Trace	....	....	....	26
Grape juice, bottled............. 1 cup	254..	83	165	1	Trace	....	....	....	42
Lemons, raw, medium, 2 1/5-inch-diameter, size 150...... 1 lemon.........	106..	90	20	1	Trace	....	....	....	6
Lemon juice:									
Fresh .... 1 cup	246..	91	60	1	Trace	....	....	....	20
1 tablespoon..	15..	91	5	Trace	Trace	....	....	....	1

FRUITS AND FRUIT PRODUCTS—Continued

Food, approximate measure, and weight (in grams)		Water	Food energy	Protein	Fat (total lipid)	Saturated (total)	Unsaturated		Carbohydrate
							Oleic	Linoleic	
	Grams	Percent	Calories	Grams	Grams	Grams	Grams	Grams	Grams
Lemon juice—Continued									
Canned, unsweetened...... 1 cup	245..	92	60	1	Trace	....	....	....	19
Lemonade concentrate, frozen, sweetened:									
Undiluted, can, 6 fluid ounces............. 1 can	220..	48	430	Trace	Trace	....	....	....	112
Water added............... 1 cup	248..	88	110	Trace	Trace	....	....	....	28
Lime juice:									
Fresh............... 1 cup	246..	90	65	1	Trace	....	....	....	22
Canned............ 1 cup	246..	90	65	1	Trace	....	....	....	22
Limeade concentrate, frozen, sweetened:									
Undiluted, can, 6 fluid ounces............. 1 can	218..	50	405	Trace	Trace	....	....	....	108
Water added...... 1 cup	248..	89	105	Trace	Trace	....	....	....	27
Oranges, raw:									
Navel, California (winter), size 88, 2 4/5-inch diameter ...... 1 orange	180..	85	60	2	Trace	....	....	....	16
Other varieties, 3-inch diameter ...... 1 orange	210..	86	70	1	Trace	....	....	....	18
Orange juice:									
Fresh:									
California, Valencia, summer............. 1 cup	249..	88	120	2	1	....	....	....	26

Food, approximate measure, and weight (in grams)		Water	Food energy	Protein	Fat (total lipid)	Fatty Acids			Carbohydrate
						Saturated (total)	Unsaturated Oleic	Linoleic	
	Grams	Percent	Calories	Grams	Grams	Grams	Grams	Grams	Grams
FRUITS AND FRUIT PRODUCTS—Continued									
Orange juice—Continued									
Florida varieties:									
Early and midseason... 1 cup	247..	90	100	1	Trace	....	....	....	23
Late season, Valencia... 1 cup	246..	88	110	1	Trace	....	....	....	26
Canned, unsweetened,...... 1 cup	249..	87	120	2	Trace	....	....	....	28
Frozen concentrate:									
Undiluted, can, 6 fluid ounces... 1 can	210..	58	330	5	Trace	....	....	....	80
Water added... 1 cup	248..	88	110	2	Trace	....	....	....	27
Dehydrated:									
Crystals, can, net weight 4 ounces... 1 can	113..	1	430	6	2	....	....	....	100
Water added... 1 cup	248..	88	115	1	Trace	....	....	....	27
Orange and grapefruit juice:									
Frozen concentrate:									
Undiluted, can, 6 fluid ounces... 1 can	209..	59	330	4	1	....	....	....	78
Water added... 1 cup	248..	88	110	1	Trace	....	....	....	26
Papayas, raw, 1/2-inch cubes... 1 cup	182..	89	70	1	Trace	....	....	....	18
Peaches:									
Raw:									
Whole, medium, 2-inch-diameter, about 4 per pound.... 1 peach	114..	89	35	1	Trace	....	....	....	10
Sliced ... 1 cup	168..	89	65	1	Trace	....	....	....	16

Food, approximate measure, and weight (in grams)			Water	Food energy	Protein	Fat (total lipid)	Fatty Acids			Carbohydrate
							Saturated (total)	Unsaturated		
								Oleic	Linoleic	
		Grams	Per cent	Calories	Grams	Grams	Grams	Grams	Grams	Grams
FRUITS AND FRUIT PRODUCTS—Continued										
Peaches—Continued										
Canned, yellow-fleshed, solids and liquid:										
Sirup pack, heavy:										
Halves or slices..	1 cup	257...	79	200	1	Trace	....	....	....	52
Halves, medium, and sirup	2 halves and 2 tablespoons	117...	79	90	Trace	Trace	....	....	....	24
Water pack..	1 cup	245...	91	75	1	Trace	....	....	....	20
Strained..	1 ounce	28..	82	20	Trace	Trace	....	....	....	5
Dried:										
Uncooked..	1 cup	160...	25	420	5	1	....	....	....	109
Cooked, unsweetened, 10–12 halves and 6 tablespoons liquid..	1 cup	270...	77	220	3	1	....	....	....	58
Frozen:										
Carton, 12 ounces	1 carton	340...	79	265	1	Trace	....	....	....	69
Can, 16 ounces	1 can	454...	79	355	2	Trace	....	....	....	92
Peach nectar, canned	1 cup	250...	87	115	Trace	Trace	....	....	....	31
Pears:										
Raw, 3 by 2 1/2-inch diameter	1 pear	182...	83	100	1	1	....	....	....	25
Canned, solids and liquid:										
Sirup pack, heavy:										
Halves or slices..	1 cup	255...	80	195	1	1	....	....	....	50
Halves, medium, and sirup	2 halves and 2 tablespoons sirup	117...	80	90	Trace	Trace	....	....	....	23

FRUITS AND FRUIT PRODUCTS—Continued

Food, approximate measure, and weight (in grams)		Water	Food energy	Protein	Fat (total lipid)	Fatty Acids Saturated (total)	Fatty Acids Unsaturated Oleic	Fatty Acids Unsaturated Linoleic	Carbohydrate
	Grams	Percent	Calories	Grams	Grams	Grams	Grams	Grams	Grams
Pears, canned, solids and liquid—Continued									
Water pack ... 1 cup	243..	91	80	Trace	Trace	....	....	....	20
Strained ... 1 ounce	28..	84	15	Trace	Trace	....	....	....	4
Pear nectar, canned ... 1 cup	250..	86	130	1	Trace	....	....	....	33
Persimmons, Japanese or Kaki, raw, seedless, 2 1/2-inch-diameter ... 1 persimmon	125..	79	75	1	Trace	....	....	....	20
Pineapple:									
Raw, diced ... 1 cup	140..	85	75	1	Trace	....	....	....	19
Canned, sirup pack, solids and liquid:									
Crushed ... 1 cup	260..	78	205	1	Trace	....	....	....	55
Sliced, slices and juice ... 2 small or 1 large and 2 tablespoons juice	122..	78	95	Trace	Trace	....	....	....	26
Pineapple juice, canned ... 1 cup	249..	86	120	1	Trace	....	....	....	32
Plums, all except prunes:									
Raw, 2-inch-diameter, about 2 ounces ... 1 plum	60..	86	30	Trace	Trace	....	....	....	7
Canned, sirup pack (Italian prunes):									
Plums and juice ... 1 cup	256..	79	185	1	Trace	....	....	....	50
Plums (without pits) and juice ... 3 plums and 2 tablespoons juice	122..	79	90	Trace	Trace	....	....	....	25

Food, approximate measure, and weight (in grams)		Water	Food energy	Protein	Fat (total lipid)	Fatty Acids			Carbohydrate
						Saturated (total)	Unsaturated		
							Oleic	Linoleic	
	Grams	Percent	Calories	Grams	Grams	Grams	Grams	Grams	Grams
FRUITS AND FRUIT PRODUCTS—Continued									
Prunes, dried:									
Medium, 50-60 per pound:									
Uncooked.................. 4 prunes	32..	24	70	1	Trace	....	....	....	19
Cooked, unsweetened, 17-18 prunes and 1/3 cup liquid........ 1 cup	270..	65	305	3	1	....	....	....	81
Prune juice, canned....... 1 ounce	28..	73	25	Trace	Trace	....	....	....	7
Canned, strained........... 1 cup	240..	80	170	1	Trace	....	....	....	45
Raisins, dried .... 1 cup	160..	18	460	4	Trace	....	....	....	124
Raspberries, red:									
Raw .... 1 cup	123..	84	70	1	1	....	....	....	17
Frozen, 10-ounce carton... 1 carton	284..	74	280	2	1	....	....	....	70
Rhubarb, cooked, sugar added .... 1 cup	272..	63	385	1	Trace	....	....	....	98
Strawberries:									
Raw, capped .... 1 cup	149..	90	55	1	1	....	....	....	13
Frozen, 10-ounce carton... 1 carton	284..	72	300	2	1	....	....	....	75
Frozen, 16-ounce can...... 1 can	454..	72	485	3	2	....	....	....	121
Tangerines, raw, medium, 2 1/2-inch-diameter, about 4 per pound............. 1 tangerine...	114..	87	40	1	Trace	....	....	....	10
Tangerine juice:									
Canned, unsweetened .... 1 cup	248..	89	105	1	Trace	....	....	....	25
Frozen concentrate:									
Undiluted, can, 6 fluid ounces .... 1 can	210..	58	340	4	1	....	....	....	80
Water added.................. 1 cup	248..	88	115	1	Trace	....	....	....	27

FRUITS AND FRUIT PRODUCTS—Continued

Food, approximate measure, and weight (in grams)		Water	Food energy	Protein	Fat (total lipid)	Fatty Acids			Carbohydrate
						Saturated (total)	Unsaturated		
							Oleic	Linoleic	
	Grams	Percent	Calories	Grams	Grams	Grams	Grams	Grams	Grams
Watermelon, raw, wedge, 4 by 8 inches (1/16 of 10- by 16-inch melon, about 2 pounds with rind) .... 1 wedge.........	925..	92	120	2	1	....	....	....	29
GRAIN PRODUCTS									
Barley, pearled, light, uncooked............... 1 cup	203..	11	710	17	2	Trace	1	1	160
Biscuits, baking powder, with enriched flour, 2 1/2-inch-diameter......... 1 biscuit	38..	28	130	3	4	1	2	Trace	18
Bran flakes (40 percent bran) with added thiamine .... 1 ounce	28..	4	85	3	1	....	....	....	22
Breads:									
Boston brown bread, made with degermed corn-meal, slice, 3 by 3/4 inch............. 1 slice	48..	45	100	3	1	....	....	....	22
Cracked-wheat bread:									
Loaf, 1-pound, 20 slices................ 1 loaf	454..	35	1,190	39	10	2	5	2	236
Slice .... 1 slice	23..	35	60	2	1	....	....	....	12
French or vienna bread:									
Enriched, 1-pound loaf .... 1 loaf	454..	31	1,315	41	14	3	8	2	251
Unenriched, 1-pound loaf .... 1 loaf	454..	31	1,315	41	14	3	8	2	251

Food, approximate measure, and weight (in grams)		Grams	Water Per-cent	Food energy Calories	Protein Grams	Fat (total lipid) Grams	Fatty Acids			Carbohy-drate Grams
							Satu-rated (total) Grams	Unsaturated Oleic Grams	Linoleic Grams	
GRAIN PRODUCTS—Continued										
Breads—Continued										
Italian bread:										
Enriched, 1-pound loaf	1 loaf	454..	32	1,250	41	4	1	1	2	256
Unenriched, 1-pound loaf	1 loaf	454..	32	1,250	41	4	1	1	2	256
Raisin bread:										
Loaf, 1-pound, 20 slices		454..	35	1,190	30	13	3	8	2	243
Slice	1 slice	23..	35	60	2	1	....	....	....	12
Rye bread:										
American, light (1/3 rye, 2/3 wheat):										
Loaf, 1-pound, 20 slices		454..	36	1,100	41	5	1	2	2	236
Slice	1 slice	23..	36	55	2	Trace	....	....	....	12
Pumpernickel, dark, loaf, 1 pound	1 loaf	454..	34	1,115	41	5	1	2	2	241
White bread, enriched:										
1 to 2 percent nonfat dry milk:										
Loaf, 1-pound, 20 slices		454..	36	1,225	39	15	3	9	2	229
Slice	1 slice	23..	36	60	2	1	....	....	....	12
3 to 4 percent nonfat dry milk:										
Loaf, 1-pound	1 loaf	454..	36	1,225	39	15	3	9	2	229

GRAIN PRODUCTS—Continued

Food, approximate measure, and weight (in grams)	Water	Food energy	Protein	Fat (total lipid)	Fatty Acids Saturated (total)	Unsaturated Oleic	Unsaturated Linoleic	Carbohydrate
Grams	Percent	Calories	Grams	Grams	Grams	Grams	Grams	Grams
Breads—3 to 4% nonfat dry milk—Continued								
Slice, 20 per loaf, 1 slice .... 23..	36	60	2	1	....	....	....	12
Slice, toasted, 1 slice .... 20..	24	60	2	1	....	....	....	12
Slice, 26 per loaf, 1 slice .... 17..	36	45	1	1	....	....	....	9
5 to 6% nonfat dry milk:								
Loaf, 1-pound, 20 slices............. 454..	35	1,245	41	17	4	10	2	228
Slice, 1 slice .... 23..	36	65	2	1	....	....	....	12
White bread, unenriched:								
1 to 2% nonfat dry milk:								
Loaf, 1-pound, 20 slices............. 454..	36	1,225	39	15	3	9	2	229
Slice, 1 slice .... 23..	36	60	2	1	....	....	....	12
3 to 4% nonfat dry milk:								
Loaf, 1-pound .... 454..	36	1,225	39	15	3	9	2	229
Slice, 20 per loaf, 1 slice .... 23..	36	60	2	1	....	....	....	12
Slice, toasted, 1 slice .... 20..	24	60	2	1	....	....	....	12
Slice, 26 per loaf, 1 slice .... 17..	36	45	1	1	....	....	....	9
5 to 6% nonfat dry milk:								
Loaf, 1-pound, 20 slices............. 454..	35	1,245	41	17	4	10	2	228
Slice, 1 slice .... 23..	35	65	2	1	....	....	....	12
Whole-wheat, graham, entire-wheat bread:								
Loaf, 1-pound, 20 slices............. 454..	36	1,105	48	14	3	7	4	216
Slice, 1 slice .... 23..	36	55	2	1	....	....	....	11
Toast, 1 slice .... 19..	25	55	2	1	....	....	....	11

GRAIN PRODUCTS—Continued

Food, approximate measure, and weight (in grams)		Water	Food energy	Pro-tein	Fat (total lipid)	Satu-rated (total)	Fatty Acids Unsaturated Oleic	Lino-leic	Carbo-hy-drate
	Grams	Per-cent	Calo-ries	Grams	Grams	Grams	Grams	Grams	Grams
Breadcrumbs, dry, grated .... 1 cup	88..	6	345	11	4	1	2	1	65
Cakes:									
Angel food cake; sector 2-inch (1/12 of 8-inch-diameter cake) .... 1 sector	40..	32	110	3	Trace	....	....	....	23
Chocolate cake, fudge icing; sector, 2-inch (1/16 of 10-inch-diameter layer cake) .. 1 sector	120..	24	420	5	14	5	7	1	70
Fruitcake, dark; piece, 2 by 2 by 1/2 inch ... 1 piece	30..	23	105	2	4	1	2	Trace	17
Gingerbread; piece, 2 by 2 by 2 inches ...... 1 piece	55..	30	180	2	7	2	4	Trace	28
Plain cake and cupcakes, without icing:									
Piece, 3 by 2 by 1 1/2 inches .... 1 piece	55..	27	180	4	5	1	3	Trace	31
Cupcake, 2 3/4-inch-diameter .... 1 cupcake	40..	27	130	3	3	1	2	Trace	23
Plain cake and cupcakes, with icing:									
Sector, 2-inch (1/16 of 10-inch layer cake).. 1 sector	100..	25	320	5	6	2	3	Trace	62
Cupcake, 2 3/4-inch-diameter...... 1 cupcake	50..	25	160	3	3	1	1	Trace	31
Pound cake; slice, 2 3/4 by 3 by 5/8 inch.......... 1 slice	30..	19	130	2	7	2	4	1	15

Food, approximate measure, and weight (in grams)		Water	Food energy	Protein	Fat (total lipid)	Fatty Acids			Carbohydrate
						Saturated (total)	Unsaturated		
							Oleic	Linoleic	
	Grams	Percent	Calories	Grams	Grams	Grams	Grams	Grams	Grams
GRAIN PRODUCTS—Continued									
Cakes—Continued									
Sponge cake; sector, 2-inch; sector (1/12 of 8-inch-diameter cake)............ 1 sector........	40..	32	115	3	2	1	1	Trace	22
Cookies:									
Plain and assorted, 3-inch-diameter ...... 1 cooky........	25..	5	110	2	3	1	2	Trace	19
Fig bars, small ...... 1 fig bar	16..	14	55	1	1	....	....	....	12
Corn-cereal mixture (mainly degermed corn-meal), puffed, with added thiamine, niacin, and iron. 1 ounce........	28..	3	115	2	1	....	....	....	23
Corn flakes, with added thiamine, niacin, and iron:									
Plain ...... 1 ounce	28..	4	110	2	Trace	....	....	....	24
Presweetened...... 1 ounce	28..	3	110	1	Trace	....	....	....	26
Corn grits, white, degermed, cooked:									
Enriched...... 1 cup	242..	87	120	3	Trace	....	....	....	27
Unenriched ...... 1 cup	242..	87	120	3	Trace	....	....	....	27
Cornmeal, white or yellow, dry:									
Whole ground...... 1 cup	118..	12	420	11	5	1	2	2	87
Degermed, enriched ...... 1 cup	145..	12	525	11	2	Trace	1	1	114
Corn muffins, made with enriched, degermed corn-meal; muffin, 2 3/4-inch-diameter ...... 1 muffin........	48..	30	155	4	5	2	2	Trace	22

GRAIN PRODUCTS—Continued

Food, approximate measure, and weight (in grams)		Water	Food energy	Protein	Fat (total lipid)	Fatty Acids			Carbohydrate
						Saturated (total)	Unsaturated Oleic	Unsaturated Linoleic	
	Grams	Per cent	Calories	Grams	Grams	Grams	Grams	Grams	Grams
Corn, puffed, presweetened, with added thiamine, riboflavin, niacin, and iron.. 1 ounce	28..	3	110	1	Trace	....	....	....	26
Corn and soy shreds, with added thiamine and niacin........ 1 ounce	28..	4	100	5	Trace	....	....	....	21
Crackers:									
Graham........ 4 small or 2 medium..	14..	6	55	1	1	....	....	....	10
Saltines, 2 inches square.. 2 crackers....	8..	5	35	1	1	....	....	....	6
Soda, plain:									
Cracker, 2 1/2 inches square .... 2 crackers....	11..	6	45	1	1	....	....	....	8
Oyster crackers........ 10 crackers....	10..	6	45	1	1	....	....	....	7
Cracker meal........ 1 tablespoon..	10..	6	45	1	1	....	....	....	7
Doughnuts, cake type........ 1 doughnut....	32..	19	135	2	7	2	2	3	17
Macaroni, cooked:									
Enriched:									
Cooked 8-10 minutes (undergoes additional cooking in a food mixture)........ 1 cup	130..	64	190	6	1	....	....	....	39
Cooked until tender...... 1 cup	140..	72	155	5	1	....	....	....	32
Unenriched:									
Cooked 8-10 minutes (undergoes additional cooking in a food mixture)........ 1 cup	130..	64	190	6	1	....	....	....	39

Food, approximate measure, and weight (in grams)		Water	Food energy	Protein	Fat (total lipid)	Fatty Acids			Carbohydrate
						Saturated (total)	Unsaturated Oleic	Unsaturated Linoleic	
	Grams	Per-cent	Calo-ries	Grams	Grams	Grams	Grams	Grams	Grams
GRAIN PRODUCTS—Continued									
Macaroni—Unenriched—Continued									
Cooked until tender...... 1 cup	140..	72	155	5	1	....	....	....	32
Macaroni, enriched, and cheese, baked............ 1 cup	220..	58	475	18	25	14	8	1	44
Muffins, with enriched white flour; muffin, 2 3/4-inch-diameter ...... 1 muffin	48..	39	135	4	5	1	3	Trace	19
Noodles (egg noodles), cooked:									
Enriched............. 1 cup	160..	70	200	7	2	1	1	Trace	37
Unenriched .... 1 cup	160..	70	200	7	2	1	1	Trace	37
Oat-cereal mixture, mainly oats, with added B-vita-mins and minerals........... 1 ounce	28..	3	115	4	2	Trace	1	1	21
Oatmeal or rolled oats, regular or quick-cooking, cooked .... 1 cup	236..	85	150	5	3	1	1	1	26
Pancakes (griddlecakes), 4-inch-diameter:									
Wheat, enriched flour (home recipe) .... 1 cake	27..	53	60	2	2	Trace	1	Trace	8
Buckwheat (buckwheat pancake mix) .... 1 cake	27..	62	45	2	2	1	1	Trace	6
Piecrust, plain, baked:									
Enriched flour:									
Lower crust, 9-inch shell............. 1 crust.........	135..	10	655	10	36	8	24	3	72
Double crust, 9-in. pie.. 1 double crust	270..	10	1,315	20	73	17	47	5	143

GRAIN PRODUCTS—Continued

Food, approximate measure, and weight (in grams)		Water	Food energy	Protein	Fat (total lipid)	Fatty Acids			Carbohydrate
						Saturated (total)	Unsaturated Oleic	Unsaturated Linoleic	
	Grams	Percent	Calories	Grams	Grams	Grams	Grams	Grams	Grams
Piecrust, plain, baked—Continued									
Unenriched flour:									
Lower crust, 9-inch shell ... 1 crust	135	10	655	10	36	8	24	3	72
Double crust, 9-inch pie ... 1 double crust	270	10	1,315	20	73	17	47	5	143
Pies; sector, 4-inch, 1/7 of 9-inch-diameter pie:									
Apple ... 1 sector	135	48	330	3	13	4	7	1	53
Cherry ... 1 sector	135	46	340	3	13	4	7	1	55
Custard ... 1 sector	130	58	265	7	11	4	6	1	34
Lemon meringue ... 1 sector	120	47	300	4	12	4	6	1	45
Mince ... 1 sector	135	43	340	3	9	2	6	1	62
Pumpkin ... 1 sector	130	59	265	5	12	5	6	1	34
Pizza (cheese). 5 1/2-inch-sector, 1/8 of 14-inch-diameter pie ... 1 sector	75	47	180	8	6	3	3	Trace	23
Popcorn, popped ... 1 cup	14	4	55	2	1	....	....	....	11
Pretzels, small stick ... 5 sticks	5	8	20	Trace	Trace	....	....	....	4
Rice, cooked:									
Parboiled ... 1 cup	176	72	205	4	Trace	....	....	....	45
White ... 1 cup	168	71	200	4	Trace	....	....	....	44
Rice, puffed, with added thiamine, niacin, and iron ... 1 cup	14	5	55	1	Trace	....	....	....	12
Rice flakes, with added thiamine and niacin ... 1 cup	30	5	115	2	Trace	....	....	....	26

Food, approximate measure, and weight (in grams)		Water	Food energy	Protein	Fat (total lipid)	Fatty Acids			Carbohydrate
						Saturated (total)	Unsaturated Oleic	Unsaturated Linoleic	
	Grams	Per-cent	Calories	Grams	Grams	Grams	Grams	Grams	Grams
GRAIN PRODUCTS—Continued									
Rolls:									
Plain, pan; 12 per 16 ounces:									
Enriched................ 1 roll	38..	31	115	3	2	1	1	Trace	20
Unenriched............ 1 roll	38..	31	115	3	2	1	1	Trace	20
Hard, round; 12 per 22 ounces............ 1 roll	52..	25	160	5	2	1	1	Trace	31
Sweet, pan; 12 per 18 ounces .... 1 roll	43..	31	135	4	4	1	2	Trace	21
Rye wafers, 1 7/8 by 3 1/2 inches ...... 2 wafers	13..	6	45	2	Trace	....	....	....	10
Spaghetti, cooked until tender:									
Enriched .... 1 cup	140..	72	155	5	1	....	....	....	32
Unenriched .... 1 cup	140..	72	155	5	1	....	....	....	32
Spaghetti in tomato sauce with cheese .... 1 cup	250..	80	210	6	5	2	1	2	36
Waffles, with enriched flour, 1/2 by 4 1/2 by 5 1/2 inches .... 1 waffle	75..	34	240	8	9	3	5	1	30
Wheat, puffed:									
With added thiamine, niacin, and iron .... 1 ounce	28..	4	100	4	Trace	....	....	....	22
With added thiamine and niacin; presweetened.... 1 ounce	28..	3	105	1	Trace	....	....	....	26
Wheat, rolled; cooked .... 1 cup	236..	80	175	5	1	....	....	....	40

Food, approximate measure, and weight (in grams)		Water	Food energy	Protein	Fat (total lipid)	Saturated (total)	Unsaturated		Carbohydrate
							Oleic	Linoleic	
	Grams	Per cent	Calories	Grams	Grams	Grams	Grams	Grams	Grams
GRAIN PRODUCTS—Continued									
Wheat, shredded, plain (long, round, or bite-size)	1 ounce	28	6	100	3	1	....	....	....	23
Wheat and malted barley cereal, with added thiamine, niacin, and iron	1 ounce	28	3	105	3	Trace	....	....	....	24
Wheat flakes, with added thiamine, niacin, and iron	1 ounce	28	4	100	3	Trace	....	....	....	23
Wheat flours:									
Whole-wheat, from hard wheats, stirred	1 cup	120	12	400	16	2	Trace	1	1	85
All-purpose or family flour:									
Enriched, sifted	1 cup	110	12	400	12	1	....	....	....	84
Unenriched, sifted	1 cup	110	12	400	12	1	....	....	....	84
Self-rising:									
Enriched	1 cup	110	12	385	10	1	....	....	....	81
Unenriched	1 cup	110	12	385	10	1	....	....	....	81
Wheat germ, stirred	1 cup	68	11	245	17	7	1	2	3	34
FATS, OILS									
Butter, 4 sticks per pound:									
Sticks, 2	1 cup	224	16	1,605	1	181	100	60	5	1
Stick, 1/8	1 tablespoon	14	16	100	Trace	11	6	4	Trace	Trace
Pat or square (64 per lb)	1 pat	7	16	50	Trace	6	3	2	0	Trace

| Food, approximate measure, and weight (in grams) | Grams | Water | Food energy | Protein | Fat (total lipid) | Fatty Acids | | | Carbohydrate |
| | | | | | | Saturated (total) | Unsaturated | | |
							Oleic	Linoleic	
	Grams	Percent	Calories	Grams	Grams	Grams	Grams	Grams	Grams
FATS, OILS—Continued									
Fats, cooking:									
Lard............................ 1 cup	220	0	1,985	0	220	84	101	22	0
1 tablespoon..	14	0	135	0	14	5	6	1	0
Vegetable fats............ 1 cup...	200	0	1,770	0	200	46	130	14	0
1 tablespoon..	12.5	0	110	0	12	3	8	1	0
Margarine (ordinary), 4 sticks per pound:									
Sticks, 2..................... 1 cup	224	16	1,615	1	181	47	103	16	1
Stick, 1/8.................... 1 tablespoon..	14	16	100	Trace	11	3	6	1	Trace
Pat or square (64 per pound) .... 1 pat	7	16	50	Trace	6	1	3	1	Trace
Oils, salad or cooking:									
Corn............................ 1 tablespoon..	14	0	125	0	14	1	4	7	0
Cottonseed.................. 1 tablespoon..	14	0	125	0	14	3	3	7	0
Olive........................... 1 tablespoon..	14	0	125	0	14	2	11	1	0
Soybean .... 1 tablespoon..	14	0	125	0	14	2	3	7	0
Salad dressings:									
Blue cheese .... 1 tablespoon..	16	28	90	1	10	2	2	5	1
Commercial, plain mayonnaise type .... 1 tablespoon..	15	48	60	Trace	6	1	1	3	1
French .... 1 tablespoon..	15	42	60	Trace	6	1	1	3	2
Home cooked, boiled........ 1 tablespoon..	17	68	30	1	2	1	1	Trace	3
Mayonnaise................. 1 tablespoon..	15	14	110	Trace	12	2	3	6	Trace
Thousand Island......... 1 tablespoon..	15	38	75	Trace	8	1	2	4	1

SUGARS, SWEETS

Food, approximate measure, and weight (in grams)	Grams	Water Per-cent	Food en-ergy Calo-ries	Pro-tein Grams	Fat (total lipid) Grams	Satu-rated (total) Grams	Fatty Acids Unsaturated Oleic Grams	Lino-leic Grams	Carbo-hy-drate Grams
Candy:									
Caramels .... 1 ounce	28..	7	120	1	3	2	1	Trace	22
Chocolate, sweetened, milk............. 1 ounce	28..	1	145	2	9	5	3	Trace	16
Fudge, plain .... 1 ounce	28..	5	115	Trace	3	2	1	Trace	23
Hard candy .... 1 ounce	28..	1	110	0	0	....	....	....	28
Marshmallow .... 1 ounce	28..	15	90	1	0	....	....	....	23
Chocolate sirup .... 1 tablespoon..	20..	39	40	Trace	Trace	....	....	....	11
Honey, strained or extracted, 1 tablespoon..	21..	20	60	Trace	0	....	....	....	17
Jams, marmalades, pre-serves .... 1 tablespoon..	20..	28	55	Trace	Trace	....	....	....	14
Jellies .... 1 tablespoon..	20..	34	50	0	....	....	....	....	13
Molasses, cane:									
Light (first extraction)..... 1 tablespoon..	20..	24	50	....	....	....	....	....	13
Blackstrap (third extrac-tion) .... 1 tablespoon..	20..	24	45	....	....	....	....	....	11
Sirup, table blends .... 1 tablespoon..	20..	25	55	0	0	....	....	....	15
Sugar:									
Granulated, cane or beet... 1 cup	200..	Trace	770	0	0	....	....	....	199
1 tablespoon..	12..	Trace	50	0	0	....	....	....	12
Lump, 1 1/8 by 5/8 by 1/8 inch .... 1 lump	7..	Trace	25	0	0	....	....	....	7
Powdered, stirred before measuring............. 1 cup	128..	Trace	495	0	0	....	....	....	127
1 tablespoon..	8..	Trace	30	0	0	....	....	....	8
Brown, firm-packed .... 1 cup	220..	3	815	0	0	....	....	....	210
1 tablespoon..	14..	3	50	0	0	....	....	....	13

Food, approximate measure, and weight (in grams)	Grams	Water Per cent	Food energy Calories	Protein Grams	Fat (total lipid) Grams	Saturated (total) Grams	Unsaturated Oleic Grams	Unsaturated Linoleic Grams	Carbohydrate Grams
MISCELLANEOUS ITEMS									
Beer (average 4 percent alcohol).............. 1 cup	240..	90	100	1	Trace	......	......	......	11
Beverages, carbonated:									
Ginger ale.............. 1 cup	230..	91	80	......	......	......	......	......	21
Kola type.............. 1 cup	230..	88	105	......	......	......	......	......	28
Bouillon cube, 5/8 inch .... 1 cube	4..	5	2	Trace	Trace	......	......	......	0
Chili powder. See Vegetables, Peppers.									
Chili sauce (mainly tomatoes) 1 tablespoon...	17..	69	15	Trace	Trace	......	......	......	4
Chocolate:									
Bitter or unsweetened..... 1 ounce	28..	2	145	2	15	8	6	Trace	8
Sweetened............. 1 ounce	28..	1	135	1	8	5	3	Trace	18
Cider. See Fruit, Applejuice.									
Gelatin, dry:									
Plain .... 1 tablespoon..	10..	13	35	9	Trace	......	......	......	0
Dessert powder, 3-ounce package......1/2 cup	85..	2	325	8	Trace	......	......	......	76
Gelatin dessert, ready-to-eat:									
Plain .... 1 cup	239..	83	155	4	Trace	......	......	......	36
With fruit .... 1 cup	241..	81	170	3	Trace	......	......	......	42
Olives, pickled:									
Green.................. 12 Extra Large or 7 Jumbo.	66..	78	65	1	7	1	5	Trace	1
Ripe: Mission; other varieties, such as Ascolano, Manzanillo, and Sevillano............. 12 Extra Large or 7 Jumbo..	66..	76	85	1	9	1	7	1	2

MISCELLANEOUS ITEMS—Continued

Food, approximate measure, and weight (in grams)		Grams	Water (Per-cent)	Food energy (Calories)	Protein (Grams)	Fat (total lipid) (Grams)	Fatty Acids Saturated (total) (Grams)	Unsaturated Oleic (Grams)	Unsaturated Linoleic (Grams)	Carbohydrate (Grams)
Pickles, cucumber:										
Dill, large, 4 by 1 3/4 inches	1 pickle	135	93	15	1	Trace	....	....	....	3
Sweet, 2 3/4 by 3/4 inch	1 pickle	20	70	20	Trace	Trace	....	....	....	5
Popcorn. See Grain Products.										
Sherbet, factory packed	1 cup	193	68	235	3	Trace	....	....	....	58
Soups, canned; ready-to-serve:										
Bean	1 cup	250	82	190	8	5	2	2	Trace	30
Beef	1 cup	250	92	100	6	4	2	2	Trace	11
Bouillon, broth, consomme	1 cup	240	95	10	2	....	....	....	....	0
Chicken	1 cup	250	94	75	4	2	1	1	Trace	10
Clam chowder	1 cup	255	91	85	5	2	Trace	Trace	1	12
Cream soup (asparagus, celery, mushroom)	1 cup	255	85	200	7	12	7	4	Trace	18
Noodle, rice, barley	1 cup	250	90	115	6	4	1	2	1	13
Pea	1 cup	245	86	140	6	2	1	1	Trace	25

Food, approximate measure, and weight (in grams)		Grams	Water, Per-cent	Food en-ergy, Calo-ries	Pro-tein, Grams	Fat (total lipid), Grams	Satu-rated (total), Grams	Unsaturated Oleic, Grams	Unsaturated Lino-leic, Grams	Carbo-hy-drate, Grams
MISCELLANEOUS ITEMS—Continued										
Soups, canned—Continued										
Tomato	1 cup .... 245..		91	90	2	2	1	Trace	1	18
Vegetable	1 cup .... 250..		92	80	4	2	1	1	Trace	14
Starch, pure, including arrowroot, corn, etc.	1 cup .... 128..		12	465	1	Trace	....	....	....	111
	1 tablespoon.. 8..		12	30	Trace	Trace	....	....	....	7
Tapioca, quick-cooking granulated, dry; stirred before measuring	1 cup .... 152..		13	545	1	Trace	....	....	....	131
Vinegar	1 tablespoon.. 10..		13	35	Trace	Trace	....	....	....	8
	1 tablespoon.. 15..		....	2	0	....	....	....	....	1
White sauce, medium	1 cup .... 265..		73	430	10	33	18	11	1	23
Yeast:										
Baker's:										
Compressed	1 ounce........ 28..		71	25	3	Trace	....	....	....	3
Dry active	1 ounce........ 28..		5	80	10	Trace	....	....	....	11
Brewer's, dry	1 tablespoon.. 8..		5	25	3	Trace	....	....	....	3

Yoghurt. *See* Milk, Cream, Cheese; Related Products.

YIELD OF COOKED MEAT PER POUND OF RAW MEAT

Meat as purchased	Description	Yield of cooked meat (without drippings) Approximate weight per pound of raw meat
		Ounces
Chops or steaks for broiling or frying:		
With bone and relatively large amount of fat, such as: Pork or lamb chops; beef rib, sirloin, or porterhouse steaks	With bone and fat.	10-12
	Without bone, with fat.	7-10
	Lean only.	5-7
Without bone and with very little fat, such as: Round of beef; veal steaks	Lean and fat.	12-13
	Lean only.	9-12
Ground meat for broiling or frying, market type, such as: Hamburger; lamb or pork patties	Patties.	9-13
Roasts for oven cooking (no liquid added):		
With bone and relatively large amount of fat, such as: Beef rib, loin, chuck; lamb shoulder, leg; pork, fresh or cured.	With bone and fat.	10-12
	Without bone, with fat.	8-10
	Lean only.	6-9
Without bone.	Lean and fat.	10-12
	Lean only.	7-10
Cuts for pot-roasting, simmering, braising, stewing:		
With bone and relatively large amount of fat, such as: Beef chuck; pork shoulder.	With bone and fat.	10-11
	Without bone, with fat.	8-9
	Lean only.	6-8
Without bone and with relatively small amount of fat, such as: Trimmed beef; veal.	Lean with small amount of adhering fat.	9-11

INDEX

INDEX

310

311

CHOCOLATE
candy, fats and nutrients in, 54, 302
cholesterol content of, 21
fats and nutrients in, 21, 54, 303
Cholesterol, 14, 17, 18-23
in average diet, 12
content in foods, 19-23
fat intake in diet and, 48-50
heart disease and, 9, 10, 14, 15, 22, 42-43
importance in body chemistry, 28-29
iodine numbers of fat and, 51
levels in blood
age and, 38-39
emotion and, 38
exercise and, 39-40
fats and, 27
heredity and, 35-36
linoleic acid and, 28
lipoproteins and, 29
measurement of, 22, 43
obesity and, 34
oleic acid and, 28
sex differential and, 32
stress and, 38
unsaturated fats, effect on, 45-46
Chopped Chicken Liver Spread, 72
Chowder. See SOUPS
Cigarette smoking and heart disease, 9, 41
CLAMS
Baked, 114
Cheese Dip, 74
chowder, Manhattan, 90
fats and nutrients in, 272
Manhattan, Chowder, 90
COCOA
saturated fat content of, 54
COCOA BUTTER
effect on cholesterol level, 51
iodine value of, 50
saturated and unsaturated fats in, 50
COCONUT
fats and nutrients in, 54, 274
COCONUT OIL
cholesterol content of, 21
effect on cholesterol level in blood, 51
iodine number of, 27, 50
fats in, 21, 50, 54
saturation degree of, 27
Coffee Frozen Dessert, 221
COD
Creole Casserole, 108
Salad, 114
Cola (Kola) drinks, nutrients in, 303
COOKIES, 236, 244-52
Almond Drop, 247

Anise Cakes, 244
Applesauce, 248
Brown Sugar Slices, 252
Butterscotch Brownies, 237
Drop Nut, 245
fats and nutrients in, 53, 295
Fruit-Nut Bars, 251
Hermits, 250
Italian Anise Crescents, 245
Lady Fingers, 236
Oatmeal Drops, 246
Molasses, 246
Nut Kisses, 249
Sesame, 250
Spice Bars, 251
Sugar Balls, 248
CORN
Bread, 212
Chinese, Soup, 88
CORN OIL, 52
effect of addition to diet, 45-46
effect on cholesterol level in blood, 51
fats in, 50, 54, 301
iodine number of, 27, 50
linoleic acid content of, 27-28, 50, 301
oleic acid content of, 50, 301
saturation degree of, 27
Coronary heart disease, 10. See also Heart disease
Coronary occlusion, 13, 16. See also Heart disease
Coronary thrombosis, 16. See also Heart disease
COTTAGE CHEESE. See CHEESE, cottage
COTTONSEED OIL, 52
effect on cholesterol level in blood, 51
iodine number of, 27, 50
linoleic acid content of, 28, 50, 301
oleic acid in, 50, 301
saturated fat in, 50, 54, 301
saturation degree of, 27
Cowpeas, fats and nutrients in, 277
CRABMEAT
cholesterol content of, 20
Ravigote, 115
Seafood Soufflé, 120
Spread, 70
CRACKERS
Poppy Seed Cocktail Wafers, 68
CREAM
cholesterol content of, 22
fats and nutrients in, 22, 53, 265
French Dessert, 222
Special, 259
Special "Whipped," 260

313

320